ETIQUETTE WITH THE QURAN

Al-Tibyān fī Ādāb Ḥamalat al-Qur'an

ETIQUETTE WITH THE QURAN

Al-Tibyān fī Ādāb Ḥamalat al-Qur'an

IMĀM AL-NAWAWĪ

Translation & Notes by

MUSA FURBER

Foreword by

NUH HA MIM KELLER

ISLAMOSAIC

ISBN 978-0-9858840-3-1 (paper)
ISBN 978-0-9858840-1-7 (epub)

Published by:
Islamosaic
islamosaic.com
publications@islamosaic.com

بسم الله الرحمن الرحيم

All praise is to Allah alone, the Lord of the Worlds
And may He send His benedictions upon
our master Muhammad, his Kin
and his Companions
and grant them
peace

AUTHORIZATION

بسم الله الرحمن الرحيم

أروي بالإجازة العامة كتاب التبيان في آداب حملة القرآن عن عدد من المشايخ منهم الشيخ أحمد جابر جبران وعن الشيخ ياسين الفاداني وهو عن شيخه محمد علي المالكي وهو عن شيخه السيد بكري عن أحمد زيني دحلان وهو عن عثمان بن حسن الدمياطي عن العلامة محمد بن عبد القادر الأمير عن علي بن محمد العربي السقاط عن عبد الله بن سالم البصري عن عيسى الجعفري الثعالبي عن علي الأجهوري عن السراج عمر الجائي عن الحافظ جلال الدين أبي الفضل عبد الرحمن بن أبي بكر السيوطي عن شيخ الإسلام علم الدين البلقيني عن أبيه سراج الدين عمر البلقيني عن الحافظ أبي الحجاج يوسف بن عبد الرحمن المزي عن المؤلف الإمام الرباني أبي زكريا يحيى بن شرف النووي وقد أجزت الأخ الشيخ موسى فربر بهذا السند كما أجازني بذلك مشائخي الفضلاء ممن أجازوني إجازة عامة وخاصة وأوصي المجاز ونفسي بتقوى الله ونشر العلم مستمدا من الله التوفيق للجميع وصلى الله على سيدنا محمد وعلى آله وصحبه وسلم.

كتبه الفقير إلى ربه وراجي عفوه
عبد الله بن حسين القاضي
غفر الله له ولوالديه ولجميع المسلمين

In the Name of God, Most Merciful and Compassionate

I relate *al-Tibyān fī Ādāb Ḥamalat al-Qur'ān* by way of general authorization from a number of shaykhs, including Shaykh Aḥmad Jābir Jibrān and Sheikh Yāsīn al-Fādānī. And he relates it from his Shaykh Muḥmmad 'Alī al-Mālikī who relates it from his sheykh al-Sayyid Bikrī, who relates it from Aḥmad Zaynī Daḥlān, who relates it from 'Uthmān Ibn Hasan al-Damyāṭī, from the eminent scholar Muḥammad Ibn 'Abd al-Qādir al-Amīr, from 'Alī Ibn Muḥammad al-'Arabī al-Saqāt, from 'Abdullah Ibn Sālim al-Baṣrī, from 'Īsā al-Ja'farī al-Tha'ālabī, from 'Alī al-Ujhūri, form al-Sirāj 'Umar Ibn al-Jā'ī, from al-Ḥāfiẓ Jalāl al-Dīn Abī al-Faḍl 'Abd al-Raḥmān Ibn Abī Bakr al-Suyuṭī, from the Shaykh of Islam 'Alam al-Dīn al-Bulqīnī, from his father Sirāj al-Dīn 'Amr al-Bulqīnī, from al-Ḥāfiẓ Abī al-Ḥallāj Yūsuf Ibn 'Abd al-Raḥmān al-Mizzī, from the author: al-Imām al-Rabbānī Abū Zakariyā Yaḥyā Ibn Sharaf al-Nawawī. I have authorized Shaykh Musa Furber with this chain [of transmission], just as my distinguished shaykhs authorized it to me with general and specific authorizations. I enjoin the one being authorized—and myself—to fear God and to draw upon success from God in spreading knowledge to all. May the blessings and peace of God be upon our master Muḥammad, and upon his family and companions.

Written by one needy of his Lord and a seeker of His pardon,
'Abd Allāh bin Hussein al-Kadi
God forgive him, his parents, and all Muslims
[*Signed and dated 25 Ṣafar 1424 AH (27 April 2003 CE)*]

TRANSLITERATION KEY

ء	’[1]	ر	r[6]	ف	f
ا	ā, a	ز	z	ق	q[13]
ب	b	س	s	ك	k
ت	t	ش	sh	ل	l
ث	th[2]	ص	ṣ[7]	م	m
ج	j	ض	ḍ[8]	ن	n
ح	ḥ[3]	ط	ṭ[9]	ه	h[14]
خ	kh[4]	ظ	ẓ[10]	و	ū, u, w
د	d	ع	‘[11]	ي	ī, i, y
ذ	dh[5]	غ	gh[12]		

1. A distinctive glottal stop made at the bottom of the throat. It is also used to indicate the running of two words into one, e.g., *bismi’Llāh*.
2. Pronounced like the *th* in *think*.
3. Hard *h* sound made at the Adam’s apple in the middle of the throat.
4. Pronounced like *ch* in Scottish *loch*.
5. Pronounced like *th* in *this*.
6. A slightly trilled *r* made behind the upper front teeth.
7. An emphatic *s* pronounced behind the upper front teeth.
8. An emphatic *d*-like sound made by pressing the entire tongue against the upper palate.
9. An emphatic *t* sound produced behind the front teeth.
10. An emphatic *th* sound, like the *th* in *this*, make behind the front teeth.
11. A distinctive Semitic sound made in the middle throat and sounding to a Western ear more like a vowel than a consonant.
12. A guttural sound made at the tope of the throat resembling the untrilled German and French *r*.
13. A hard *k* sound produced at the back of the palate.
14. This sound is like the English *h* but has more body. It is made at the very bottom of the throat and pronounced at the beginning, middle, and ends of words.

CONTENTS

FOREWORD XI
PREFACE TO THE SECOND EDITION XIII
TRANSLATOR'S INTRODUCTION XV
BRIEF BIOGRAPHY OF IMĀM AL-NAWAWĪ XX
IMĀM AL-NAWAWĪ'S INTRODUCTION 1

1 The Merit of Reciting & Bearing the Quran 5
2 The Precedence of Recitation & of Reciters 8
3 Honoring the Folk of the Quran 9
4 The Etiquette of Teachers & Students of the Quran 11
5 The Etiquette of the Bearers of the Quran 26
6 The Etiquette of Recitation 35
7 The Etiquette of All People With the Quran 96
8 Recommended Times & Circumstances for Recitation 104
9 Writing the Quran & Respecting the *Muṣḥaf* 110
10 Imām al-Nawawī's Lexicon 119
11 Concluding Remarks 131

TRANSLATOR'S NOTES 132
APPENDIX ONE: SUPPLICATIONS 148
APPENDIX TWO: VERSES OF PROSTRATION 153
APPENDIX THREE: BRIEF BIOGRAPHIES 156
BIBLIOGRAPHY 190

DETAILED TABLE OF CONTENTS 194
INDEX 200
ABOUT THE TRANSLATOR 206

FOREWORD

The translation of *Al-Tibyān fī Ādāb Ḥamalat al-Qur'ān* is a welcome and valuable contribution to the English library of great Islamic literature. Its author, Imām al-Nawawī, needs no introduction to Western Muslims, and the translator, Musa Furber, is indeed to be congratulated on his choice of this work and its felicitous rendering into English. Its publication is a long-awaited event for both traditional Islamic knowledge and the point of that knowledge, which is practice.

Allah Himself has used the word *tibyān* to describe the Holy Quran, the source of all knowledge, which He says He revealed *tibyānan li kulli shay'* or as a clarification of everything. That is, it exposits in detail the things no human being can know, not the mere physical and intellectual dimensions of man in the world, which anyone can find out, but the very context of man and his reality, the "why" of being itself, whence man came, why he exists, runs his full term, dies, and what he shall meet on the other side of the impenetrable veil of death. In the Quran, our reality itself is a sign, an *ayah,* something that points beyond itself for those who realize what it signifies, namely the *tawḥīd* or Oneness of Allah. The exposition of these facts in the form of a divine scripture, which no human being could possibly produce, makes it the Supreme Book for mankind.

The present work was designed and written to explain to men and women how best to benefit from the Book of Allah. The blessing of the Quran is that whoever recites it as it should be recited is changed by it, and brought by imperceptible degrees to see why everything is the way it is. The seed of this knowledge is a humble intention to draw nearer to the Divine, the soil in which it takes root are reverence, awe, and love, and its fruit is the certitude in the eternal truths of faith that bring felicity in this world and the next.

It is well known to everyone conversant with the Islamic disciplines that the learning of many things does not teach wisdom, and that traditional books do not reveal their secrets or bestow their benefits to those without the key to them. This key is *adab*, the "right way of doing things," rendered in the title as "etiquette," but in its comprehensiveness a perennial difficulty to translate into English. Books, especially sacred ones, give their knowledge to those of *adab*, and Westerners who know something about the sciences of Islam have been waiting for a book like this in English for a long time.

NUH HA MIM KELLER
AMMAN
10 JUNE 2003

PREFACE TO THE SECOND EDITION

In the Name of God, Most Merciful and Compassionate

This edition is *Etiquette With the Quran* includes the same contents as the first edition published by Starlatch Press in 2003. Due to negligent backups on my part, the text here had to be recovered from a manuscript that was one or two revisions before the final one printed in the first edition. While I have done my best to duplicate Starlatch's masterful editorial work and to enter in all known mistakes to the first edition, no human—save the Prophets (peace and blessings of God be upon them)—is saved from erring, and no book—save the Quran—is free from errors.

MUSA FURBER
ABU DHABI, UAE
20 RAMADAN 1433 AH
8 AUGUST 2012 CE

TRANSLATOR'S INTRODUCTION

In the Name of God, Most Merciful and Compassionate

Throughout Islamic history, a Muslim's education started with the Quran. This education consisted of the student reciting the entire Quran aloud to an instructor. Early on, the recitation would be from memory, and only later would the student read the text first and then memorize, for the norm at the beginning of Islamic educational history was for students to have the Quran recited to them and for them to memorize it that way, with their instruction entirely aural. In either case, the process takes months, even years. During this time, though, the instructor has duties to his or her students beyond the task of correcting the recitation and checking the memorization. The instructor also has the responsibility of teaching the student about the Quran itself: its history, how to carry it, how and when to recite it, and how to apply it. He also has the task of nurturing the student's spiritual and ethical growth, so that his heart and limbs are made ready to transform this knowledge into righteous deeds and spiritual ascendance. In short, the instructor is responsible for teaching his pupil the required and recommended etiquette befitting the bearers of the Quran and making him one of their honored ranks.

Scholars have written many books on what one must know about the Quran and the etiquette one must show the Book. Early works include *Akhlāq Ḥamalat al-Qur'ān* (*The Refined Character of the Bearers of the Quran*) by Imām Abū Bakr Muḥammad ibn al-Ḥusayn al-Ajūrī (d. 360 AH) and *al-Tidhkār fī Afḍal al-Adhkār* (*The Reminder of the Most Beautiful of Litanies*) by Abū 'Abdallāh Muḥammad ibn Aḥmad Faraḥ al-Qurṭubī (d. 671 AH). Earlier works tended to be quite comprehensive—often too long and detailed to benefit most readers. Seeing the need for a shorter book on the subject, Imām al-Nawawī (d. 676 AH) set out to write a condensed treatise suitable for novices and masters alike. He titled his work *al-Tibyān fī Ādāb Ḥamalat al-Qur'ān* (*An Exposition on the Etiquette of the Bearers of the Quran*). Like so many of the Imām's works, it gained universal acceptance and became the standard reference for later books of its genre. Imām al-Nawawī included an abridged version of the *Tibyān* in his book *al-Adhkār,* in a chapter titled "Reciting the Quran" ("*Kitāb Tilāwat al-Qur'ān*"). In his commentary on this chapter in *al-Adhkār*, Ibn 'Allān mentions that Shaykh Abū al-Ḥasan al-Bakrī wrote a condensed version of the *Tibyān* and that Ibn 'Imād al-Aqfaḥshī set the main points of the *Tibyān* into metered poetry. The *Tibyān* was also the basis for the 35th chapter of Imām al-Suyūṭī's encyclopedia of the Quranic sciences, *al-Itqān fī 'Ulūm al-Qur'ān* (1:359–91), and was abridged by Qāḍī Yūsuf al-Nabhānī in his 1,000 page encyclopedia on the miracles of the Prophet (God bless him and give him peace), titled *Ḥujjat Allāh 'alā'l-'Ālamīn*. In part 3, chapter 1, he says, "A glimpse of the immense merit of the glorious Quran and the merit and etiquette of its recitation, being a summary of the book *al-Tibyān fī Ādāb Ḥamalat al-Qur'ān* by the major Imām Muḥyī al-Dīn al-Nawawī in which I changed nothing except the order of presentation."

Although the *Tibyān* has been published numerous times, no one has yet produced a critical edition. In Damascus alone, at least four different editions are in print, four of which deserve mention. Shaykh 'Abd al-Qādir al-Arna'ūṭ's edition (Dār al-Bayān, 1983 CE) gives detailed references for the hadiths mentioned in the book. Bashīr Muḥammad 'Uyūn's edition (Dār al-Bayān, 2000 CE) gives more extensive references for the hadiths and adds biographical information for all but a few of the people mentioned in the book. Both of these editions made reference to manuscript number 326 in the Ẓāhiriyya Library in Damascus, a manuscript of 151 pages, scribed by Muḥammad 'Alī al-Basyūnī in 891 AH (1486 CE). Shaykh Muḥammad al-Ḥajjār's edition (Dār Ibn Ḥazam, 1996 CE) includes notes aimed at the modern reader—particularly with matters pertaining to law (*fiqh*). There is also the edition edited by 'Abd al-'Azīz 'Izz al-Dīn al-Sayrawān (Beirut: Dār al-Nafā'is, 1992 (3rd printing).

Introduction to the Translation

There are a few things the reader should know in order to derive the greatest benefit from the *Tibyān*. This book is the work of a polymath. Imām al-Nawawī's mastery of transmitted sources shows in his numerous citations of Quranic verses, prophetic hadiths, and narrations from Companions, Successors (*Tābi'ūn*), and the Righteous Forebears (*Salaf*) after them. His encyclopedic mastery of *fiqh* and jurisprudence is manifest in his handling of rulings from his own legal school (*madhhab*) and other *madhhab*s that are still extant or now extinct. His mastery of biographies, geography, and Arabic philology are also demonstrated throughout the text, particularly in the final chapter of the book.

A good portion of the *Tibyān* is devoted to *fiqh,* that is, to legal rulings. For most issues, the Imām gives the various scholarly opinions, the evidence for each, and then supports the strongest opinion. As an aid to Ḥanafī readers, I have included references to works of their school for further study pertaining to some topics raised in this book. While the individual rulings are of particular importance to Shafi'īs, there are still vital lessons for us all. Imām al-Nawawī does not promote his *madhhab,* the Shāfi'ī school, at the expense of others. He does not intentionally weaken other opinions so as to gain victory for his own. The Imām, a scrupulous scholar of the highest order, does not treat this casually, which, in and of itself, is a vital lesson in *fiqh*.

Section titles are sparse in short Arabic texts, especially those like the *Tibyān* which were intended to be memorized. To serve the needs of English readers, I have added section titles to make the text more accessible and easier to follow.

Even though the *Tibyān* is for laymen, its language, style, and concepts may be foreign to many English readers. Much of this is remedied through translation, though explanatory notes are necessary in a few cases.

Imām al-Nawawī quotes at least 115 individual prophetic hadiths. I have documented the sources of each, most of which is adapted from Bashīr Muḥammad 'Uyūn's edition of the *Tibyān*. No effort has been made to judge the hadiths since Imām al-Nawawī was himself qualified to do this, and he clearly defines his scholarly parameters for the transmitted evidence he includes. In short, his inclusion of a hadith indicates that he judged it to be sound enough for citation, whether it be for *fiqhī* rulings or morals and merits.

The Imām mentions some two hundred individuals. I added an appendix with brief biographies for all but a few of the people mentioned. The biographies come in alphabetical order (*Al-* and *'ayn* are ignored). There are many cross-references since individuals are referred to in many ways. Whenever a name is preceded by an agnomen ("Abū..."), the biography comes under the name—not the agnomen.

The last chapter of the *Tibyān* is Imām al-Nawawī's lexicon of problematic names and places, organized in the order of their appearance in the text. Translation, transliteration, and biographies have rendered superfluous the lexicon and similar material mentioned elsewhere in the text. It was my decision nonetheless to keep this material intact. While the content itself may now be of minor utility, its inclusion, at the very least, demonstrates the meticulous care that scholars took to be sure that everything was as clear as possible without ambiguity or potential for misinterpretation.

For the initial translation, I used Shaykh 'Abd al-Qādir al-Arna'ūṭ's edition. I compared later drafts to Bashīr Muḥammad 'Uyūn's edition. The hadith references and biographies are largely adapted from this latter edition.

On a personal note, this is my first published translation and I admit that in the art of translation I am a novice. Where I have succeeded, it is only through the blessing and grace of God; and where I have faltered it is from my own shortcomings. If the reader finds mistakes, I would like to know about them and correct them for future editions, and I hope that he or she bears in mind that it is noble to overlook the weak when they falter, and that good deeds cancel out the bad. So here presented is the translation of the entire text of *Tibyān,* with the exception of two paragraphs I chose to abridge.

The people who helped me with this project are too numerous to mention. I owe a great debt for the help I received from students further along in their studies, especially Hedaya, Omar, Talal, Zahir, Zaid, and M. Afifi for help with the manuscript. I especially owe much to my wife and children for their constant support. This project would be markedly different without the aid of two individuals: Shaykh Nuh Keller, who suggested translating the *Tibyān* in 1999 and allowed me to benefit from his experience; also Gibril Haddad, who helped with two thorough revisions of the work, added notes to my biographies, and provided the material for Imām al-Nawawī's biography.

May God reward Imām al-Nawawī and the people he mentioned in the *Tibyān.* And may God make us worthy of being among the honored bearers of the Quran.

MUSA FURBER
DAMASCUS
MARCH 30, 2003

BRIEF BIOGRAPHY OF IMĀM AL-NAWAWĪ

Yaḥyā ibn Sharaf, Muḥyī al-Dīn Abū Zakariyyā al-Nawawi[1] (631–676 AH) the pious, ascetic, most learned, scrupulously Godwary, accomplished jurisprudent and hadith master, the impeccable Shaykh al-Islām by the unanimity of the people of the Sunna of the Prophet (Allah bless him and give him peace), fearless before kings, lordly and chaste, who died young yet, in a short life of 45 years, produced works of learning that made him the principal authority in the later Shāfiʿī school. He is the "the standard-bearer of the Friends of God" (al-Dhahabī); and he himself said, "God has blessed me in the right use of my time," in reference to Imām al-Nawawī's remarkable scholarly output and achievements. Imām al-Nawawī is named after his hometown of Nawa near Damacsus. He is "the Spiritual Pole of the noble Friends of God, the Legist of Humankind, the Reviver of the Sunna and the Slayer of Innovation" (al-Sakhāwī). May God bestow great and endless mercy on him, bless him, and reward him on behalf of every Muslim!

Early Education and Teachers

Imām al-Nawawī came to Damscus in 649 and lived in the Madrasa al-Rawwāḥiyya. In four and a half months, he memorized Abū Isḥāq al-Shīrāzī's manual of Shāfiʿī *fiqh* entitled *al-Tanbīh* and a quarter of Abū Isḥāq ibn Aḥmad *al-Muhadhdhab fī'l-Madhhab* with his shaykh Isḥāq ibn Aḥmad al-Maghribī, after which he went on the Pilgrimage with his father—ailing during most of the trip—and took up residence in Madinah for a month and a half and then returned to Damascus.

In his early studies, the Imām said, "It occurred to me to study medicine, so I bought the *Qānūn* of Ibn Sīnā, whereupon darkness filled my heart and I remained unable to work for several days. Then I came to my senses and sold the *Qānūn*, after which light filled my heart." Shaykh 'Abd al-Fattāḥ Abū Ghudda commented: "In this way does God Most High create in souls attraction for one type of knowledge and aversion to another, proficiency in one, and deficiency in another; and in this there are great examples of wisdom, both hidden and manifest."[2]

Imām al-Nawawī's teacher include: al-Raḍī ibn al-Dahhān; Shaykh al-Shuyūkh 'Abd al-'Azīz ibn Muḥammad al-Anṣārī; Zayn al-Dīn ibn 'Abd al-Dā'im; 'Imād al-Dīn 'Abd al-Karīm ibn al-Harastānī; Zayn al-Dīn Khālid ibn Yūsuf; Taqī al-Dīn ibn Abī al-Yusr; Jamāl al-Dīn ibn al-Ṣayrfī; and Shams al-Dīn ibn Abī 'Umar. With Abū Isḥāq Ibrāhīm ibn 'Īsā al-Murādī, Imām al-Nawawī studied al-Bukharī's and Muslim's compendiums of sound (*ṣaḥīḥ*) hadiths; with al-Taflīsī, he studied jurisprudence (*uṣūl*); with Aḥmad al-Miṣrī he studied grammar; and with Imām Ibn Mālik, the author of the *Alfiyya*, he studied the finer aspects of Arabic language.

Curriculum and Daily Schedule

Al-Nawawī's student 'Alā al-Dīn Abū al-Ḥasan Ibn al-'Aṭṭār said that the Imām every day read before his shaykhs the following: two sessions in Imām al-Ghazalī's *al-Waṣīṭ*; one in Abū Isḥāq's *al-Muhadhdhab* (both in Shāfi'ī jurisprudence); one in Ibn al-Ginnī's *al-Luma'* in grammar; one in *al-Jam' bayn al-Ṣaḥīḥayn* in hadith;[3] one in *Ṣaḥīḥ Muslim*; one in Abū Isḥāq's *al-Luma'* and al-Fakhr al-Rāzī's *al-Muntakhab* in the principles of jurisprudence; one in Ibn al-Sikkīt's *Iṣlāḥ al-Manṭiq* in philology; one in morphology; one in the principles of jurisprudence; one in hadith narrator-criticism; and one in Islamic doctrine.

Imām al-Nawawī's students include: the orator Ṣadr al-Dīn Sulaymān al-Ja'farī; Shihāb al-Dīn al-Irbidī; Ibn Abī al-Fatḥ; and the hadith master Imām al-Mizzī.

During his period of study, the Imām said that he spent six years during which he wasted absolutely no time, whether day or night. He was completely devoted to his studies, even when walking in the street. Only after this did he begin writing and teaching.

His Asceticism and Extremely Simple Living

Imām al-Nawawī was a strict ascetic in the manner of the early Muslims, neither eating nor sleeping except out of necessity. He fasted continually throughout the year, eating a simple dish at nightfall and drinking some water before dawn. This he did once every twenty-four hours. He avoided moist foods, such as fruits and cucumber, in order not to induce drowsiness. He dressed austerely, owning only one long shirt and a small turban. He divided his time between worship and learning.

Asked why he never allowed himself to eat food grown in Damascus, he said: "Damascus abounds in endowments [*awqāf*] and properties restricted to those under legal guardianship, and to make use of them is impermissible except in the most appropriate and beneficial manner. In addition, the normal procedure in Damascus is to use one-crop sharecropping contracts, and there is disagreement [among the legists] about it [being lawful]: how then can I rest happy eating from this?"

His Superlative Mastership in Hadith and Jurisprudence

"In addition to his perseverance in the struggle against the ego, his application in scrupulous Godfearingness, watchfulness over his soul, the purification of the soul from its defects, and its discipline, he was also an accomplished master in hadith and its sciences, its narrators, the authentic and the defective, and a foremost authority in the [Shāfi'ī] school." A recent study shows that Imām al-Nawawī's verdict on narrator-commendation and generally identical to those of Imām Ibn Ḥajar al-'Asqalānī, a remarkable assessment in view of Ibn Ḥajar's position as the greatest of all the hadith masters after the luminaries of the early centuries.[4]

His Fearless Admonishing of Princes

Imām al-Nawawī used to address those in power and admonish them for the sake of God, in accordance with the obligation of "admonishing [*naṣīḥa*] princes" which he himself defined: "Admonishing the leaders of the Muslims consists in ... appraising them of any remiss of which they are unaware concerning the rights of Muslims." He did this several times in the palace of al-Mālik al-Ẓāhir who once exclaimed: "I am frightened of him!"

Headmastership of Dār al-Ḥadīth al-Ashrafiyya in Damascus

He took up the headmastership of Dār al-Ḥadīth al-Ashrafiyya in Damascus after the death of his Shaykh Abū Shāma in 665 AH and held it until his own death eleven years later, never accepting any compensation for his needs.

In the time of Imām al-Nawawī, Dār al-Ḥadīth had the Noble Sandal of the Prophet (God bless him and give him peace) in its possession. The Sandal was kept in a wooden box above the *Miḥrāb* in its mosque. The mosque, however, was burnt by the Tatars and the relic disappeared, but the *Miḥrāb* remains to this day in the mosque of Dār al-Ḥadīth's preparatory school (headed by Shaykh Abū al-Khayr al-Mīdānī), near the Umawī Mosque in Damascus.

Select Bibliography of Shaykh al-Islām

In his brief but blessed life, Imām al-Nawawī authored nearly fifty books. These volumes are—like their author—among the treasures of Islam and contain an immense blessing (*baraka*) bestowed by God. They are characterized by great diligence and scholarship. They are among the most relied-upon works of Islamic law and hadith in Islam. Some of them are listed below: *Al-Arbaʿūna Ḥadīth* (*The Forty Hadiths*) is the most widely read collection of its kinds, in which the Imām chose forty of the most important hadith that pertain to the spiritual and social life of the

Muslims. It is a mark of divine approval of Imām al-Nawawī that God Most High has made him famous through this small booklet, as the *Arba'ūn* has been blessed for seven hundred years with unreserved approval and acceptance among Muslims worldwide. *Riyāḍ al-Ṣāliḥīn* (*Garden of the Righteous*), one of the most widely read anthologies of the prophetic traditions focusing on personal ethics. It is comprised of 372 chapters spread over nineteen books, each chapter citing the verses of Quran and authentic hadiths that pertain to the subject at hand. The Imām finished compiling the work in mid-Ramadan of 670 AH.

Al-Adhkār al-Muntakhaba min Kalām Sayyid al-Abrār (*Supplications Chosen from the Discourse of the Master of the Pious*) is a model in the genre unequaled by any similar work. It contains 349 chapters treating every situation Muslims face in their private and public life and adducing the supplication appropriate to each as related from the Prophet (God bless him and give him peace), with sound, fair, or weak chains of transmission. Imām Ibn Ḥajar al-'Asqalānī held six hundred and sixty classes devoted to the documentation of the *Adhkār*, some of which was recently published in three volumes. Imām Ibn 'Allān al-Ṣiddiqī wrote a nine-volume commentary on the *Adhkār*, titled *al-Futūḥāt al-Rabbāniyya 'ala'l-Adhkār al-Nawawiyya*.

Sharḥ Ṣaḥīḥ Muslim ranks among the great masterpieces of Muslim literature. The Imām titled it *al-Minhāj fī Sharḥ Ṣaḥīḥ Muslim ibn al-Ḥajjāj* (*The Method: A Commentary on Ṣaḥīḥ Muslim ibn al-Ḥajjāj*). The work is built on previous scholarship by the Mālikī scholars al-Qāḍī 'Iyāḍ and al-Māzarī. It numbers about twenty volumes in print.

Al-Tarkhīṣ fi'l-Ikrām bi'l-Qiyām li Dhawī al-Faḍli wa'l-Maziyyati min AHl'l-Islām 'alā Jihati al-Birri wa'l-Taqwīri wa'l-Iḥtirām lā 'alā Jihati al-Riyā'i wa'l-I'ẓām (*The Permissibility of Dignifying by Standing for Those Who Possess Excellence and Distinction Among the People of Islam: In the Spirit of Piousness, Reverence, and Respect, Not in the Spirit of Display and Aggrandizement*).[5]

Wird al-Imām al-Nawawī is the Imām's daily devotional supplications and invocations.

Bustān al-ʿĀrifīn fī'l-Zuhr wa'l-Taṣawwuf (*The Garden of the Knowers in Asceticism and Self-Purification*) is a slim compendium of narrations which Imām al-Nawawī did not complete.

Irshād Ṭullāb al-Ḥaqā'iq ilā Maʿrifat Sunan Khayr al-Khalā'iq (*Guiding Seekers of Truths to Knowing the Ways of the Best of All Creation*), known simply as *al-Irshād*, is Imām al-Nawawī's concise abridgment of Ibn al-Ṣalāḥ's *Muqaddima fī ʿUlūm al-Ḥadīth*, which he then condensed in the shorter *al-Taqrīb wa'l-Taysīr li Maʿrifat Sunan al-Bashīr al-Nadhīr* (*Access and Facility to Knowing the Ways of the Bearer of Glad Tidings and Warner*). *Taqrīb* received an illustrious commentary by Imām al-Suyūṭī in two volumes, *Tadrīb al-Rāwī*.

Al-Majmūʿ Sharḥ al-Muhadhdhab (*The Compendium: Commentary of the Muhadhdhab*) is al-Nawawī's unfinished magnum opus of Shāfiʿī *fiqh*. Ibn Kathīr said: "I do not know in all the books of *fiqh* any that excels it."[6] (The Imām died—God have mercy on him and grant him Paradise!)—when he reached the chapters on usury, the Shaykh al-Islām al-Subkī continued the work, which grew to about eighteen volumes.)

Rawḍat al-Ṭālibīn (*The Seeker's Garden*), a medium-sized reference manual in Shāfiʿī *fiqh*, and the smaller *Minhāj al-Ṭālibīn* (*The Seeker's Road*) are, respectively, abridgments of Imām al-Rāfʿī's *Sharḥ al-Wajīz* (also known as *Sharḥ al-Kabīr*) and *al-Muḥarrar*.

Al-Iḍāh fī Manāsik al-Ḥajj (*Elucidation of the Rites of the Pilgrimage*) is a detailed explanation of the rites of Pilgrimage according to the Shāfiʿī school, one of four such manuals he wrote and which he epitomized in *al-Ijāz fī Manāsik al-Ḥajj*.

Al-Manthūrāt fī'l-Fiqh, better known as his *Fatāwā*, is a single volume collected and published by his student Ibn al-ʿAṭṭār.

Tahdhīb al-Asmā' wa'l-Lughāt (*Precise Rendition of Names and Dialects*) is a four-volume reference manual containing a biography of the Prophet (God bless him and give him peace) and brief biographies of some of the figures of the first three Islamic centuries and the four principal Imāms of the schools of Sacred Law. It also includes geographical and lexical information. It is more extensive than what is included in the last chapter of the *Tibyān*.[7]

Imām al-Nawawī's Death

Returning to Nawā from a trip to Jerusalem and Hebron, the Imām and Friend of God died in his father's house after a short illness. Al-Dhahabī said, "His grave in Nawā is a place of visitation," and the late Mufti of Lebanon, Shaykh Ḥasan Khālid, said, "God Most High responds to supplication at the grave of Imām al-Nawawī." Al-Dhahabī's shaykh, Ibn Faraḥ, said, "Shaykh Muḥyī al-Dīn reached three high stations, each of which would suffice to make its possessor someone people would travel to see: knowledge, asceticism, and command good and forbidding evil." In truth, for these three reasons and more, Imām al-Nawawī is most deserving of the title of Great Master (*al-Shaykh al-Akbar*) and Authority of Islam (*Shaykh al-Islām*).

(This brief biography has been abridged and reworked from *The Righteous Life and Words of the Pious Sheikh al-Islām: Imām Muḥyī al-Dīn Yaḥyā ibn Sharaf al-Nawawī*, by G. F. Haddad. His main sources were: al-Dhahabī, *Ṭabaqāt al-Ḥuffāẓ* (4:1470–74); Ibn al-Subkī, *Ṭabaqāt al-Shāfiʿīyya al-Kubrā* (8:395–400 #1288); and Ibn Qāḍī Shuhba, *Ṭabaqāt al-Shāfiʿīyyah* (3:9–13 #454).)

Notes to the Biography

1. Pronounced both *Nawawī* and *Nawāwi*, the latter after his native town of Nawā, the former according to the autograph spelling of his name.
2. ʿAbd al-Fattāḥ Abū Ghudda, *al-ʿUlamāʾ al-ʿUzzāb*. p. 147.
3. Abū ʿAbdullāh al-Ḥumaydī al-Andalūsī's (d. 488 AH) *al-Jamʿ bayn al-Ṣaḥīḥayn*. There is also Ibn al-Qaysarānī's (d. 507 AH) *al-Jamʿ bayn Rijāl al-Ṣaḥīḥayn*.
4. See Ḥusayn Ismāʿīl al-Jamāl's introduction to al-Nawawī's *Khulaṣat al-Aḥkām fī Muhimmāt al-Sunan wa Qawāʿid al-Islām*, 2 vols. (Beirut: Muʾassasa al-Risāla, 1997).
5. *Al-Tarkhīṣ*, edited by Kīlānī Muḥammad Khalīfa (Beirut: Dār al-Bashāʾir al-Islāmiyya, 1988). See Gibril Haddad's extensive transla-

tions from al-Nawawī's *Tarkhīṣ* and his *Sharḥ Ṣaḥīḥ Muslim* together with Ibn al-Ḥājj's objections to *al-Tarkhīṣ*, in the *Encyclopedia of Islamic Doctrine* (5:33–41). See also, in this issue, chapter 26 on standing out of respect in al-Bayhaqī's *al-Madkhal ilā al-Sunan*.

6. Ibn Kathīr, *al-Bidāya wa'l-Nihāya*, 13:279.
7. *Tahdhīb al-Asmā' wa'l-Lughāt* (Cairo: Idārat al-Ṭibā'at al-Munīriyya, 1927).

IMĀM AL-NAWAWĪ'S INTRODUCTION

The shaykh, legist, and knowledgeable Imām, the scrupulous ascetic, the precise and skillful, Abū Zakariyyā Yaḥyā Muḥyī al-Dīn ibn Sharaf ibn Ḥazām al-Ḥazamī al-Nawawī (God Most High have mercy upon him) said:

Praise be to God, the Noble Benefactor, Possessor of Infinite Power, Superiority, and Perfection, who guided us to belief and who has made our religion superior to all the rest. He graced us by sending us the one most noble unto Him, the most superior of His creation, His beloved and intimate Friend, His servant and Messenger, Muḥammad (God bless him and grant him peace), through whom He effaced idol-worship. He honored him with the miraculous Quran which endures the passing of time. With it He challenges humankind and jinn in their entirety; and with it He silences the misguiders and transgressors. He made it a comfort for the hearts of the insightful and perceptive. It does not wear out with frequent repetition and the changing of time. He made it easy to remember so that even young children may memorize it. He guaranteed its protection from being compromised by alterations and accidents. And it is indeed protected—by the praise of God and His exaltedness—for so long as night and day endure. He made it well suited for the cultivation of His sciences for the ones whom He chooses to have skill and mastery, and He gathered therein from every discipline that which opens the hearts of those who have certainty.

I praise Him for this and for His other innumerable graces, especially for the grace of belief. I ask Him for the generous bestowal of [His] good favor for myself, all my loved ones, and all other Muslims. I testify that there is no deity other than God, One without partner: a testimony which attains forgiveness, saves from the Fire anyone who testifies it, and brings one to reside in Paradise.

I testify that Muḥammad is His servant and Messenger, the caller to belief. God bless him and give him peace—and his Folk and Companions—and honor, ennoble, and extol them until the end of time.

To commence:

God, Sublime and Most High, has graced this nation (God Most High increase it and its people in honor) with the religion that He has chosen, the religion of Islam.[1] He has graced them by sending Muḥammad, the best of His creation, may the most eminent of blessings, bounties, and peace be conferred upon him. And He honored them with His Book, the best of all speech. God, Sublime and Most High, gathered in it all that is needed; it includes stories of the first people and the last, spiritual counsel, similitudes, etiquette, and rulings of all types. And it includes clear, sure proofs indicating His absolute unity, and other things that His messengers (God bless them and give them peace) brought: irrefutable arguments against the followers of ignoble heresies. He multiplied the reward for reciting it; ordered us to heed it and give it veneration, to adhere to it through proper conduct, and to spend generously in honoring it.

Groups of the exemplary and outstanding [scholars] have written about the excellence of reciting the Quran—books known to people of reason and discernment. But the resolve to memorize—even peruse—these books has waned so no one benefits from them, except for some exceptionally intelligent individuals.

Reasons for Writing the Book and Its Structure

I have seen the people of our land, Damascus (God Most High protect and preserve it, and all other lands of Islam), concentrating on reciting the Mighty Quran: studying, instructing, reading, and learning—in groups and individually. They spend enormous effort in this—day and night (God increase their desire for it and for all kinds of obedience), desiring thereby the pleasure of God, the Possessor of Majesty and Honor.

This called me to put together a concise treatise concerning the proper etiquette to be observed by the bearers of the Quran, and the characteristics of its memorizers and students. This is because God Most High has prescribed showing good will towards His Book, which includes illuminating the proper conduct of its bearers and students, instructing them therein, and calling their attention to it. I favor brevity and am wary of prolixity. I limit each chapter to one subject of etiquette; and for each subject, I point to a number of its categories. Most of what I mention proceeds by omitting chains of transmission—even though I have the chains of transmission readily present and have the authorization to transmit them. But my goal is to call attention to its source. And what I mention alludes to what I omitted. The reason for preferring brevity is my desire that it be memorized and that it be fully useful and disseminated. I singled out unfamiliar vocabulary and diction that occur in the chapters [and provided] a clear summarized explanation and voweling, which I have placed at the end of the book in the order of their occurrence in the chapters. The purpose of this is to complete the book's benefit to its possessor and to remove doubt from its seeker. Included within the chapters themselves are groups of principles and invaluable lessons. [See IMĀM AL-NAWAWĪ'S LEXICON at the end of the translation.]

Using Weakly Authenticated Hadiths

I clarify the strongly and weakly authenticated hadiths, and ascribe each to whichever Imām related it. In some circumstances, they have overlooked hadiths, though this is rare. Know that the scholars of hadith and others permit working with weakly authenticated hadiths concerning the merits of actions. In spite of this, I restrict myself to those that are rigorously authenticated and do not mention the weakly authenticated ones except in a few circumstances.

My trust and reliance is upon God Most Noble and to Him is my unbridled resignation and upon Him is my utter dependence. I ask Him that I travel the path of guidance, for protection from the people of heresy and insolence, and that I constantly be upon this and other good things with continual increase. I humbly beseech God Most Sublime that He grant me good deeds that I may gain His pleasure; that He make me among those who fear Him and properly observe His rights; that He guide me to perfect intentions; that He facilitate for me all types of good; that He assist me in all excellent qualities; that He keep me steadfast in this until death; and that He does all of this for all of my loved ones and all other Muslims—male and female. He is our sufficiency and the best reliance. And there is no power and strength except by God, the High, Most Great.

I

THE MERIT OF RECITING AND BEARING THE QURAN

God, Mighty and Majestic, says: *Those who read the Book of God, and establish Prayer, and spend, secretly and openly, from that which He has bestowed on them, they look forward to imperishable gain, so that He will fully recompense them their wages and increase them of His grace. Indeed, He is all-forgiving, thankful* (Quran, 35:29–30).

We relate that ʿUthmān ibn ʿAffān (God be pleased with him) stated that the Messenger of God (God bless him and grant him peace) said, "The best among you is one who learns the Quran and teaches it."[1] (Abū ʿAbdallāh Muḥammad ibn Ismāʿīl ibn Ibrāhīm al-Bukhārī related it in his *Ṣaḥīḥ*, which is the most authentic book after the Quran.)

ʿĀʾisha (God be pleased with her) stated that the Messenger of God (God bless him and grant him peace) said, "The one who recites the Quran and is skillful therein will be with the obedient, noble, recording angels; and the one who reads the Quran stammering, it being difficult for him, has two rewards."[2] (Bukhārī and Abū al-Ḥusayn Muslim ibn al-Ḥajjāj ibn Muslim al-Qushayrī al-Nīsābūrī related it in their *Ṣaḥīḥayn*.[3])

Abū Mūsā al-Ashʿarī (God be pleased with him) stated that the Messenger of God (God bless him and grant him peace) said, "The likeness of a believer who recites the Quran is like that of a citron: its scent is fragrant and its taste delicious. The likeness of a believer who does not recite the Quran is like that of a date: it has no fragrance and its taste is delicious. The likeness of a hypocrite who recites the Quran is like a water lily: its scent is fragrant and its taste is bitter. And the likeness of a hypocrite who does not recite the Quran is like a bitter colocynth: it is scentless and its taste is bitter."[4] (Bukhārī and Muslim related it.)

'Umar ibn al-Khaṭṭāb (God be pleased with him) stated that the Prophet (God bless him and grant him peace) said, "God Most High exalts some groups with this Book, and debases others."[5] (Muslim related it.)

Abū Umāma al-Bāhilī (God be pleased with him) said, "I heard the Messenger of God (God bless him and grant him peace) say, 'Recite the Quran, for on the Day of Judgment it will come to intercede for its companion.'"[6] (Muslim related it.)

Ibn 'Umar (God be pleased with them both) stated that the Prophet (God bless him and grant him peace) said, "There is no envy except concerning two: a person to whom God has given the Quran and he conforms with it night and day; and a person to whom God has given wealth from which he spends [charitably] night and day."[7] (Bukhārī and Muslim related it. We also relate it from 'Abdallāh ibn Mas'ūd (God be pleased with him) but with the phrase: "There is no envy except concerning two: a person to whom God has given wealth and he expended it all for the sake of God, and a person to whom God has given wisdom and he judges according to it and teaches it."[8])

'Abdallāh ibn Mas'ūd (God be pleased with him) stated that the Messenger of God (God bless him and grant him peace) said, "Whoever recites one letter from the Book of God has one reward, and rewards are [multiplied] by ten of their kind. I do not say that '*Alif Lām Mīm*' is a [single] letter, rather '*Alif*' is a letter, '*Lām*' is a letter, and '*Mīm*' is a letter.'"[9] (Abū 'Īsā Muḥammad ibn 'Īsā al-Tirmidhī related it and said that it is a well-rigorously authenticated [*ḥasan ṣaḥīḥ*] hadith.[10])

Abū Sa'īd al-Khudrī (God be pleased with him) stated that the Prophet (God bless him and grant him peace) said, "God, Sublime and Most High, says, 'Whomever the Quran and My remembrance preoccupy him from beseeching Me, I give [him] the best of what the beseechers are given. The superiority of the Word of God, Sublime and Most High, over all others is like the superiority of God Most High over His creation.'"[11] (Tirmidhī related it and said that it is a well-authenticated hadith.)

Ibn 'Abbās (God be well pleased with him and his father) stated that the Messenger of God (God bless him and grant him peace) said, "Someone without Quran in his heart is like a ruined house."[12] (Tirmidhī related it and said it was a well-rigorously authenticated hadith.)

'Abdallāh ibn 'Amr ibn al-'Āṣ (God be pleased with them both) stated that the Prophet (God bless him and grant him peace) said, "To the person with the Quran, it is said, 'Recite and ascend! Recite measuredly just as you used to recite in the world! Your station will be at the last verse you recite.'"[13] (Abū Dāwūd, Tirmidhī, and Nasā'ī related it; Tirmidhī said that it is a well-rigorously authenticated hadith.)

Mu'ādh ibn Anas (God be pleased with him) stated that the Messenger of God (God bless him and grant him peace) said, "Whoever recites the Quran and acts according to what it contains, God will adorn his parents with a crown on the Day of Judgment, its radiance more beautiful than the radiance of the sun in the abode of this world. So what do you presume [the reward will be] for the one who acts according to it?"[14] (Abū Dāwūd related it.)

Al-Dārimī related with his chain of transmitters that 'Abdallāh ibn Mas'ūd (God be pleased with him) stated that the Prophet (God bless him and grant him peace) said, "Recite the Quran, since God Most High will not chastise a heart that has memorized the Quran. This Quran is the banquet of God: whoever enters it is safe and whoever loves the Quran rejoices."[15]

'Abd al-Ḥamīd al-Ḥammānī said, "I asked Sufyān al-Thawrī about a man who engages in battles: Is that more beloved to you or that he recite the Quran? He answered, 'That he recite the Quran because the Prophet (God bless him and grant him peace) said, "The best among you is one who learns the Quran and teaches it."'"[16]

2

THE PRECEDENCE OF RECITATION AND OF RECITERS OVER OTHERS

It is established that Abū Mas'ūd al-Anṣārī al-Badrī (God be pleased with him) stated that the Messenger of God (God bless him and grant him peace) said, "Whosoever is the best in reciting the Book of God Most High[1] should lead the people [in Prayer]."[2] Ibn 'Abbās (God be pleased with them both) said, "The reciters were the companions of the assembly of 'Umar (God be pleased with him) and his council, whether middle-aged or young."[3] (Related in Bukhārī's *Ṣaḥīḥ*.) [Some] hadiths included in this chapter will be related in the next.

Know that the soundest position, the one followed by the scholars, who themselves are relied upon, is that reciting the Quran is superior to saying, "*Subḥān Allāh*" ["Sublime and Perfect is God"], "*Lā ilāha illa' Allāh*" ["There is no deity except God"], and other litanies. The evidence for this has been shown.

And God knows best.[4]

3

HONORING THE FOLK OF THE QURAN AND THE PROHIBITION OF ANNOYING THEM

God Most High says, *And he who reveres the rites of God, it is from Godfearingness in the heart* (Quran, 22:32); *and He who reveres what God has deemed sacred, that is better for him with his Lord* (Quran, 22:30); *And lower your wing [in kindness] to those believers who follow you* (Quran, 26:215); *And those who malign believing men and believing women undeservedly, they bear the guilt of slander and manifest sin* (Quran, 33:58).

This chapter includes the hadiths of Abū Mas'ūd al-Anṣārī (God be pleased with him) and Ibn 'Abbās (God be pleased with him) that preceded in the second chapter.

Abū Mūsā al-Ash'arī (God be pleased with him) stated that the Prophet (God bless him and grant him peace) said, "Exalting God Most High includes giving honor to the gray-haired Muslim, to whomever bears the Quran without exceeding its proper bounds or shunning it, and any person of authority who acts justly."[1] (Abū Dāwūd related it. It is a well-authenticated [*ḥasan*] hadith.)

'Ā'isha (God be pleased with her) said, "The Messenger of God (God bless him and grant him peace) ordered us to treat people according to their due station."[2] (Abū Dāwūd related it in his *Sunan*, and al-Bazzār related it in his *Musnad*. Al-Ḥākim—Abū 'Abdallāh—said in *'Ulūm al-Ḥadīth* that it is a rigorously authenticated hadith.[3])

Jābir ibn 'Abdallāh (God be pleased with them both) said that the Prophet (God bless him and grant him peace) would gather two casualties from Uḥud and then say, "Which of the two [deceased] has amassed the most Quran?" If one of them was indicated, he would put him first in the *laḥd* [the portion of the gravesite closest to the *qibla*]."[4] (Bukhārī related it.)

Abū Hurayra (God be pleased with him) stated that the Prophet (God bless him and grant him peace) said, "Indeed, God Mighty and Glorious says, 'Whoever shows enmity to a friend of mine, I have declared war upon him.'"[5] (Bukhārī related it.) It is established in the *Ṣaḥīḥayn* that the Prophet (God bless him and grant him peace) said, "Whoever prays the Morning Prayer is under the guardianship of God Most High, and God Most High does not demand of you something that is under His guardianship."[6]

The two venerable shaykhs, Abū Ḥanīfa and al-Shāfiʿī (God Most High have mercy upon them both), said, "If the scholars are not the Friends [*Awliyā'*] of God, then God has no Friends."

The Imām, the hadith master, Abū al-Qāsim ibn ʿAsākir (God have mercy upon him) said, "Know, my brother (and may God make you and us suitable for His pleasure, make us among those who fear Him and observe His duty with right observance) that the flesh of scholars is a poison, and God's custom with those who disparage them is well known: whoever utters defamation regarding the scholars with his tongue, God Most High afflicts him before his death with the death of his heart. *And let those who go against His command beware lest an affliction befall the more painful torment* (Quran, 24:63)."

4

THE ETIQUETTE OF TEACHERS AND STUDENTS OF THE QURAN

This chapter, combined with the two that follow, is essentially the aim of this book itself. It is quite long and wide ranging. I do, however, concisely point out its objectives in sections, facilitating its memorization and accuracy, if God Most High wills.

The Intention of the Bearers of the Quran

First, the teacher and the reciter should engage in the recitation [of the Quran] for the purpose of gaining the pleasure of God Most High. God Most High says, *And they were ordered no more than to worship God sincerely, keeping religion pure for Him, being upright, to establish the Prayer, and to give obligatory charity. And that is the worthy religion* (Quran, 98:5), ["worthy religion" here] meaning the undeviating creed.

It is related in the *Ṣaḥīḥayn* that the Messenger of God (God bless him and grant him peace) said, "Actions are only [valued] according to their intentions, and each person has only what he has intended."[1] This hadith is one of the foundations of Islam.[2] We relate that Ibn 'Abbās (God be pleased with them both) said, "A man is protected only to the degree of his intention." Another [has said], "People are only given to the degree of their intentions."

We relate that the master Abū al-Qāsim al-Qushayrī (God Most High grant him mercy) said, "Sincerity is to single out the Real [God] in obedience with full intention: meaning, through obedience, [a worshipper] desires only to draw near to God Most High—nothing else: not ostentation for the sake of others, gaining praise with people, loving praise from them, or something else that shows [an objective] other than drawing closer to God Most High." He said, "It is correct to say that *sincerity* is purifying the action from being observed by people."

Ḥudhayfa al-Mar'ashī (God Most High grant him mercy) said, "Sincerity is the worshiper's actions being identical in what is manifest and what is hidden."

Dhū'l-Nūn (God Most High grant him mercy) said, "Three signs of sincerity are when praise and censure from the masses are equal; forgetting to see your involvement in deeds; and wanting reward for one's action in the Hereafter."

Al-Fuḍyl ibn 'Iyāḍ (God be pleased with him) said, "Leaving an action for the sake of others is showing off. Acting for the sake of others is [a kind of] idolatry. Sincerity is God protecting you from the two."

Sahl al-Tustarī (God Most High grant him mercy) said, "The astute have looked into the meaning of *sincerity* and have found none other than this: that one's motion and stillness, in what is secret and what is public, be solely for God Most High. He mixes nothing with it: not ego nor whim—nothing of this world."

Al-Sarī (God grant him mercy) said, "Do not do anything for the sake of others, and do not abandon anything for their sake. Do not cover anything for them, and do not reveal anything for them." Al-Qushayrī said, "The most superior truthfulness is when the secret and public are equal."

Al-Ḥārith al-Muḥāsibī (God grant him mercy) said, "The truthful one is he who has no concern if the estimation people have for him were to depart from their hearts—so as to maintain the soundness of his own heart. He does not like people inspecting an atom's weight of his excellent actions; but he does not mind people inspecting his evil deeds. If he were to dislike the latter, this would indicate that he loves greater esteem on their part, and this is not the proper behavior of the truthful and trusting saints [*ṣiddiqīn*]." Another said, "If you seek God Most High through truthfulness, He would give you a mirror by which you could see every wonder of this world and the next."

The sayings of the Righteous Forebears [*Salaf*] concerning this are many. We have referred to some of them so as to point out the objective here. I have mentioned most of them with their commentary in the beginning of [the book] *Sharḥ al-Muhadhdhab,* in addition to some of the etiquette of the teacher and the student, and the legist and his student, which no student of knowledge can do without.

And God knows best.

Not Seeking a Worldly Objective

The teacher must not make his intentions [to teach] for the purpose of attaining some worldly objective, such as wealth, leadership, influence, rising above his peers, gaining people's praise, or drawing their attention to himself. One does not dishonor his teaching of [the Quran] by hoping to obtain some favor—by way of an [influential] student who recites to him—whether the favor is in the form of property or some service, however small, or even a gift that he would not have received had it not been for [his] student reciting to him.

God Most High says, *Whoever seeks the harvest of the Hereafter, We shall increase his harvest; and whoever seeks the harvest of this world, We shall give him of it here, but in the Hereafter he will have no portion* (Quran, 42:20); *Whoever desires the immediate [gains of this world], We hasten what We will to whomever We will* (Quran, 17:18).[3]

Abū Hurayra (God be pleased with him) stated that the Messenger of God (God bless him and grant him peace) said, "Whoever learns knowledge by which one [customarily] seeks the pleasure of God Most High but learns it in order to obtain one of this world's riches, he will not find the scent of Paradise on the Day of Judgment."[4] (Abū Dāwūd related it with a rigorously authenticated chain; there are many hadiths similar to it.)

Anas, Ḥudhayfa, and Ka'b ibn Mālik (God be well pleased with them all) stated that the Messenger of God (God bless him and grant him peace) said, "Whoever seeks knowledge so that he can contest fools, vie with the scholars, or attract attention toward himself[5] occupies his seat in the Fire."[6] Tirmidhī related it from the account of Ka'b ibn Mālik (God be pleased with him) that states, "...it puts him into the Fire."

Not Objecting to Students Reciting With Others

The teacher takes every precaution from boasting because of the many people under his tutelage and who patronize him. He is cautious of disliking his students reciting with someone else who offers them benefit. These afflictions put some ignorant teachers to the test, and they are clear indications of the evil intention and corrupt innermost mettle of whoever possesses them. Indeed, they are sure proof of [the teacher's] lack of desire to teach for the sake of the noble pleasure of God Most High, since if he were to desire God Most High by teaching [the Quran], he would not have disliked [his students reading with others]. Instead he should say to himself, "I sought [God's] obedience by teaching, and it has thus been achieved. [The student] sought an increase in knowledge by reciting with someone else." And he should not censure the student.

We relate in the *Musnad* of Imām Abū Muḥammad al-Dārimī (God grant him mercy)—about whom there is consensus on his profound learning and leadership—that 'Alī ibn Abī Ṭālib (God be pleased with him) said, "O bearers of knowledge! Act according to [your knowledge], since the scholar is the one who acts according to what he has learned and whose knowledge corresponds to his action. There will be groups who possess knowledge that does not go beyond their collar bones. Their action contradicts their knowledge; their inward state contradicts their outward. They sit in circles vying with one another, until a man becomes angry with the one he sits with, and so he sits with someone else, leaving the other behind. Their actions in these assemblies of theirs do not ascend to God Most High."[7]

It is rigorously authenticated that Imām al-Shāfi'ī (God Most High have mercy upon him) said, "I hope that people learn this knowledge," meaning his knowledge and books, "with the condition that they not attribute a single letter of it to me."

Molded by Good Qualities

The scholar should be molded by the good qualities mentioned in the Revelation, and the praiseworthy inner qualities and the pleasing habits that God Most High guided to.

They include: abstinence in this world, thinking little of it, and lacking concern for it and its worldly people. They include: generosity, openhandedness, noble character, and a cheerful face but without becoming immodest. They include: discernment, self-control, and being above vile acquisition. They include: adhering to scrupulousness, humility, tranquility, dignity, modesty, submission, and avoiding laughter and frequent play. They include: adhering to religious tasks, such as, cleanliness, removing filth and hair that the legislation mentions removing; trimming the mustache, trimming the nails and combing the beard; and removing offensive smells and offensive clothing.

The scholar should take every precaution from envy, showing off, pride, and thinking little of others—even if [they are] beneath him.

Invocations and Supplications

The teacher should implement the hadiths that were related concerning saying "*Subḥān Allāh*" ["Sublime and Perfect is God"], "*Lā ilāha illa'Allāh*" ["There is no deity except God"], and other litanies [*adhkār*] and supplications. The teacher should be constantly conscious of God Most High, when alone and when in public, and his reliance in all of his affairs should be upon God Most High.

Being Kind and Accommodating

The teacher should be kind to whomever recites to him, welcoming him and well mannered with him in accordance to his circumstances.

We related that Abū Hārūn al-'Abdī said, "We would come to Abū Sa'īd al-Khudrī (God be pleased with him), and he would say, 'Welcome to the beneficiaries of the Messenger of God (God bless him and grant him peace). The Prophet (God bless him and grant him peace) said, "People rely upon you. Men will come to you from the earth's regions to acquire religious knowledge. When they come to you, make them your concern.""[8] (Tirmidhī, Ibn Mājah, and others related it. Something like it was related to us in *Musnad al-Dārimī* by way of Abū al-Dardā' (God be pleased with him).)

Sincerity Toward Students

The teacher should make every effort to be sincere with whomever recites to him, since the Messenger of God (God bless him and grant him peace) said, "Religion is sincerity:[9] towards God, His Book, His Messenger, the leaders of the Muslims, and their common folk."[10] (Muslim related it.)

Sincerity towards God and His Book includes, honoring its reciter and its student, guiding him to his best interest; being kind to him; assisting him in his studies with all that one can. It includes harmonizing the student's heart; being openhanded by teaching him gently, being kind towards him, and encouraging him to learn.

The teacher should mention the superiority of learning to the student, so that it causes him to be eager and increases his desire, makes him abstinent in this world, and changes him from being inclined towards [the world] and from being deluded by it. The teacher should mention to him the superiority of being occupied with the Quran and all other religious sciences. This is the path of those who have knowledge of God [*'ārifīn*], the resolute, and the righteous worshipers of God. And it is the rank of the prophets (God bless them and grant them peace).

The teacher should feel compassion for the student and pay attention to his well-being, just as he pays attention to his own well-being and his son's. The teacher assumes the role of the student's father by having compassion for him, concern for his well-being, and patience with his roughness and ill manners; and he pardons him for his poor behavior in some circumstances—since he is prone to shortcomings, especially if [he is] young in age.

The teacher—without exception—should like for [his student] what he likes for himself, and dislike for him the shortcomings that he dislikes for himself. It has been firmly established in the

Ṣaḥīḥayn that the Messenger of God (God bless him and grant him peace) said, "None of you believes until he loves for his brother what he loves for himself."[11] Ibn 'Abbās (God be pleased with them both) said, "The one I must respect the most is the one sitting before me—he who stepped over people's necks until he sat before me.[12] If I were capable of preventing a single fly from landing on his face, I would have done so!" And in one narration [it reads], "...and flies land on his face and it bothers me!"

Not Possessed of Arrogance

The teacher should not be arrogant towards his students. Instead, he should be gentle and humble. Many well-known accounts have been related about the importance of having humility with ordinary individuals; so how is it with those who are like one's own children, especially given what they are doing—occupied with the Quran? All of this is in addition to what they hold over him already, including the right of companionship and their right to go to him repeatedly. It has been related that the Prophet (God bless him and grant him peace) said, "Be gentle with your student and with your teacher."[13]

Ayyūb al-Sakhtiyānī (God Most High grant him mercy) said, "The teacher should put dirt on his head out of humbleness towards God Mighty and Majestic."

Disciplining the Student

The teacher should gradually discipline the student in order that he have excellent manners and a pleasing disposition; that he struggle against his lower-self [*nafs*] applying subtle ways. The teacher should habituate him so as to safeguard all of his student's affairs, both private and public. The teacher should urge him repeatedly, in words and in deeds, to have sincerity and perfect intentions, and to be vigilant of God Most High at all times. The teacher should inform him that through all of this, the lights of spiritual knowledge will open to him, his heart will be opened also; and the wellsprings of wisdom and subtleties will gush forth from his heart and God will bless him in his work and state and give him success in what he says and does.

The Communal Obligation of Teaching

Teaching is a communal obligation. If only one individual is right for the task, then it becomes his personal obligation. But in the context of a community, in which there is a group of people through whom [the duty of education] may be discharged, [they are all obliged]. If all of them refuse, then all have sinned; if some of them establish [education], then the sin falls from the rest. If one of them is requested to teach but refuses, the preponderant of two opinions is that he is not a sinner, although it is offensive for him to [refuse] without excuse.

Resolved to Teach

It is recommended that the teacher be fully committed to teaching [his students], preferring it over his personal worldly matters that are not critical. It is recommended that he empty his heart of all preoccupying matters—and they are many and known—while sitting for their recitation. It is recommended that he be resolved to making them understand.

He should give each student what is suitable for him, that is, he should not give a greater [workload] to one who cannot bear the increase, nor should he lessen the load for one who can indeed bear the addition.

He should request the students to repeat what they have memorized. Moreover, he should praise a student whose excellence is manifest, as long as there is no problem with conceit or something else that may be feared of him. He should gently admonish whoever falls short in his studies, as long as he does not fear alienating him.

Never should a teacher envy a student for excelling, nor harbor thoughts that what God has bestowed upon him is excessive. This is because envying even strangers is strictly unlawful. How is it, then, with envying a student who is like one's own son, and whose excellences shall cause his teacher to reap abundant reward in the Hereafter and excellent praise in this world?

God alone brings success.

Teaching in Order of Arrival

When there are many students, the teacher gives precedence in instructing [his students] according to the order in which they arrive. If the first [student] approves that another be given precedence, it is duly given. He should show them joy and a cheerful face. He should inquire about their circumstances, and ask about someone who is absent.

Students with Unsound Intentions

The scholars (God be well pleased with them) said, "Do not deny anyone instruction because of unsound intentions." Sufyān [al-Thawrī] and others have said, "Their seeking knowledge is intention in itself." They said, "We sought knowledge for reasons other than God, but the knowledge refused to be other than for the sake of God," meaning that its purpose be for God Most High.

Not Fidgeting During Recitation

During recitation, the teacher should not fidget with his hands, and he should keep his eyes from needlessly glancing about. He sits, while having ritual purification, facing the *qibla* [direction of Prayer]. And he sits with dignity, his clothes white and clean.

When he reaches the place in which he sits [to teach], he prays two *rak'as* before actually sitting, whether or not the location is a mosque. This practice is more emphatic if it is in a mosque, since it is offensive to sit in a mosque before praying. Also, he may sit cross-legged. Abū Bakr al-Sajistānī relates with his chain of transmission that 'Abdallāh ibn Mas'ūd (God be pleased with him) would have people recite to him in the mosque while kneeling.

Not Disgracing Knowledge

It is an emphasized etiquette that the teacher not disgrace the status of knowledge by teaching in a place associated with his student—whether the student is the caliph or a lesser person.[14] Instead, he safeguards the knowledge from this, just as the Righteous Forebears [*Salaf*] did (God be well pleased with them). Their statements concerning this are well known and many.

Having a Spacious Assembly

The teacher's assembly should be spacious enough to accommodate his audience. The Prophet (God bless him and grant him peace) said, "The best assemblies are the most spacious";[15] (Abū Dāwūd related this hadith in his *Sunan* at the beginning of "The Book of Etiquette" with a rigorously authenticated chain of narrators from the narration of Abū Sa'īd al-Khudrī (God be pleased with him).)

The Student's Etiquette

All of the teacher's etiquette that we have mentioned—in and of itself—are the student's etiquette also. The student's etiquette includes moreover avoiding any concerns that preoccupy him from achieving [his objectives], except that which is unavoidable because of necessity. He should purify his heart from any impurity so that it is fit for receiving the Quran, memorizing it, and profiting from it.

It is rigorously authenticated that the Messenger of God (God bless him and grant him peace) said, "In the body there is a morsel: when it is sound, the whole body is sound; and when it is corrupt, the whole body is corrupt. [This morsel] is the heart."[16] The one who said the following has done well in saying: "The heart is made wholesome for knowledge, just as the earth is made wholesome for cultivation."

The student should show humility towards his teacher and be well behaved with him, even if the teacher is younger than him, less famous, of lower lineage, less righteous, and so on. He shows humility with regard to knowledge, and attains it by means of his humility. Some have said in verse:

> Knowledge destroys the arrogant youth,
> like the torrent erodes high ground.

The student should be obedient to his teacher, consult him in his affairs, and accept his opinion. An ill person who is rational accepts the opinion of a practiced and sincere physician. [With religious knowledge] this is even more appropriate.

Studying from the Best

The student does not study except from someone whose competence is complete, his religiosity visible, has achieved *ma'rifa*,[17] and is well known as a person free of [debilitating] problems. Muḥammad ibn Sīrīn, Mālik ibn Anas, and other Righteous Forebears have said, "This knowledge is religion, so examine well he from whom you take your religion."[18]

Respecting the Teacher

The student must look to his teacher with the eye of respect, believe in his competence completely, and his superiority over his contemporaries, since this makes it more likely that one will benefit from him. One scholar from the earlier generations would give something in charity whenever he went to his teacher and say: "O God, cover my teacher's faults from me, and do not take the spiritual blessing of his knowledge away from me."

Rabī', the companion of al-Shāfi'ī (God have mercy on them both), said, "I did not venture to drink water while al-Shāfi'ī was looking at me out of veneration for him."

We relate that the commander of the faithful, 'Alī ibn Abī Ṭālib (God be pleased with him), said:

> The rights the teacher has over you include that you give greetings to people in general but single him out with greetings to the exclusion of the rest. [They include:] sitting in front of him; not pointing with your hand in his company; not winking your eye at someone; not citing a position contrary to his; not backbiting anyone when in his presence. [And they include:] not conferring with someone sitting near you while in his audience; not grabbing his garment; not being insistent when he has reservations [about something]; and not being inharmonious, such that you become fed up with accompanying him after a length of time."[19]

The student should discipline himself with these characteristics that 'Alī referred to (God ennoble his face). Also, the student rebuts any backbiting of his shaykh whenever he is able, and leaves that assembly if he is unable to do so.

Entering and Exiting the Lesson

The student visits his shaykh [with] most excellent traits, keeping himself tidy with everything we have just mentioned concerning the teacher: cleanliness, regular use of the toothstick, and a heart free of preoccupying matters. He does not enter without seeking permission when the shaykh is in a place that requires permission. The student greets the attendees upon entering, and [then] singles out his teacher with his greeting. Likewise, he bids farewell to him and [the assembly in general] when he departs, just as it is related in the hadith: "The first [greeting] is no more deserving than the second."[20] The student does not step over people, and sits wherever the assembly's perimeter happens to be, unless the shaykh gives him permission to come forward, or he knows from the behavior [of the other students] that they prefer it. He does not let someone rise from his place [out of deference], and if someone does give him preference he declines it still, following the example of Ibn 'Umar (God be pleased with him), unless his coming forward is in the welfare of those present or if the shaykh requested him to do so. He does not sit in the middle of the circle, except out of necessity. He does not sit between two companions except with their permission; and if they make room for him, he sits and squeezes himself in.

Sitting During the Lesson

The student should also have good etiquette with his companions and those attending the assembly of the shaykh, since this is also having good etiquette with the shaykh and preserves [the dignity of] his assembly. He sits in the presence of the shaykh in the manner of a student, not that of a teacher. He does not raise his voice exaggeratedly, laugh, or speak much without need. He does not fidget with his hands or the like. He does not turn right and left without need; rather he faces the shaykh, attentive to his words.

A Moody Shaykh

Among the things the student is advised to heed is that he not recite to the shaykh while the shaykh's heart is preoccupied or bored, or while he is reluctant, distressed, overjoyed, hungry, thirsty, tired, troubled, or anything that makes it difficult for him or prevents him from having complete presence of heart or from being energetic. The student should take full advantage of the times in which the teacher is energetic.

The student's etiquette includes bearing with the shaykh's coarseness and bad aspects of his character, and not being dissuaded from remaining with him and believing in his aptness. The student proffers valid excuses for his shaykh's actions and utterances that outwardly seem flawed. Who is incapable of this, except for someone with little or no accomplishment? If the shaykh is coarse with him, he takes the initiative to apologize to the shaykh, and outwardly shows that the offense is his and he deserves the reprimand. This is more beneficial for him in this world and the next, and purer for the heart of the shaykh.

It has been said, "Whoever is impatient with the humiliation of learning will spend his life in the blindness of ignorance. And whoever is patient with it, it will eventually lead to the glory of this life and the next." The student's etiquette encompasses the famous statement from Ibn 'Abbās (God be pleased with them both). "I was humble [when] I studied, so I was respected when I was sought." How excellent is the one who said: "Whoever does not experience the taste of humility for an hour will spend eternity humiliated."

Between Lessons

The student's etiquette includes [his] determination to study—incessantly doing so any time the opportunity arises. He is not satisfied with a little when much is possible. Yet he does not burden himself with what is overbearing to him out of fear of boredom and losing what he has gained. This varies according to different people and conditions.

If the student reaches the place where the shaykh usually sits and does not find him there, he waits patiently for him and stays close to his door. The student does not skip his daily lesson unless out of concern that the shaykh has an aversion [to a given lesson for some reason], since he knows [the shaykh's] preference for being read to at one time and not another. If he finds the shaykh sleeping or occupied with something important, he does not seek permission to enter. Instead, he waits until the shaykh awakens or completes his tasks. Otherwise, he simply departs. It is better to be patient, just as Ibn 'Abbās (God be pleased with them both) and others were.

The student should take it upon himself to strive hard to achieve [all he can] while he is free of responsibility and energetic, the body strong, mind alert, and occupied by few things—before the hurdles of heroism and high rank come. The commander of the faithful, 'Umar ibn al-Khaṭṭāb (God be pleased with him), has said, "Become learned [*faqīh*] before you become a master,"[21] meaning, strive to attain complete competence while you are subordinates, before you become masters. When you become masters with a following [of students], you will be prevented from further learning because of your high rank and numerous preoccupations. This is the meaning of Imām al-Shāfi'ī's statement (God be pleased with him): "Become a *faqīh* before you become a leader, since when you are a leader there is no path to becoming a *faqīh*."

When to Study

The student should make his recitation with the shaykh early, at the beginning of the day, because of the hadith of the Prophet (God bless him and grant him peace): "O God, bless my nation in its earliness."[22]

The student should be mindful to recite what he has memorized. He should not give someone else his turn, since it is offensive to give preference to someone else when it comes to deeds that draw one close to God, although it is recommended to give such preference when it comes to personal interests. If the shaykh sees advantage in preferring certain times [over others] because of a legal reason and he alludes to it, his order should be followed.

Treating Envy and Pride

A student is obliged—and is highly advised to heed—that he not harbor envy toward his peers, or anyone else for that matter, because of some good quality that God the Generous has given one. Likewise, the student should not wax proud over what he himself achieves. We explained before that this is also part of the teacher's etiquette.

The way for the student to remove pride is by remembering that his achievement did not occur through his own power and strength; rather it was only through God's grace. As such, the student should not be proud of something he did not produce—something that God Most High placed in him.

The way to remove envy is to know with certainty that it was the wisdom of God Most High that brought a good trait to a person. So one should never object to it; nor should one dislike wisdom that God Most High willed and, thus, He Himself did not dislike.

5

THE ETIQUETTE OF THE BEARERS OF THE QURAN

Much of this etiquette has been mentioned in the previous chapter. It includes being in the most complete of states and having the most honorable of qualities, avoiding everything the Quran prohibits out of respect for the Quran. [It includes] being preserved from low means of income; having dignity; rising above the tyrants and vulgar people of this world; being humble with the righteous, the well-doers, and the poor; being fearful [of God]; and having tranquility and respect.

It has been related that ʿUmar ibn al-Khaṭṭāb (God be pleased with him) said, "O fellowship of reciters! Lift your heads! The path has been laid for you, so advance towards the good, and do not be dependant on people!"

ʿAbdallāh ibn Masʿūd (God be pleased with him) said, "The bearer of the Quran should be known by his night when the people are sleeping; by his day when the people are awake; by his sadness when people are joyous; by his weeping when people are laughing; by his silence when people are engrossed [in conversation]; and by his fear when people are pompous."

Al-Ḥasan al-Baṣrī (God Most High grant him mercy) said, "The people before you considered the Quran to be correspondence from their Lord, so they would ponder it by night and perform it by day."

Al-Fuḍayl ibn ʿIyāḍ (God Most High grant him mercy) said, "The bearer of the Quran should have no need of any caliph or any lesser person." He also said, "The bearer of the Quran is the bearer of the banner of Islam. He should not distract himself with someone who distracts himself, nor talk about nonsense with those who talk nonsense—all out of due veneration of the Quran."

Reciting for Livelihood

It is important to take every precaution not to use the Quran for livelihood and to earn income with it. ʿAbd al-Raḥmān ibn Shibl (God be pleased with him) stated that the Messenger of God (God bless him and grant him peace) said, "Recite the Quran. Do not eat from it; do not be averse to it; and do not exceed proper bounds with it."[1]

Jābir (God be pleased with him) stated that the Prophet (God bless him and grant him peace) [said], "Recite the Quran before a people come who misuse it. They are hasty with it, and do not recite it slowly."[2] Abū Dāwūd related a [statement similar in] meaning from the narration of Sahl ibn Saʿd: "The meaning is being hasty with its reward, either seeking worldly reward or reputation or the like."

Al-Fuḍayl ibn ʿAmr (God be pleased with him) said, "Two companions of the Messenger of God (God bless him and grant him peace) entered a mosque. When the imām gave his salutations, a man stood, recited a verse from the Quran, and then begged. One of the two men [lamented], 'Verily we belong to God, and to Him is our return! I heard the Messenger of God (God bless him and grant him peace) say: "A people will come who use the Quran to beg. Do not give to someone who uses the Quran to beg."'"[3] (This narration is considered a broken-chain [*munqaṭiʿ*] report, since al-Fuḍayl ibn ʿAmr himself did not hear it from the Companions).

Taking Wages

The scholars disagree about the issue of taking wages for teaching the Quran. Imām Abū Sulaymān al-Khaṭṭābī related that a group of scholars prohibited taking wages from [teaching the Quran], including al-Zuhrī and Abū Ḥanīfa.[4] He related, however, that it is permissible if one does not make it a stipulation. This is the opinion of al-Ḥasan al-Baṣrī, al-Shaʿbī, and Ibn Sīrīn.

'Aṭā, Mālik, al-Shāfi'ī, and others held the view that it is permissible even if he stipulates it. So if [the teacher] is hired it is a valid contract. And rigorously authenticated hadith have been related indicating its permissibility.

Those who prohibit [taking wages] justify it with the hadith that reports: 'Ubāda ibn al-Ṣāmit taught Quran to one of the [indigent] men from among the People of the Shelter[5] and so he gave him a bow as a gift. The Prophet (God bless him and grant him peace) then said [to 'Ubāda], "If having fire wrapped around your neck pleases you, then accept the [gift]."[6] (It is a well-known hadith; Abū Dāwūd and others related it.) They also justify their positions with many accounts from the Righteous Forebears [*Salaf*].

Those who permit [taking wages] respond to the hadith of 'Ubāda ibn al-Ṣāmit with two answers. First, there is something to be said about [the soundness of] its chain. Second, he had donated his teaching and thus did not merit any [payment]; but then [the bow] was given to him as a gift as a form of compensation, thus rendering it illicit to take. This is different than one who makes a contract for wages with [a student] before giving instruction.

And God knows best.

Continually Completing the Quran

A person should maintain his recitation and do much of it. The Righteous Forebears (God Most High be well pleased with them) had different habits regarding the time in which they would finish [the Quran]. Ibn Abī Dāwūd related from the Righteous Forebears (God Most High be well pleased with them) that some of them would finish the Quran once every two months or every month; once every ten nights or every eight; most of them every seven nights; some every six nights, every five, or every four; many every three nights; some every two days, every day-and-night, twice every day-and-night, twice each day, and eight times [each day]—four by night and four by day.

EVERY DAY: Those who completed the recitation of the Quran every day include 'Uthmān ibn 'Affān, Tamīm al-Dārī, Sa'īd ibn Jubayr, Mujāhid, al-Shāfi'ī, and others.

THREE TIMES PER DAY: Those who completed the Quran three times daily include Sulaym ibn 'Itr (God be pleased with him), the judge of Egypt when Mu'āwiya (God be pleased with him) was the caliph. Abū Bakr ibn Abī Dāwūd related that he would complete [the Quran] three times each night, and Abū Bakr al-Kindī relates in his book about the judges of Egypt that he would complete [the Quran] four times in a night.

EIGHT TIMES IN 24 HOURS: The righteous shaykh Abū 'Abd al-Raḥmān al-Sulamī (God be pleased with him) said, "I heard Shaykh Abū 'Uthmān al-Maghribī say, 'Ibn al-Kātib would complete [the Quran] four times by day and four times by night.'" This is the most that reached us for a single day and a night.

DURING RAMADAN: The illustrious shaykh Aḥmad al-Dawraqī relates, with his chain of narration, from Manṣūr ibn Zādhān, who was among the devotees of the Successors (God Most High be well pleased with them), that he would complete the Quran in the time between the Noon [*Ẓuhr*] and Afternoon [*'Aṣr*] Prayers, and complete it again in the time between the Sunset [*Maghrib*] and Nightfall [*'Ishā'*] Prayers, and during Ramadan two complete times and some. And they delayed the Nightfall Prayer during Ramadan until a quarter of the night had passed.

Ibn Abī Dāwūd related, with his sound chain of narration, that Mujāhid would complete the Quran during Ramadan every night between the Sunset and Nightfall Prayers. Manṣūr said, "'Alī al-Azdī would complete it during Ramadan every night between the Sunset and Nightfall Prayers." Ibrāhīm ibn Sa'd said, "My father would sit, shins up, and continue sitting that way until completing the Quran."

IN A SINGLE RAK'A: Those who completed the Quran during one *rak'a* [of Prayer] are too numerous to count. The early generations include 'Uthmān ibn 'Affān, Tamīm al-Dārī, and Sa'īd ibn Jubayr (God Most High be well pleased with them), who completed it every *rak'a* inside the Ka'ba.

ONCE A WEEK: There are many who completed it once a week, as it is conveyed from 'Uthmān ibn 'Affān, 'Abdallāh ibn Mas'ūd, Zayd ibn Thābit, Ubay ibn Ka'b (God Most High be well pleased with them), and a group among the Successors, such as ʿAbd al-Raḥmān ibn Yazīd, ʿAlqama [ibn Qays ibn ʿAbdallāh], and Ibrāhīm [ibn Yazīd ibn Qays al-Nakhaʿī] (God Most High grant him mercy).

THE GENERAL RULE: The preferred opinion is that [the amount one reads] may vary from person to person. If one finds subtleties and experiences [insight] by way of intricate reflection, then he should limit [himself] to the amount [of reading] in which he obtains full understanding of what he reads. This applies to anyone occupied with spreading knowledge or something else important to religion and the general welfare of Muslims: he limits [himself] to that which does not disrupt what he is capable of. Yet if one is not among these, then he should do as much as possible but not to the point of tedium and discontinuing his recitation.

LESS THAN THREE DAYS BEING OFFENSIVE: A group of the early generations of scholars disliked the idea of completing [the recitation of the whole Quran] in a single day and night. This is supported by the rigorously authenticated hadith in which ʿAbdallāh ibn ʿAmr ibn al-ʿĀṣ (God be pleased with them both) stated that the Messenger of God (God bless him and grant him peace) had said, "Whoever reads the Quran in less than three days does not understand [what he recited]."[7] (Abū Dāwūd, Tirmidhī, Nasāʾī, and others related it; Tirmidhī said that it is a well-rigorously authenticated hadith.)[8]

And God knows best.

RECITING THE WHOLE QURAN WEEKLY: As for the start and finish times of the person who completes [the recitation] each week, Ibn Abī Dāwūd related with his chain of narration that ʿUthmān ibn ʿAffān (God be pleased with him) would start the Quran Friday night and complete it Thursday night.[9] Imām Abū Ḥāmid al-Ghazālī (may God Most High grant him abundant mercy) said in *al-Iḥyāʾ* that it is best to complete [the recitation] once by night and another time by day. As for completing it by day, let it be Tuesday during the two *rakʿas* of the Morning Prayer or afterwards; and as for completing it by night, let it be the night of Friday during the two [*sunna*] *rakʿas* of the Sunset Prayer or afterwards. This way [one] greets the beginning and the end of the day.[10]

Ibn Abī Dāwūd related that the Successor [*Tābi'ī*] 'Amr ibn Murra said, "We loved to complete the Quran at the beginning of the night or at the beginning of the day." The illustrious Successor Ṭalḥa ibn Muṣarrif said, "Whoever completes the Quran during the day, the angels will pray for him until dawn. If his completion coincides with the end of the night, the angels pray for him until [the following] night."[11] Al-Dārimī said that this is well authenticated from Sa'd [ibn Abī Waqqāṣ]. [It is related that] the successor Ḥabīb ibn Abī Thābit would complete [the Quran's recitation] before prostrating. Ibn Abī Dāwūd stated that Aḥmad ibn Ḥanbal (God Most High grant him mercy) said the same.

The remainder of such matters as presented in this section will come in the forthcoming chapter (if God Most High wills).

Reciting at Night

One should take care to recite the Quran mostly at night, and mostly during Prayer at night. God Most High has said, *Among the People of the Book is an upright community that recites the verses of God during the night and fall prostrate before Him. They believe in God and the Last Day, enjoin what is right and forbid what is evil, and vie with one another in good works. They are the righteous* (Quran, 3:113–14).

It is established in the *Ṣaḥīḥayn* that the Messenger of God (God bless him and grant him peace) said, "What an excellent man 'Abdallāh [ibn 'Umar] would be if he were to pray at night."[12] In another hadith in the *Ṣaḥīḥ* the Prophet (God bless him and grant him peace) said, "O 'Abdallāh, do not be like so-and-so who used to pray at night and then neglected it."[13] Al-Ṭabarānī and others related that Sahl ibn Sa'd (God be pleased with him) stated that the Messenger of God (God bless him and grant him peace) said, "A Muslim's nobility is praying at night." There are many prophetic hadiths and other accounts concerning this.

It has been related that Abū al-Aḥwaṣ al-Jushamī said, "If a person were to approach the camp at night"—meaning to reach it at night—"he would hear a sound from its people like the buzzing of bees." He said, "So what makes these people [today] feel safe from what those [before them] feared?"[14]

Ibrāhīm al-Nakha'ī would say, "Read at night, even [for the time it takes] milking a sheep." Yazīd al-Raqāshī said, "If I slept, then woke, and then slept: my eyes did not sleep."

I [Imām al-Nawawī] say: Praying and reciting at night are preponderant because [at that time] they are most primed for the collectedness of the heart; removed from preoccupations, entertainment, and attending to needs; and more safe-guarded from ostentation and other things that reduce reward—in addition to what the Sacred Law has deemed about the great good that can be found at night. Indeed, the Messenger's (God bless him and grant him peace) Miraculous Journey was at night.

The hadith states, "Every night your Lord descends to the lowest heaven when half of the night has passed and says: 'Is there anyone praying so I may answer his prayer.'"[15] And in a rigorously authenticated hadith, the Messenger of God (God bless him and grant him peace) said, "At night there is an hour in which God answers every supplication. It is every night."[16]

The author of *Bahjat al-Asrār*[17] relates with his chain of narration that Salmān al-Anmāṭī said, "I saw 'Alī ibn Abī Ṭālib (God be pleased with him) in my dream say:

> If not for those who have a *wird* [litany] that they do
> And others who have a contiguous fast,
> Your ground would be flattened out beneath you before dawn
> Because you are a wicked people who do not obey us.

Know that the advantage of praying at night and reciting [the Quran] is attained with little or much [recitation]. The more you increase, though, the better [it is], unless it completely fills the night, since it is offensive to always do so and may cause harm to oneself.

One of the indications of achieving [spiritual ascendance] with just a minimal [devotion at night] is the hadith of 'Abdallāh ibn

'Amr ibn al-'Āṣ (God be pleased with them both) that the Messenger of God (God bless him and grant him peace) said, "Whoever stood [at night] for ten verses will not be written among the heedless. Whoever stood for one hundred verses is written among the obedient. Whoever stood for one thousand verses is written among the ones with intense riches."[18] (Abū Dāwūd and others related it.) Al-Tha'labī conveyed that Ibn 'Abbās (God be pleased with them both) said, "Whoever prays two *rak'as* at night has spent the night prostrating and standing for God."

The Importance of Retaining the Quran

It is established that Abū Mūsā al-Ash'arī (God be pleased with him) stated that the Prophet (God bless him and grant him peace) said, "Retain this Quran. By He in whose Hand is Muḥammad's soul, it escapes more easily than a camel escapes its tether."[19] (Bukhārī and Muslim related it.)

Ibn 'Umar (God be pleased with them both) stated that the Messenger of God (God bless him and grant him peace) said, "The likeness of one who has the Quran is like one who has a tethered camel: if you tether it, you retain it, and if you let it roam, it departs."[20] (Bukhārī and Muslim related it.)

Anas ibn Mālik (God be pleased with him) stated that the Messenger of God (God bless him and grant him peace) said, "The rewards of my nation were shown to me—even the litter a man removes from the mosque. And the sins of my nation were shown to me. I did not see a sin greater than a sura [chapter] or verse of the Quran given to a person who then forgot it."[21] (Abū Dāwūd and Tirmidhī related it, and spoke about it.[22])

Sa'd ibn 'Ubāda stated that the Prophet (God bless him and grant him peace) said, "Whoever reads the Quran and then forgets it meets God Mighty and Majestic on the Day of Judgment [while he is] disfigured."[23] (Abū Dāwūd and Dārimī related it.)

Sleeping Through One's Wird (or Ḥizb)[24]

'Umar ibn al-Khaṭṭāb (God be pleased with him) relates that the Messenger of God (God bless him and grant him peace) said,

"Whoever slept through all or part of his nightly *ḥizb* [litany of recitation] but read it between the Morning and Afternoon Prayers, it is written for him as if he had read it at night."[25] (Muslim related it.) Sulaymān ibn Yasār said, "Abū Usayd [Mālik ibn Rabīʿa ibn al-Budn] (God be pleased with him) said, 'Yesterday I slept without doing my litany until I woke. When I woke up I said [in lament], "Verily we belong to God, and to Him is our return." My *wird* was [Sūrat] al-Baqara, and in my sleep I saw a cow goring me."' (Ibn Abī Dāwūd related it.)

Ibn Abī Dunya related from one of the masters of the Quran that he slept one night without doing his *ḥizb* and in his sleep he saw as if someone was saying to him:

> I am amazed at a body and health,
>   and at one who sleeps until dawn,
> while there is death, from which none is safe from its sudden snatch
>   in the darkness of night, when its due time comes.

6

THE ETIQUETTE OF RECITATION

This chapter is the [main] point of this book, and it is wide ranging. I allude to the essence of its objectives for my dislike of lengthiness and for fear of boring the reader.

The first things that are obligatory for the reciter are sincerity, as previously stated, and observing proper etiquette with the Quran. One should bring to mind that he is addressing God Most High and therefore should read as if one sees God Most High; and [even] if he does not see God, verily God Most High sees him.[1]

The Toothstick [Miswāk]

If one wants to recite the Quran, he should clean his mouth with a toothstick [*miswāk*] or the like. The preference is for the toothstick to be a twig from the *arak* tree. It is permissible to use all other twigs and to use anything that cleans, such as a coarse cloth or saltwort.

As for accomplishing this with a coarse finger, the companions of al-Shāfiʿī (God grant him mercy) have three opinions. The most well known is that this does not accomplish the task; the second is that it does; the third is that this [is acceptable] if nothing else is available—but not when there is.

One uses the toothstick laterally, beginning from the right side. He makes intention to perform the *sunna*. Some scholars have said that when using the toothstick one should say, "O God! bless me in it! O Most Merciful of the merciful!"

Al-Māwardī, one of al-Shāfi'ī's later followers, said, "It is recommended to use toothstick on the outer and inner portions of the teeth. One gently passes the toothstick over the edges of his teeth, bicuspids, and molars, and the roof of his palate. They said that one should use an ordinary toothstick, not [one] extremely dry or wet." He said, "If it is extremely dry, then one should soften it with water. There is no problem with using someone else's toothstick with his permission."

When the mouth is filthy

When one's mouth is filthy with blood or the like, it is offensive to recite the Quran before rinsing it. But is it unlawful? Al-Ruwyanī, one of the later followers of al-Shāfi'ī, conveyed from his father that two opinions are conceivable[2] the soundest one being that it is not unlawful.

Ritual purity

MINOR RITUAL IMPURITY: It is recommended to be in a state of ritual purity when reciting the Quran. It is permissible to recite in a state of minor ritual impurity, according to the consensus of the Muslims; the hadiths concerning it are many and well known. Imām al-Ḥaramayn [al-Juwaynī] said that one should not say that one has committed something offensive [if he recites with minor ritual impurity]; rather, he has neglected what is best. If one does not find water, he should make *tayammum* [dry ablution]. The ruling concerning a woman with abnormal vaginal bleeding when she is otherwise considered pure, is similar to that of anyone with minor ritual impurity.

MAJOR RITUAL IMPURITY: It is unlawful for a person in a state of major ritual impurity or during menstruation to recite the Quran, whether it is a verse or even less.[3] It is permissible for them to [silently] peruse the Quran in their hearts without uttering it, and to look in the actual written text of the Quran [*muṣḥaf*] and go over it in the heart.

The Muslims have consensus that it is permissible for a person in a state of major ritual impurity or during menstruation to say

"Subḥān Allāh," "Lā ilāha illa'Allāh," "al-ḥamdulillāh," "Allāhu akbar," to offer prayers of salutation upon the Messenger of God (God bless him and grant him peace), and other litanies. Our Shāfi'ī companions said that it is the same if one says to a person, *"O Yaḥyā! Hold fast to the Book"* (Quran, 19:12), or the like, but not intending by it the Quran per se. This is permissible. It is likewise permissible for them both [the person with major ritual impurity and the woman in menses] to say, *"We belong to God, and surely to Him we shall return"* (Quran, 2:156), in response to some calamity, if they do not intend it as a recitation [of the Quran per se].

Our Shāfi'ī companions from Khurasān said that it is permissible for them, when mounting a riding beast, to say, *"Glory be to Him who has subjugated this for us, otherwise we could not have subdued them"* (Quran, 43:13), and when supplicating, *"Lord! Give us what is good in this world and what is good in the Hereafter; and keep us from the torment of the Fire"* (Quran, 2:201), again, if they do not intend it as a recitation.

Imām al-Ḥaramayn [al-Juwaynī] said that when a person in major ritual impurity says, "In the name of God," and "Praise be to God" intending it to be [recitation of] the Quran, he has transgressed. But if he intended thereby the remembrance [of God] or nothing in particular, then he did not sin. It is permissible for them to recite something whose recitation has been abrogated [like]: "When a married man or a married woman commits adultery, their punishment shall be stoning as retribution."[4]

Dry Ablution

An individual with major ritual impurity or menstruation may make dry ablution [*tayammum*] in the absence of water. Then it is lawful to recite Quran, pray, and perform other things [that require ritual purity]. But if thereafter one were to have minor ritual impurity, it is unlawful to pray, but not unlawful to recite [Quran], sit in a mosque, or other things lawful for someone in a state of minor ritual impurity. He is considered a person who made the purificatory bath and then had minor ritual impurity. This is an issue that is asked about and considered rare. It is said: What is a scenario in which a person in major ritual impurity is barred from praying but not barred from reciting the Quran or sitting in the mosque without necessity? [The foregoing] is such a scenario. Regarding this issue, there is no difference between making dry ablution while resident or traveling. Some of the followers of Imām al-Shāfi'ī have mentioned that if one makes dry ablution while resident, it is lawful to pray, but he may not recite [Quran] outside the Prayer nor sit in the mosque. But the sound position is that [reciting] is permissible, as we previously mentioned.

If one were to make dry ablution, pray, recite, and then saw water, he must use it [for a purification bath], since it is unlawful for him to recite or perform anything unlawful for one with major ritual impurity until making the purificatory bath.

If one were to make dry ablution, then pray, recite, and then wanted to make dry ablution again because of major ritual impurity—to prepare for another obligatory Prayer or something else—it is not unlawful for him to recite Quran according to the sound preferred opinion. Some of the [later] companions of al-Shāfi'ī hold the opinion that it is not permissible, but the well-known is the former.

In the Absence of Water and Earth

When someone with major ritual impurity finds neither earth nor water [with which to attain purification], he may perform Prayer because of the constriction of the [Prayer's] time range. He does so whatever his circumstances may be. It is unlawful, however, for him to recite [Quran] outside of the bounds of Prayer; and during the Prayer itself it is unlawful for him to recite more than al-Fātiḥa.

Yet is it unlawful for him to recite al-Fātiḥa? There are two opinions concerning this. The sound and preferred opinion is that it is not unlawful. In fact, it is obligatory [to recite al-Fātiḥa] since Prayer is invalid without it. Just as it is permissible to perform Prayer in spite of major ritual impurity—because it became critical at that moment—it is likewise permissible to recite [al-Fātiḥa].

The second opinion is that it is not permissible; rather one says the litanies that an incapacitated person who has not memorize anything from the Quran would say; the former is incapable, according to Sacred Law, [to perform Prayer] and has become analogous to someone disabled. The correct opinion is the first.

These details that we have just mentioned are needed, and thus I alluded to them with the most concise expressions. They have evidence and numerous supplements, which are well known in the books of *fiqh*.

And God knows best.

The Place of Recitation

A CLEAN PLACE: It is recommended that recitation [of the Quran] be in a carefully chosen and clean place. Because of this, a group of scholars recommended reciting in the mosque, since it combines cleanliness and nobility; and it achieves another benefit: spiritual retreat [*i'tikāf*]. Anyone who sits in a mosque should intend spiritual retreat whether he sits for a short or long duration. Upon entering the mosque, he should intend such a spiritual retreat. This etiquette should be given attention and disseminated widely so that the young and the general public know of it, for it is one of the things that is now ignored.

BATH HOUSES: The righteous forebears disagreed over whether or not it is offensive to recite in a bathhouse. Our Shāfi'ī companions said that it is not offensive. Imām Abū Bakr ibn al-Mundhir, whose illustriousness is agreed upon, relates this in *al-Ishrāf* from Ibrāhīm al-Nakha'ī and Mālik. It is also the opinion of 'Aṭā.

However, one group of scholars declared it offensive, including 'Alī ibn Abī Ṭālib (God be pleased with him). (Ibn Abī Dāwūd related this position from him. Ibn Mundhir related it from many of the Successors, including Abū Wā'il Shaqīq ibn Salama, al-Sha'bī, al-Ḥasan al-Baṣrī, Makhul, and Qubisata ibn Dhu'ayb. He also related from Ibrāhīm al-Nakha'ī. Our Shāfi'ī companions related it from Abū Ḥanīfa.[5] God be well pleased with them all.)

Al-Sha'bī said that it is offensive to read the Quran in three locations: bathhouses, lavatories, and mill-houses while the stone is turning. Abū Maysara said, "Do not make remembrance of God except in a wholesome place."

And God knows best.

ON THE ROAD: As for reciting on the road, the preferred opinion is that it is permissible and not offensive if the reciter is not distracted. But it is offensive if the reciter is distracted. This is analogous to the Prophet (God bless him and grant him peace) disliking it when a person recites while he is tired, out of concern that he may make a mistake.

Ibn Abī Dāwūd related that Abū Dardā' (God be pleased with him) would recite on the path, and that 'Umar ibn 'Abd al-'Azīz (God grant him mercy) declared it permissible.

Ibn Abī Dāwūd relates, by way of Abū al-Rabī', that Ibn Wahb said, "I asked Mālik about a person who prays during the last part of the night and then goes out to the mosque while having not completed his recitation. He said, 'I do not know about reciting on the road,' and he disliked it." (This is a rigorously authenticated chain from Mālik (God grant him mercy).)

Facing the Qibla

It is recommended for the reciter to face the *qibla*, even when not in Prayer. It has been related in hadith: "The best way to sit is facing the *qibla*."[6] One sits with humility, tranquility, and dignity, lowering his head. He sits alone to perfect his etiquette and humbleness, like sitting before his teacher. This is the most complete way to do so. If he were to read while standing, reclining on his side, in bed, or in some other bearing, it is permissible, and he has reward, though less than the former [postures]. God Mighty and Majestic said, *In the creation of the heavens and the earth, and in the alternation of night and day, there are signs for men of understanding: those who remember God while standing, sitting, and lying down, and meditate upon the creation of the heavens and the earth* (Quran, 3:190–1).

It is established in a rigorously authenticated hadith that 'Ā'isha (God be pleased with her) said, "The Messenger of God (God bless him and grant him peace) would recline in my lap reading the Quran while I was menstruating."[7] (Bukhārī and Muslim related it, and in one narration [it reads] "...*reciting* the Quran while his head was in my lap.")

Abū Mūsā al-Ash'arī (God be pleased with him) said, "I read the Quran in my Prayer and in my bed." 'Ā'isha (God be pleased with her) said, "I read my *ḥizb* while laying on my side in bed."

Seeking Protection

When one intends to begin recitation, he first seeks protection saying: *"A'ūdhu billāhi min al-shayṭān al-rajīm"* ["I seek protection by God from the accursed Devil"], as the majority of the scholars said. Some of the righteous forebears have said that one should seeks protection *after* reciting, because God Most High says, *When you recite the Quran, seek refuge from the accursed Devil* (Quran, 16:98). The interpretation of this verse—according to the majority of scholars—is that if you have determined to recite, seek refuge.

ITS DESCRIPTION: The description of seeking protection is as we mentioned. A group of the Righteous Forebears, however, would say: "I seek protection in God, the All-Hearing, the All-Knowing, from the accursed Devil." There is nothing wrong with this, but the preferred one is the first.

ITS RULING: Seeking protection is recommended but not obligatory. It is recommended for every reciter, whether in Prayer or not. It is recommended in Prayer in each *rak'a*, according to the sound opinion of our Shāfi'ī companions. According to the second opinion, it is only recommended in the first *rak'a*, and if one neglected it in the first, then he says it in the second. It is recommended to seek refuge after the inagural *"Allāhu akbar"* is said in the Funeral Prayer, according to the soundest opinion.

Saying "Bismillāhi al-Raḥmān al-Raḥīm"

One should take care to recite *"Bismillāhi al-Raḥmān al-Raḥīm"* ["In the name of God, Most Merciful and Compassionate"] in the beginning of each chapter [of the Quran] except for Sūrat al-Barā' (9) [or al-Tawba].[8] Most scholars consider [the *basmala*] a verse [of the Quran] since it is written in the text of the Quran [*muṣḥaf*], and has been written in the beginning of all chapters except al-Barā': so if one recites it he affirms a complete recitation [of the whole Quran] or a whole chapter, and if one omits it, then—according to the majority of scholars—he is neglecting part of the Quran. If the recitation is part of a service that involves wages—such as reciting a seventh of the Quran [*subu'*] or a thirtieth [*juz'*] that comprises endowments and sustenance—more care must be taken to read [the *basmala*] so as to be certain that the reciter deserves [the wage] he is taking, for if he left it out he would not deserve anything from the endowment, according to those who say that the phrase *"Bismillāhi al-Raḥmān al-Raḥīm"* is a verse at the beginning of the chapter. This fine point merits additional attention and prominence.

Humility and Pondering

At the beginning and during recitation, one's state should be that of humility and reflection. There is boundless evidence for this—very well known and too obvious to be mentioned here. [This state] is the sought-after objective, through which breasts are opened and hearts illuminated.

God Mighty and Majestic said, *Will they not reflect upon the Quran?* (Quran, 4:82); [*This is*] *a Book that We have sent down to you, full of blessing, that they may reflect upon its signs* (Quran, 38:29). The hadith concerning this topic are numerous, and the sayings of the Righteous Forebears are well known.

Once a number of Righteous Forebears spent the night reciting a single verse, pondering and repeating it until the morning. A number of them were overwhelmed when reciting [it], and some actually died.

We related that Bahz ibn Ḥakīm said that the noble Successor Zurār ibn Awfā (God be well pleased with them), led them in the morning Prayer; he recited [Sūra 74] until he reached the passage, *For when the trumpet sounds, surely that day will be a day of distress* (Quran, 74:8–9), at which point he fell to the ground dead. Bahz said, "I was among those who carried him."[9]

Aḥmad ibn Abī al-Ḥawārī (God be pleased with him), the splendor of Syria, was just as Abū al-Qāsim al-Junayd (God grant him mercy) had said: when the Quran was recited to him he would cry out and faint. Ibn Abī Dāwūd said that al-Qāsim ibn 'Uthmān al-Jū'ī (God grant him mercy) would scold Ibn Abī al-Ḥawārī for this. Al-Jū'ī, one of Damascus' outstanding hadith specialists, whose superiority is put before Ibn Abī al-Ḥawārī, said, "Abū al-Jawzā', Qays ibn Ḥabtar, and others likewise scolded him." I say that it is correct not to scold them, except for someone who admits behaving this way artificially. And God knows best.

Ibrāhīm al-Khawwāṣ (God be pleased with him), the noble master of spiritual gifts and experiences, said: "There are five medicines for the heart: reciting the Quran with pondering, emptying the stomach, standing at night [in Prayer], supplicating during the last part of the night, and sitting with the righteous."

Repeating a Verse

We have mentioned previously the importance of pondering [the Quran]—making clear its [elevated] station—and the sensitivity of the Righteous Forebears. We related that Abū Dharr (God Most High be well pleased with him) said that the Prophet (God bless him and grant him peace) stood repeating a verse until dawn. The verse was *If You punish them, they are Your servants...* (Quran, 5:118).[10]

Tamīm al-Dārī (God Most High be well pleased with him) said that he repeated the following verse until daybreak: *Or do those who commit evil deeds suppose that We shall make them as those who believe and do good works?*[11] (Quran, 45:21).

'Abbād ibn Ḥamza said, "I visited Asmā' [bint Abī Bakr] (God be pleased with them borth) while she was reciting: *But God has been gracious to us, and delivered us from the torment of the breath of Fire* (Quran, 52:27). I stood there with her and she began repeating it and supplicating. This grew long for me, so I went to the market and took care of my needs. I then returned and she was still repeating and supplicating." We related this [same] story from 'Ā'isha (God Most High be well pleased with her).

Ibn Mas'ūd (God be pleased with him) repeated, *My Lord, increase me in knowledge* (Quran, 20:114). Sa'īd ibn Jubayr repeated [the verses], *And guard yourselves against a day in which you will be brought back to God* (Quran, 2:281), *They will soon know when shackles and chains shall be round their necks* Quran, 40:70–1), and *What has deceived you as regards your generous Lord* (Quran, 82:6).

Whenever Ḍaḥḥāk recited, *They shall be covered with layers of fire from above and from beneath more layers* (Quran, 39:16), he would repeat it until the end of night.

Weeping During Recitation

What incites someone to weep while reciting the Quran was explained in the two previous sections. It is an attribute of those with profound knowledge of God [*'ārifīn*], and a distinguishing feature of God's righteous devotees. God Most High said, *They fall down upon their faces weeping, and it increases them in humility* (Quran, 17:109).

Many hadiths and accounts from the Righteous Forebears have been related concerning this. Among them is from the Prophet (God bless him give and him peace): "Read the Quran and weep. If you do not weep, cause yourself weep."[12]

'Umar ibn al-Khaṭṭāb (God be pleased with him) prayed the Morning Prayer in congregation and read Sūrat Yūsuf (12). He wept until his tears flowed over his collarbone. In another version [of the report], it was in the Nightfall Prayer, affirming that this happened repeatedly, and in one version he wept until the people in the rows behind him heard his weeping.

Abū Rajā' said, "I saw Ibn 'Abbās and below his eyes were tracks wet from tears." Abū Ṣāliḥ said, "A group of people from Yemen came to Abū Bakr al-Ṣiddīq (God be pleased with him) and began reciting the Quran and they wept. Abū Bakr al-Ṣiddīq (God be pleased with him) said, 'This is how we were.'" Hishām said, "I sometimes heard Muḥammad ibn Sīrīn's crying at night while he was praying."

The accounts concerning this are innumerable. What we have just alluded to suffices. And God knows best.

Al-Imām Abū Ḥāmid al-Ghazālī said, "Weeping is recommended while reciting [the Quran] or witnessing [its recitation]." He said, "The way to achieve this is by bringing sadness to mind by pondering the threats and warnings, the covenants and agreements that it contains, and then contemplating one's shortcomings with regard to them. If this does not bring to mind sadness and weeping, as it does with the elite worshippers, then one should weep from the lack of it, since it is among the greatest of calamities."[13]

Distinctly Reciting

One should recite distinctly. The scholars (God be well pleased with them) are in agreement that distinct recitation is recommended. God Most High said, *And recite the Quran distinctly* (Quran, 73:4).

It is established that Umm Salama (God be pleased with her) described the recitation of the Messenger of God (God bless him and grant him peace) as being distinct, letter by letter.[14] (Abū Dāwūd, Nasā'ī, and Tirmidhī related it. Tirmidhī said that it is a well-rigorously authenticated hadith.)

Mu'āwiyya ibn Qurra [related] that 'Abdallāh ibn Mughaffal (God be pleased with him) said, "On the day that Mecca was conquered, I saw the Messenger of God (God bless him and grant him peace) on his camel reciting Sūrat al-Fatḥ (48). He recited distinctly in a vibrant tone."[15] (Bukhārī and Muslim related it.) Ibn 'Abbās (God be pleased with him) said, "It is more beloved to me to distinctly recite one chapter than to recite the entire Quran." Mujāhid said that he was asked about two men, one of them recited Sūrat al-Baqara and Sūrat Āl 'Imrān and the other recited only al-Baqara, [while] their time spent in bowing, prostrating, and sitting were precisely equal. He said, "The one who read only Sūrat al-Baqara is better."

Reciting Rapidly

Reciting rapidly with excessive haste, called *hadhrama*, is prohibited. It is established that 'Abdallāh ibn Mas'ūd (God be pleased with him) said that a man told him: "I read the short chapters in a single *rak'a*." 'Abdallāh ibn Mas'ūd said, "This is like poetry recited rapidly. There are people who recite the Quran and it does not pass their throats. But if it descends into the heart and becomes firmly set therein, it will provide benefit."[16] (Bukhārī and Muslim related [the hadith], and this is the wording of one of Muslim's narrations.)

The scholars said that reciting slowly is recommended for the sake of understanding. As for others, it is recommended for a foreigner who does not understand its meanings to recite slowly, since this is closer to veneration and respect, and has much more impact on the heart.

Supplicating While Reciting

Whenever one passes by a verse containing the mention of mercy, it is recommended that he ask God Most High from His bounty. Whenever he passes by a verse containing the mention of "chastisement," he seeks protection with God from evil or from chastisement or he says, *"Allāhumma innī as'aluka al-'āfiyyah"* ["O God, I ask You for safe-being"], "[*Allāhumma innī*] *as'aluka al-mu'āfa min kulli makrūh"* ["I ask You for exemption from every disliked thing"], or similar [supplications].

When he passes by a verse declaring God Most High transcendent beyond any imperfection, he should declare Him transcendent beyond imperfection and say: *"Subḥānahu wa ta'ālā"* ["He is Transcendent and Most High"], *"Tabārak wa ta'ālā"* ["He is Blessed and Most High"], or *"Jallat 'aẓamatu rabbinā"* ["Glorified is our Lord's greatness"].

It is rigorously authenticated that Ḥudhayfa ibn al-Yamān (God be well pleased with him and his father) said, "I prayed with the Prophet (God bless him and grant him peace) one night. He started with Sūrat al-Baqara. I said [to myself]: 'He will bow at the one hundredth verse.' He then passed it, and I said, 'He will pray one full *rak'a* with [the whole sura],' but then he passed it. He then started Sūrat al-Nisā' and read it. I said, 'He will bow with its [completion].' He then started Sūrat Āl 'Imrān and read it. He read leisurely. Whenever he passed by a verse where God is declared transcendent beyond imperfection, he would say *"Subḥān*

Allāh"; whenever he passed by a verse where something is asked for, he would ask for it; and whenever he passed by a verse where protection is sought with God from the Devil, he would seek it."[17] Muslim related it in his *Ṣaḥīḥ*. At the time, Sūrat al-Nisā' came before Sūrat Āl 'Imrān.

Our Shāfi'ī companions (God Most High grant them mercy) said that asking, seeking protection, and saying *"Subḥān Allāh"* are recommended for everyone listening [to the Quran's recitation], whether or not they are praying. They said that this is recommended for the one leading a congregation [in Prayer], following an *imām*, or praying individually, since they are supplications and are all equal in it, like saying "*āmīn*" after the recitation of Sūrat al-Fātiḥa.

Differences of Opinion

What we mentioned regarding the recommended nature of asking and seeking protection [during the recitation] is part of the *madhhab* of Imām al-Shāfi'ī (God be pleased with him) and the majority of the scholars (God grant them mercy). However, Abū Ḥanīfa (God be pleased with him) said that this is not recommended, rather it is disliked in Prayer.[18] The correct position is the opinion of the majority based on all that we have mentioned.

Things from which to protect the Quran

Among the things that should be emphasized is protecting the Quran from matters that some heedless reciters may neglect when gathered together. [The emphasized etiquette] includes avoiding laughing, clamor, and conversing during a recitation—with the exception of absolutely necessary words. This complies with the example in the statement of God Most High: *And when the Quran is recited, listen to it and pay heed, that you may obtain mercy* (Quran, 7:204).

The reciter should follow what Ibn Abī Dāwūd related about Ibn 'Umar (God be well pleased with him and his father both), "Whenever he recited the Quran [outside of Prayer], he would not speak until he had finished what he wanted to recite." Bukhārī related this in his *Ṣaḥīḥ*, and said, "He did not talk until finishing [his recitation]." He mentioned it in the "Book of Tafsīr" where God Most High says: *Your wives are a tillage for you*[19] (Quran, 2:223).

Fidgeting, Distractions, and the Unlawful

Other things [to avoid] include fidgeting with the hands or the like. Since one is addressing his Lord, Sublime and Most Great, he should not fidget when in His presence. And these matters include looking at what distracts and scatters the mind. More abhorrent than all of these is looking at what is impermissible to look at in general, though it is permissible—out of need—to look about when selling and buying; taking and giving; regarding medical attention; teaching and the like; and other areas of need. In these circumstances, the one looking limits himself to only what is necessary and does not look on unnecessarily.

In all situations, it is unlawful to look with lust, whether a man or woman, and whether the woman is unmarriageable kin or not—except looking at one's spouse. Some of our Shāfiʿī companions said that it is unlawful to look with lust at his unmarriageable kin, such as his daughter or mother.

And God knows best.[20]

Enjoining Right and Forbidding Wrong

Someone attending an assembly for recitation and who sees one of these censured things we mentioned or the like, he must forbid it to whatever extent possible: with the *hand* for someone who is able, with the *tongue* for someone unable with the hand but able with words, and if not [with the hand or tongue] then he censures it with his heart. And God Most High knows best.

Reciting in a Foreign Language

It is not permissible to recite the Quran in a [non-Arabic] language, whether or not the reciter is proficient with Arabic, and whether or not it takes place during Prayer. If one recites the Quran in a foreign language during Prayer, his Prayer is invalid. This is our school and the school of Mālik, Aḥmad, Dāwūd, and Abū Bakr ibn Mundhir. Abū Ḥanīfa said that it is permissible and it is valid to pray using [a foreign language].[21] Abū Yūsuf said that this is permissible for someone who is not versed in Arabic, but impermissible for someone who is.

Permissible Recitations

It is permissible to recite [the Quran] using the seven agreed upon recitations.[22] It is not permissible using anything else, or using the *shādh* [anomalous] accounts transmitted from the seven reciters. This will come in CHAPTER VII (if God Most High wills), in which [we] elucidate on how the jurists agree that one who recites in [an unlawful manner] should seek repentance.

Our Shāfiʿī companions and others said that if one were to recite with the *shādh* in his Prayer, his Prayer would be invalid if he knew [the ruling forbidding it]. If he was ignorant of it, then the Prayer is valid, but he is not rewarded for this recitation.

Imām Abū ʿAmr ibn ʿAbd al-Barr, the hadith master, reports that there is consensus among the Muslims that it is impermissible to recite with a *shādh* recitation, and that one does not pray behind someone reciting as such. The scholars said that whoever recites with a *shādh* recitation while ignorant of [the recitation itself] or of it being impermissible and is then duly informed, but still he repeats it, he should be reproached until he refrains. [This holds true] if he knew [from the start] that it was not permissible. It is obligatory that anyone able to censure and prevent him [from this] should indeed do so.

Switching Recitations

If one begins to recite using one accepted recitation, he should not interrupt it as long as the words [he recites] remain connected. He may, however, recite with another of the seven recitations when the words are no longer connected [at a natural pause]. But it is better for him to continue with the first recitation throughout the sitting.

Reciting in Order

The scholars said that it is better to recite following the order of the *muṣḥaf* [the text of the Quran]. [For example], one recites al-Fātiḥa (1), then al-Baqara (2), then Āl ʿImrān (3), then what follows, according to the order—whether or not one recites during Prayer. Some of our Shāfiʿī companions even said that if he recited al-Nās (114) in the first *rakʿa* he should read al-Baqara (2) in the second after al-Fātiḥa (1).

Some of our Shāfiʿī companions have said it is recommended that when one recites a chapter he should read what follows it immediately. Support for this is in the fact that the *muṣḥaf*'s order was arranged this way purely out of divine wisdom. So one should preserve [the order], with the exceptions mentioned in the the *Sharīʿa*, such as the Morning Prayer on Friday, in which one recites Sūrat al-Sajda (32) in the first *rakʿa* and in the second Sūrat al-Insān[23] (76);[24] the Eid Prayer, in which Sūrat Qāf (50) is recited in the first *rakʿa* and in the second Sūrat al-Qamr (54);[25] the two *sunna rakʿāt* of the Morning Prayer, in which Sūrat al-Kāfirūn (109) is recited in the first *rakʿa* and in the second Sūrat al-Ikhlāṣ (112); the *rakʿāt* of *Witr* Prayer, in which Sūrat al-Aʿlā (87) is recited in the first *rakʿa*, Sūrat al-Kāfirūn (109) in the second, and, in the third, Sūrat al-Ikhlāṣ (112), Sūrat al-Falaq (113),[26] and Sūrat al-Nās (114).[27]

It is permissible to forgo the order by reading a chapter that does not immediately follow or by reading a chapter and then any before it. Many accounts have been related concerning this. ʿUmar ibn al-Khaṭṭāb (God be pleased with him) recited Sūrat al-Kahf (18) in the first *rakʿa* of Morning Prayer and Sūrat Yūsuf (12) in the second.

Reciting a Chapter of the Quran Itself in Reverse Order

Some scholars disliked violating the order of the *muṣḥaf* altogether. Ibn Abī Dāwūd related from al-Ḥasan [al-Baṣrī] that he disliked violating the order of the *muṣḥaf*.[28] [He related] with his rigorously authenticated chain that ʿAbdallāh ibn Masʿūd (God be pleased with him) was informed of an individual who recites [passages of] the Quran in an inverse order: "This will invert his heart," he said.[29]

As for reciting a chapter from its end to its beginning, this is categorically forbidden, since it removes aspects of [the Quran's] inimitability [*i'jāz*] and negates the wisdom invested in the specific ordering of the verses. Ibn Abī Dāwūd related from Imām Ibrāhīm al-Nakha'ī (the honorable Successor [*Tābi'ī*]) and from Imām Mālik ibn Anas that they both disliked this, and that Mālik reprimanded the practice and said it was appalling.

Teaching children from the end of the *muṣḥaf* [moving] toward its beginning is good and is not relevant to this discussion since it is a discontinuous recitation throughout several days. In addition, it makes it easier for children to memorize.

And God knows best.

Reciting from the Muṣḥaf or from Memory

Reciting the Quran from the *muṣḥaf* [the text of the Quran] is better than reciting from memory since looking in the *muṣḥaf* is a kind of worship one seeks, for it combines recitation and looking. This is what some of our Shāfi'ī companions, al-Qāḍī Ḥusayn, Abū Ḥāmid al-Ghazālī, and groups of Righteous Forebears have said.

Al-Imām al-Ghazālī in *al-Iḥyā'* cites that many of the Companions (God be well pleased with them) recited from the *muṣḥaf* and found it reprehensible that a single day would pass without looking in the *muṣḥaf*.[30] Ibn Abī Dāwūd related accounts from many of the Righteous Forebears that they recited from the *muṣḥaf*, and I myself do not see any disagreement therein.

It may be said that this differs according to different people: reciting from the *muṣḥaf* is the choice of one who finds having veneration [of God] and pondering [the Quran] equally attainable whether reading from the *muṣḥaf* or from memory; yet reciting from memory is preferable for someone whose veneration is not complete when reading from the *muṣḥaf*, and thus his veneration and pondering are greater [when reading from he heart] than when reciting from the *muṣḥaf*. This is a good opinion. It is clear that the words and actions of the Righteous Forebears conform to these details.

Devotion to the Quran in a Group

Know that a group reciting together is a recommended act, according to clear evidence and according to the actions of the pure Righteous Forebears and their successors. It is rigorously authenticated by way of Abū Hurayra and Abū Sa'īd al-Khudrī (God be well pleased with them both) that the Prophet (God bless him and grant him peace) said, "No group remembers God except that angels encompass them, mercy envelops them, and tranquility descends upon them; and God mentions them to those in His presence."[31] (Tirmidhī said that it is a well-rigorously authenticated hadith.)

Abū Hurayra (God be pleased with him) related that the Prophet (God bless him and grant him peace) said, "A group does not gather in one of the houses of God Most High reciting the Quran and studying it together, except that tranquility descends upon them, mercy envelops them, the angels encompass them, and God mentions them to those in His presence."[32] (Muslim related it, as did Abū Dāwūd with a rigorously authenticated chain meeting the criteria of Bukhārī and Muslim.)

Mu'āwiyyah (God be pleased with him) said that the Prophet (God bless him and grant him peace) approached a circle of his Companions and asked, "What caused you to sit together?" They said, "We sat to remember God Most High and praise Him because He guided us to Islam and graced us with it." The Prophet (God bless him and grant him peace) said, "[Angel] Gabriel [peace be upon him] came to me and informed me that God boasts of you to the angels."[33] Tirmidhī and Nasā'ī related it; Tirmidhī said that it is a well-rigorously authenticated hadith. The hadiths concerning this are many.

Dārimī related with his rigorously authenticated chain that Ibn 'Abbās (God be well pleased with him and his father both) said, "Whoever listens to a verse of the Quran, it is a light for him."[34] Ibn Abī Dāwūd related that Abū Dardā' (God be pleased with him) would study the Quran with a group, all of them reciting together.

The superiority of studying gathered together is related from many among the illustrious scholars of the early generations and the grand legists of old. Ḥassan ibn ʿAṭiyya and al-Awzāʿī both said, "The first one to initiate studies in the Damascus mosque is Hishām ibn Ismāʿīl on his arrival to ʿAbd al-Mālik."

By contrast, Ibn Abī Dāwūd related from al-Ḍaḥḥāk ibn ʿAbd al-Raḥmān ibn ʿArzab that he censured these studies and said, "I did not see nor did I hear [any of this] and I have met the Companions of the Messenger of God (God bless him and grant him peace)," meaning, "I did not see anyone engaged in this." And Ibn Wahb said, "I said to Mālik, 'What do you think about a people gathering and reading a single chapter together until they finish it?' He rejected this and censured it. He said, 'This is not how people do it. Only one person would recite it to another.'"

Their censuring of [congregational recitation of the Quran] runs contrary to the actions of the early generations and contrary to what the evidence implies. So it should be disregarded, instead rely on what has preceded about congregational recitation being recommended. However, recitation in groups has conditions that we previously mentioned. And they should be given attention.

And God knows best.

There are many clear texts concerning the superiority of the one who gathers people to recite, such as the statement of the Prophet (God bless him and grant him peace): "The one who guides to good is like the one who performs it [himself]."[35] Also, "Guiding a single person [to Islam] is better for you than the best of camels."[36] The hadith concerning this are many. God Most High says, *Help one another in benevolence and piety* (Quran, 5:2). There is no doubt about the great reward in striving for this.

Reciting in Turns

This involves a gathering in which someone recites , for example, a tenth of the Quran [*ʿushūr*] *or a thirtieth* [*juz'*], and then falls silent, as another recites from where the former had left off, and so on. This is permissible and good. Mālik (God be pleased with him) was asked about this and he said, "There is no problem with it."

Reciting with a Raised Voice

This section is important and should be given particular attention. Know that there are many hadiths found in the rigorously authenticated volumes of hadith and others [hadith compendiums] indicating that it is recommended to raise one's voice when reciting; yet there is an account stating that it is recommended to hush the recitation and to lower the voice. (We will provide a small section that deals with its source, if God wills.) [See page 56.]

Imām Abū Ḥāmid al-Ghazālī[37] and other scholars have said that the way to reconcile these [seemingly] conflicting narrations and accounts is [to know] that making [one's recitation] secret is further removed from ostentatious show and is thus better for someone who fears it. If one does not fear ostentation in reciting audibly and raising the voice, then being audible and raising the voice is better, since there is more effort involved and its benefit extends to others [who may hear it]. And benefit that extends to others is better than personal benefit [alone]. Also, [audible recitation] awakens the heart of the reciter, gathers his attentiveness to thinking about [what he reads], draws his hearing to it, repels sleep, and invigorates [the mind]; and it rouses others who sleep or are inattentive and thus energizes them. Scholars have said that whenever one brings to mind all of these intentions, then being audible is better, and if these intentions are combined together then the reward is duly increased. Al-Ghazālī said, "Because of this we say that reciting from the *muṣḥaf* is better, and this is the ruling of this matter."

As for the cited accounts [on this topic], they are numerous. I will allude to the essential portions of some of them. It is established in the rigorously authenticated [hadith] that Abū Hurayra (God be pleased with him) said, "I heard the Messenger of God (God bless him and grant him peace) say, 'God does not listen attentively [*adhina*] to anything the way He listens to a prophet with a beautiful voice audibly singing the Quran.'"[38] (Bukhārī and Muslim related it.) The meaning of "*adhina*" here is to listen attentively and implies being well pleased and approving.

Abū Mūsā al-Ash'arī (God be pleased with him) stated that the Messenger of God (God bless him and grant him peace) said to him, "You have been given a *mizmār* [exceptional sense of melody] from the family of Dāwūd." (Bukhārī and Muslim related it.) In one of Muslim's narrations [of the above hadith], the Messenger of God (God bless him and grant him peace) said, "If you had [only] seen me while I was listening to your recitation yesterday." (Muslim also related it from Burayda ibn al-Ḥuṣayb.[39])

Faḍālah ibn 'Ubayd (God be pleased with him) stated that the Messenger of God (God bless him and grant him peace) said, "Surely, God listens more attentively to a man who has a beautiful voice [reciting] the Quran than an owner of a singing girl listens to his singing girl."[40] (Ibn Mājah related it.)

Abū Mūsā (God be pleased with him) stated that the Messenger of God (God bless him and grant him peace) said, "I know the voices of a group of Ash'arīs at night when they enter, and I know where they settled down because of their voices with the Quran at night, even if I did not see where they settled when they settled during the day."[41] (Bukhārī and Muslim related it.)

Al-Barā' ibn 'Āzib (God be pleased with him) stated that the Messenger of God (God bless him and grant him peace) said, "Decorate the Quran with your voices."[42] (Abū Dāwūd, Nasā'ī and others related it.)

Ibn Abī Dāwūd [relates] that 'Alī (God be pleased with him) heard people reciting Quran in the mosque at midmorning and he said, "Glad tidings to them: they are the people most beloved to the Messenger of God (God bless him and grant him peace)."

There are many hadiths affirming [the merit of] audible recitation. As for the accounts of statements and actions of the Companions and the Successors, they are too many and too well known to mention. All of this was said, however, with regard to one who does not fear ostentation, being proud, or any other repugnant defect, and does not annoy a group by confusing them in their Prayer and confounding them therein.

Reciting Quietly

The preference to conceal recitation has been conveyed from a group of the Successors out of their fear of what we have mentioned.

Al-A'mash said, "I visited Ibrāhīm [al-Nakha'ī] while he was reading from the *muṣḥaf*. A man asked him for permission [to enter]. He closed the *muṣḥaf* and said, 'I do this so he does not see that I read the Quran every hour [of the day].'" Abū al-'Āliya said, "I was sitting with the Companions of the Messenger of God (God bless him and give him peace, and be well pleased with them). One of them said, 'During the night I read such-and-such.' They said, 'That is your portion [of reward] from it.'" The hadith of 'Uqba ibn 'Āmir (God be pleased with him) provides them evidence: "One who publicly [recites] the Quran is like the one who gives voluntary charity in public. And one who conceals the Quran is like the one who gives voluntary charity in private."[43] Abū Dāwūd, Tirmidhī, and Nasā'ī related it. Tirmidhī said it is an authentic [*ḥasan*] hadith." Tirmidhī also said that the meaning of the hadith is that one who makes the Quran inaudible is superior to one who makes it audible, since the giving of voluntary charity in a concealed manner is superior to voluntary charity that is made public, according to the people of knowledge, since the former is safe from conceit, for conceit is not feared for someone who conceals works, though it is feared in someone who announces them.

Summary

I say that all of this conforms with what was previously mentioned in the foregoing sections: if one fears something offensive in [reciting the Quran] audibly, he should not make it audible; if one does not fear this, then it is recommended for him to make it audible. And if the recitation is from a group gathered together, it is emphatically recommended to raise the voice because of what we previously mentioned and because of the benefit it offers to others when doing so.

And God knows best.

Beautifying the Voice with Quran

The scholars of the earlier generations, including the Companions (God be well pleased with them), the Successors, and the scholars of various regions after them—the *imāms* of the Muslims—are in agreement that it is recommended to beautify the voice when reciting the Quran. The statements and actions are well known to the furthest extent, so there is no need or use in citing individual instances.

The evidence for this is the hadiths of the Messenger of God (God bless him and grant him peace) that are well circulated among the general public and the elite, "Adorn the Quran with your voices;" "Indeed he was given a *mizmār* [exceptional sense of melody]..." and the hadith: "Surely, God listens more attentively..." All of these were mentioned above.

In the section on the superiority of reciting distinctly, there is the hadith of ʿAbdallāh ibn Mughaffal concerning the Prophet (God bless him and grant him peace) reciting in a vibrant tone. And there is the hadith of Saʿd ibn Abī Waqqāṣ, and the hadith Abū Lubāba (God be well pleased with them) that the Prophet (God bless him and grant him peace) said, "Whoever does not sing the Quran is not one of us."[44] (Abū Dāwūd related them both with chains of transmitters that are good; there is disagreement about Saʿd's chain that does no harm.) The majority of scholars say that the meaning of "not sing" is "not beautifying his voice." Al-Barāʾ (God be pleased with him) said, "I heard the Messenger of God (God be pleased with him) recite Sūrat al-Tīn (95) in the Nightfall Prayer. I have not heard anyone with a voice more beautiful than his."[45] (Bukhārī and Muslim related it.)

The scholars (God have mercy upon them) said that it is recommended to beautify the voice and adorn it with recitation, as long as it does not exceed the proper limits of recitation by being overly stretched out. If [the recitation] is exaggerated such that a letter is added or is muffled, then it is unlawful.

Reciting with a Melodious Fashion

As for reciting in a melodious tone, Imām al-Shāfi'ī (God grant him mercy) has said in places, "I dislike it," and in [other] places, "I do not dislike it." Our Shāfi'ī companions said that this is not a matter of two opinions. Instead, it pertains to detailed rulings: if one is excessive in stretching out [the recitation] and exceeds the limits, then this is what Imām al-Shāfi'ī disliked. But if the reciter does exceed in this manner, this is what Imām al-Shāfi'ī did not dislike.

The master judge [al-Māwardī] said in his book *al-Ḥāwī*: "Recitation using modes of melody that remove the utterance of the Quran from its [original] phrasing by inserting vowelization [*ḥarakāt*] into it, removing vowelization from it, elongating what should be short, shortening what should be elongated, or stretching out [words] such that it voids its meaning or obscures it—[this recitation] is unlawful and renders its reciter morally corrupt. And one who listens to it sins, since he deviates from [the Quran's] straight manner to what is crooked. God Most High says: *It is a Quran in Arabic, without any crookedness* (Quran, 39:28)." [Al-Māwardī] said, "If the melody does not remove [the Quran] from its [original] phrasing nor the reciter from its clear recitation, it is permissible since the reciter augments its beauty with his melody." This is the statement of the master judge [al-Māwardī].

Some ignorant laymen are afflicted with the former [illicit] type of recitation using unlawful melodies, and so are ignoble fools who recite at funerals and some festivals. This is a manifestly unlawful innovation; every one listening to it sins, just as the master judge has said. And everyone capable of stopping [such recitation] or censuring it is sinful if he does not do so. Toward this end, I have expended some of my abilities, and I hope that God the Noble—from His beneficence—gives success, for the sake of its removal, to those who are qualified to do so and grant them well-being.

In al-Muzanī's *Mukhtaṣar*, al-Shāfi'ī says, "[A reciter] beautifies his voice in whatever manner it may be." He said, "I like what is recited slowly and with sadness." The lexicographers say that recitation is "slow" when it is said to be drawn out without being [unnecessarily] elongated. And it is said that "one recites with sadness" if he softens his voice.

Ibn Abī Dāwūd has narrated with his chain of narration that Abū Hurayra (God be pleased with him) read Sūrat al-Takwīr (81) making it sad, resembling a dirge. [It is related] in the *Sunan* of Abū Dāwūd that Abū Mulayka was asked, "What is your opinion if one's voice is not beautiful?" He replied, "He should beautify it as much as he is able."[46]

Seeking a Wholesome, Beautiful Recitation

Know that many among the Righteous Forebears would request those who recite with beautiful voices to recite while they listen on. There is agreement that this is recommended. It is the habit of the elite devoted worshippers and the righteous worshippers of God, and it is an established *sunna* of the Prophet (God bless him and grant him peace) himself.

It is rigorously authenticated that Ibn Mas'ūd (God be pleased with him) said, "The Messenger of God (God bless him and grant him peace) said to me, 'Recite the Quran to me.' I said, 'O Messenger of God! Shall I recite to you while it was revealed to you?' He said, 'I love to hear it from someone other than myself.' So I recited Sūrat al-Nisā' until I came to this verse, *How will it be when We bring a witness from every nation, and We bring you* [*O Muḥammad*] *as a witness against these* [*people*] (Quran, 4:41). He said, 'Enough.' I turned to him and his eyes were brimming with tears."[47] (Bukhārī and Muslim narrated it.)

Dārimī and others related with their chains of narration that 'Umar ibn al-Khaṭṭāb (God be pleased with him) would say to Abū Mūsā al-Ash'arī, "Remind us of our Lord," and Abū Mūsā would then recite [Quran] to him.[48]

The accounts concerning this are well known and many. Some among the Righteous Forebears have actually died because of the [powerful] recitations of those whom they had asked to recite. And God knows best.

Reciting at Assemblies

Some scholars recommend that an assembly gathered [to hear or study] the hadith of the Prophet (God bless him and grant him peace) should commence and conclude with a reciter possessed of a beautiful voice reciting something brief from the Quran. In these contexts, the reciter should recite what is appropriate and suitable for the assembly. His recitation should include verses in which there is hope, fear, and exhortation; having abstinence in this world, awakening a desire and arousal for the Hereafter, and diminishing vain hopes, and [the importance of] having noble character.

Reading What has Complete Meaning

When the reciter begins in the middle of a chapter or does not stop at its end, he should start from the previous words [of the sura] that are related to one another [in meaning]. The same applies when the reciter stops on words that are related to each other or that come at the end of a dialogue. When beginning and stopping, the reciter should not limit himself to [strict textual divisions of the Quran, like stopping or starting at] tenths, sixtieths, and thirtieths [of the text], since he might be in the middle of an interrelated passage, like the following thirtieths [of the Quran] containing words of the Most High [that impart meaning only when read with what is connected]: *And all the married women...* (Quran, 4:24);[49] [*Joseph said,*] *"I do not claim innocence for my soul..."* (Quran, 12:53);[50] *The answer of his people was that they said...* (Quran, 27:56);[51] *And she who is dutiful to God and His Messenger...* (Quran, 33:31);[52] *We sent not down against his people after him a host from heaven...* (Quran, 36:28);[53] *To God is referred the knowledge of the Hour...* (Quran, 41:47);[54] *There the evil results of their deeds will confront them...* (Quran, 39:48);[55] and *"What is your errand, O Messengers?" he said...* (Quran, 51:31).[56]

It is the same for sixtieths, like the phrase of the Most High: *And remember God on the Appointed Days*... (Quran, 2:203);[57] and *Say, "Shall I tell you of better than that?"*... (Quran, 3:15).[58]

The reciter should not begin or stop at any of these [places] or their like, since they are related in meaning to what came before it. People should not be deceived by reciters who ignore this etiquette and do not ponder these meanings! The reciter should follow the example of what al-Ḥākim Abū ʿAbdallāh narrated with his chain of narration that al-Fuḍayl ibn ʿIyāḍ (God be pleased with him) said, "Do not feel repelled from the paths of guidance by how small is the number of its people, nor be deceived by the large number of those who are ruined! And do not be harmed by how small is the number of those making progress!"

Because of this meaning, the scholars have said that reciting a short chapter in its entirety is better than reciting the same amount of a large chapter in part, since the interrelatedness [of its meanings] may be hidden to some people in some circumstances. Ibn Abī Dāwūd has narrated with his chain of narration that ʿAbdallāh ibn Abī al-Hudhayl, the well-known Successor, said, "They disliked it when they read part of a verse and left out a part."

When It Is Offensive to Read the Quran

Know that reciting the Quran, in general, is absolutely recommended, except for specific circumstances where the *Sharīʿa* has prohibited its recitation. I will now mention those circumstances that come to my mind, but I will not include their proofs since they are well known.

It is offensive to recite while one is bowing, prostrating, [saying the] *tashahud*, and other stations of the Prayer [*ṣalāt*] other than standing. It is offensive for someone following [the Prayer leader (*imām*)] to recite anything in addition to al-Fātiḥa during an audible Prayer, [that is, Dawn, Sunset, and Nightfall Prayers], when he hears the *imām*'s recitation. It is offensive [to recite] while relieving oneself, or while drowsy, or any similar circumstance in which the Quran becomes unintelligible to one.

During the Friday Prayer

It is offensive to recite during the Friday sermon for anyone who hears it. However, it is not offensive for someone who does not hear [the sermon], rather, it is recommended. This is the sound and preferred opinion. The verdict that this is offensive has been related from Ṭawūs, and that it is *not* offensive according to Ibrāhīm [al-Nakha'ī]. It is possible to reconcile between their two statements applying what we had said, regarding what our Shāfi'ī companions have mentioned[, namely, this is a matter of detail rather than something absolute].

Reciting While Going Around the Ka'ba [Ṭawāf]

It is not offensive to recite while going around the Ka'ba. This is our *madhhab*, and most of the scholars have iterated [this opinion]. Ibn Mundhir quoted this from 'Aṭā', Mujāhid, Ibn al-Mubārak, Abū Thawr, and the people of juridical opinion [*ahl al-ra'y*]; and he also conveys it from al-Ḥasan al-Baṣrī. But 'Urwa ibn al-Zubayr and Mālik hold that reciting while going around the Ka'ba is offensive. The sound position, however, is the former. The discussion on the difference concerning reciting in a bath-house and along a road [one travels], and concerning one's whose mouth is unclean, has preceded. [See CHAPTER VI.]

Rejected Innovations

One of the rejected innovations regarding the recitation [of the Quran] is what the ignorant do when praying Tarāwīḥ [special Ramadan Prayers] among common folk: they recite Sūrat al-An'am (6) in the final *rak'a* of the seventh night, believing that this is recommended. They combine several rejected matters, such as, their belief that this in itself is recommended; deluding lay-folk into thinking that it is indeed recommended; lengthening the second *rak'a* more than the first, while the established prophetic norm [*sunna*] is making the first longer; being lengthy [and burdensome] on the worshippers following them; and interrupting the sequence of the recitation.

Some ignorant people engage in similar innovation during the

Morning Prayer on Friday, deliberately reciting [a passage of the Quran that calls for] prostration other than Sūrat al-Sajda (32), while the *sunna* is to recite Sūrat al-Sajda in the first *rak'a*, and Sūrat al-Insān (76) in the second.

Miscellaneous Issues of Concern

If one happens to pass wind while he is reciting [outside of Prayer], then he should cease reciting until it completely exits, and then he may resume. This is how Ibn Abī Dāwūd and others related it from 'Aṭā', and it is a fine etiquette.

If one yawns, one should cease reciting until he finishes yawning and then resume. Mujāhid holds this [view], and it is acceptable. This is supported by what is established from Abū Sa'īd al-Khudrī (God be pleased with him) that the Messenger of God (God bless him and grant him peace) said, "If any of you yawns, let him press his hand against his mouth, for indeed Satan enters."[59] (Muslim related it.)

Things Said with Certain Verses

It is good etiquette that one lower his voice when reciting certain statements of God Mighty and Majestic, as in the verses: *The Jews say, "Ezra is the son of God," and the Christians say, "The Messiah is the son of God"* (Quran, 9:30);[60] *The Jews say, "God's hand is fettered"* (Quran, 5:64);[61] *They say, "The All-Merciful has begotten a son"* (Quran, 19:88).[62] This is what Ibrāhīm al-Nakha'ī (God be pleased with him) would do.

Ibn Abī Dāwūd related with a weakly authenticated chain of transmitters that al-Sha'bī was once asked, "If a person recites, *God and His angels bless the Prophet. O you who believe, bless him and salute him with a worthy salutation* (Quran, 33:56),[63] should he pray upon the Prophet (God bless him and grant him peace)?' He said, "Yes!"

It is recommended for the reciter to repeat what Abū Hurayra (God be pleased with him) related from the Prophet (God bless him and grant him peace): "Whoever recites Sūrat al-Tīn (95) and says, *Is not God the best of judges?* (Quran, 95:8),[64] he should say, *"Balā wa anā 'alā dhālika min al-shāhidīn"* ["Most certainly! And I am among those who bear witness to this!"]. (Abū Dāwūd and Tirmidhī related it with a weak chain of narration from an [unnamed] bedouin, from Abū Hurayra (God be pleased with him).[65] Tirmidhī said, "This hadith was related with this chain from a bedouin by way of Abū Hurayra," and he said, "And he was not named.")

Ibn Abī Dāwūd and others related this hadith with something added beyond the narration of Abū Dāwūd and Tirmidhī: "Whoever recites the end of Sūrat al-Qiyāma (75), *Is He then not able to raise the dead to life?* (Quran, 75:40),[66] should say, *"Balā wa anā ashhad'* ["Most certainly! And I am a witness!"].

Whoever recites, *In what words after this will they believe?* (Quran, 7:185),[67] should say, *"Amantu bi-llāh"* ["I believe in God!"].

It is related that whenever Ibn 'Abbās, al-Zubayr, and Abū Mūsā al-Ash'arī [God be well pleased with them] recited Sūrat al-A'lā (87) they would say, *"Subḥāna rabbī al-A'lā"* ["Transcendant is my Lord, Most Exalted, above all imperfections!"], and that 'Umar ibn al-Khaṭṭāb (God be pleased with him) would repeat it three times.

It is related that 'Abdallāh ibn Mas'ūd (God be pleased with him) Prayed and recited the end of Sūrat Banī Isrā'īl[68] (17) and then said, *"al-ḥamdu lillāh alladhī lam yatakhidh waladā"* ["Praise be to God who has not begotten a son!"].

Some of our Shāfi'ī companions stated that it is recommended to say during the Prayer what we have just mentioned in the hadith of Abū Hurayra (God be pleased with him) regarding the three suras. It is likewise recommended to say the other things that we mentioned and their like. And God knows best.

Reciting the Quran Intending It to Be Speech

Ibn Abī Dāwūd cited disagreement concerning this matter [of reciting the Quran intending it to be speech]. It is related from Ibrāhīm al-Nakha'ī (God grant him mercy) that he disliked explaining the Quran with some worldly incident.

'Umar ibn al-Khaṭṭāb (God be pleased with him), in Mecca, read during the Sunset Prayer, *By the fig and the olive and the Mount of Sinai* (Quran, 95:1–2)," and raised his voice [at the next verse], *And by this secure city* (Quran, 95:3).

Ḥukaym ibn Sa'd said that a member of the *Muhakkima* sect[69] came to 'Alī [ibn Abī Ṭālib] (God be pleased with him) while he was in the Morning Prayer and recited [to 'Alī], *If you were to ascribe partners to God, all your works will be vain* (Quran, 39:65), and 'Alī (God be pleased with him) responded while still in Prayer, *So have patience! God's promise is true, and let not those who have no certainty make you impatient* (Quran, 30:60).

Our Shāfi'ī companions said that if a person seeks permission [to enter] from someone who is in Prayer who then recites, *Enter it with safety and security* (Quran, 15:46)—whether he intended thereby only recitation or intending both recitation and notification [to person seeking permission]—it does not nullify his Prayer. But if he intended notification alone and the intention [for recitation] did not occur to him, his Prayer is nullified.

A Reciter Giving Greetings

If one recites while walking and then comes across people, it is recommended to interrupt the recitation, greet the people, and then resume his recitation. And if [upon resuming] he repeats the [supplication] seeking protection from God, it is excellent. And it is the same if he were sitting [as he recites] and someone passes by him.

Greeting a Reciter

Imām Abū Ḥasan al-Wāḥidī said, "It is best to omit greeting someone who is reciting because he is occupied with recitation. But if someone gives him greetings, it is sufficient for [the reciter] to reply with a gesture. And he wishes to reply with an utterance, then he may reply as such, but then repeats the [supplication] seeking protection from God, and resumes his recitation." What [Imām Abū al-Ḥasan] said is weak, however. The stronger opinion is that it is obligatory to reply [to someone's greetings] with an utterance.

Our Shāfiʿī companions said that if someone offers greetings upon entering the Friday sermon—though we hold the opinion that being silent is a *sunna*—then it is obligatory to return his greetings according to the soundest of two opinions. So in the midst of recitation, in which there is agreement that it is not unlawful to speak therein, it is even more pressing [to return the greeting], even though returning a greeting is obligatory in general. And God knows best.

Sneezing During One's Recitation

If one sneezes while reciting, it is recommended for him to say, *"al-ḥamdu lillāh"* ["Praise to God"]; it is the same if [one sneezes] during the Prayer. If a person reciting outside of Prayer [hears] someone else sneeze and say, *"al-ḥamdu lillāh"* ["Praise to God"], it is recommended for the reciter to respond and say, *"Yarḥamuka Allāh"* ["God grant you mercy"].

The Call to Prayer

If a reciter hears someone make the Call to Prayer [*Adhān*], he should interrupt his recitation and reply to the call [as established in the *sunna*] by repeating the utterance of the Call to Prayer and the Call for the Commencement of Prayer [*Iqāma*]. He then may return to his recitation. Our Shāfiʿī companions agree upon this.

Replying to a Question

If something is requested from a person reciting the Quran and it is possible for him to respond to the petitioner by way of a known gesture, and [the reciter] knows that it will not break the heart [of the petitioner] and it will not harm the friendship between them and the like, then it is better to answer by way of gesture and not interrupt the recitation. But it is permissible for [the reciter] to interrupt [his recitation].

And God knows best.

Reciting and Standing for Someone

If someone of superior knowledge, righteousness, nobility, old age (without infirmity), or prestige, from position, parentage, or some other reason, passes by someone reciting, there is no harm in the reciter standing [to greet him] out of respect and deference—but not out of ostentation or glorifying. In fact, standing is recommended. Indeed, standing out of deference has been affirmed by the action of the Prophet (God bless him and grant him peace) and the Companions (God be well pleased with them)—who did so in [the Prophet's (God bless him and grant him peace)] presence and by his order—and affirmed by the action of the Successors and those after them, including the righteous scholars.

I have composed a monograph regarding the issue of standing out of respect. I mentioned therein the hadiths and accounts that recommend it and prohibit it, and I showed the weakness of those accounts which are weakly authenticated; the authenticity of those that are rigorously authenticated; and the answer to that which implies that it is prohibited while, in fact, there is no prohibition. I elucidated all of this, by the praise of God Most High. So whoever has doubt concerning any of its hadiths and reviews it will find what removes his doubt—by the will of God Most High.[70]

Valuable Rulings Associated with Recitation During Prayer

I take great liberty in summarizing these [rulings], since they are well known in the books of *fiqh*.

Recitation is obligatory in the prescribed Prayers, according to the consensus of the scholars. Mālik, al-Shāfiʿī, Aḥmad, and the majority of the scholars said that reciting Sūrat al-Fātiḥa in every *rakʿa* is specifically obligatory for all individuals. Abū Ḥanīfa and a group of scholars said that al-Fātiḥa is never specifically obligatory [*muʿayyin*] and that reciting al-Fātiḥa in the last two *rakʿa*s is never obligatory [*wājib*].[71]

The correct opinion is the former, since evidence from the *sunna* has made this clear. It suffices as proof that the Prophet (God bless him and grant him peace) said in a rigorously authenticated hadith, "A Prayer in which *Umm al-Qur'ān* [that is, Sūrat al-Fātiḥa] has not been recited is not sufficient."[72]

An Additional Verse

There is agreement among the scholars that it is recommended to recite [verses of the Quran] after reciting Sūrat al-Fātiḥa and in the first two *rak'a*s of the other Prayers. They differ over whether or not it is recommended [to recite additional verses] in the third and fourth *rak'a*s. Al-Shāfi'ī has two opinions on this: the newer position is that it is recommended, while the older one is that it is not.[73] Our Shāfi'ī companions state that if we hold that it is recommended, then there is no difference [of opinion] that it is indeed recommended that [the recitation in the third and fourth] should be shorter than the recitation in the first two [*rak'a*s], and, they said, that the recitation in the third and fourth [*rak'a*s] should be equivalent.

Should the [recitation] in the first *rak'a* be made longer than the second? There are two opinions concerning this. The sounder opinion, according to the accomplished authorities [*muḥaqqiqīn*], is that [the recitation in the first *rak'a*] be made long. This is the preferred opinion because of the rigorously authenticated hadith stating that the Messenger of God (God bless him and grant him peace) would lengthen [his recitation in] the first *rak'a* unlike the length in the second.[74] The benefit of this practice is that someone who came late [to the Prayer] would make the first *rak'a*.

And God knows best.

The Latecomer

Al-Shāfi'ī (God grant him mercy) said that if someone joined an [obligatory] Prayer after it had already commenced but was present with the *imām* for the last two *rak'a*s of, say, the Afternoon Prayer [or another], and then he stands to finish the remaining [*rak'a*s] he owes, it is recommended that he recite a chapter [after Sūrat al-Fātiḥa]. The majority of our Shāfi'ī companions said that this matter involves two opinions. Some say that it is based on al-Shāfi'ī's statement that one should recite [Quran] in addition [to al-Fātiḥa] in the last two *rak'a*s. The other opinion is that it is

not [recommended].[75] The correct opinion is the former, so that one's Prayer is not void of the [additional] recitation.
And God knows best.

This ruling [of reciting suras in the last two *rak'as*] applies to both: someone leading the Prayer and someone praying alone.

The Follower in a Prayer

As for someone being led in Prayer and the Prayer is silent, al-Fātiḥa is obligatory and the [additional] chapter is recommended. If it is audible and he can hear the *imām*'s recitation, it is offensive for him to recite any [additional] chapter.

There are two opinions regarding al-Fātiḥa being obligatory [to recite]. The sounder opinion is that it is obligatory; the other is that it is not. If one does not hear the *imām*'s recitation, the sound opinion is that al-Fātiḥa is obligatory and the [additional] chapter is recommended. Other opinions hold that al-Fātiḥa is not obligatory; others yet say that it *is* obligatory and the [additional] chapter is not recommended.

And God knows best.

The Funeral Prayer

It is obligatory to read al-Fātiḥa after the first saying of *"Allāhu akbar"* during a funeral Prayer.

Supererogatory Prayers

As for reciting al-Fātiḥa in a supererogatory Prayer, this is considered indispensable.

Saying "Bismillāhi al-Raḥmāni al-Raḥīm"

Our Shāfi'ī companions disagree over saying *"Bismillāhi al-Raḥmāni al-raḥīm"* in al-Fātiḥa. Al-Qaffāl said that it is obligatory [*wājib*]. His companion, al-Qāḍī Ḥusayn, said that saying [the *basmala*] is a conditional [*sharṭ*] part of the Prayer. Others yet have said it is an integral [*rukn*] part of the Prayer—and this is the most preponderant opinion.

And God knows best.

Someone Unable to Recite al-Fātiḥa

Someone incapable of reciting Sūrat al-Fātiḥa in all of these contexts may recite something else in its place. He may recite something else from the Quran of the same length. If he is incapable of that, then he may repeat invocations of the same length, like, *"Subḥān Allāh"* or *"Lā illāh illa'Allāh."* If he is incapable of anything at all, he stands for the length of [time it takes to recite] al-Fātiḥa and then bows. And God knows best.

Several Suras in One Rak'a

There is no harm in joining chapters in a single *rak'a*. It has been established in the authentic books of Bukhārī and Muslim that 'Abdallāh ibn Mas'ūd (God be pleased with him) said, "I know the chapters that the Messenger of God (God bless him and grant him peace) would couple together [in recitation],"[76] and he mentioned twenty chapters from the last two parts of the Quran, each of them two chapters in one *rak'a*. We mentioned previously that a group of the Pious Forebears would often recite the complete Quran in one *rak'a*.

When a Recitation Should Be Audible

Muslims have consensus that it is recommended to recite the Quran audibly during the Morning Prayers, the Friday Congregational Prayers, the two Eid Prayers, during the first two [*rak'as*] of the Sunset and Nightfall Prayers, during *Tarāwīḥ* Prayers, and the *Witr* Prayer that follows it. This is recommended for one leading a congregational Prayer and for the individual [praying] alone. Someone who is led in Prayer does not make [his recitation] audible, according to the consensus. It is a *sunna* that the recitation be audible during the Prayer occasioned by a lunar eclipse, but not audible during the Prayer for a solar eclipse.[77] The recitation is audible in the Prayer [in which worshipers supplicate] for rain. It is not audible in a Funeral Prayer if it is performed during the day, but is [audible] when prayed during the night, according to the sound preferred opinion in the [Shāfi'ī] *madhhab*.

Supererogatory Prayers

Recitation is not audible in the supererogatory daytime Prayers, with the exception of what we have just mentioned concerning the two Eid Prayers and the Prayer for rain. Our Shāfi'ī companions disagreed concerning Night Prayer Vigil. The dominant position is that it is not audible; the second opinion is that it is indeed audible; a third position holds that one alternates his recitation between audibility and silence, and this is what al-Baghawī chose.

Making up Prayers

If one missed a Prayer normally performed at night and made it up during the day—or if one misses a Prayer normally performed during the day and made it up at night—what aspect is taken into account in order to determine whether it should be audible or silent: the time in which it was missed or the time in which it was made up? Our Shāfi'ī companions have two opinions; the preponderant one is that the time in which [the missed Prayer] is made up is taken into account.

If one were to recite audibly when he should have been silent, or silent when he should have been audible, his Prayer is valid though he has committed something offensive, but he does not need to make the "prostrations of forgetfulness."

Guidelines for Recitation in Silence and Aloud

Know that what is meant by "silence" in recitation with regard to saying *"Allāh akbar"* and other statements [of the Prayer] is that one recite them such that he hears them himself. It is indispensable to utter them such that he hears them, that is, if he is of sound hearing and there is no interference. But if one does not hear himself, his recitation [of them] is not valid and neither are other invocations.[78] There is no disagreement on this.

The Imām pausing for Silence

Our Shāfi'ī companions said that it is recommended for the *imām* leading an audible Prayer to remain silent during four periods while standing: First, silence after the opening *"Allāhu akbar,"* in order to make an opening supplication and so the followers may also say the opening *"Allāhu akbar"*; second, a very brief pause right after reciting Sūrat al-Fātiḥa and [a brief pause] between the completion of al-Fātiḥa and saying *"Āmīn"* so that *"Āmīn"* is not misconstrued to be actually part of al-Fātiḥa; third, a long pause after *"Āmīn"* so the followers themselves can [silently] read al-Fātiḥa; and fourth, after finishing [the recitation of] a sura of the Quran, in order to provide a separation between the recitation and saying *"Allāhu akbar"* before descending to bow.

Saying "Amin"

It is recommended for every reciter, whether or not it is during Prayer, to say *"Āmīn"* when finishing al-Fātiḥa. The rigorously authenticated hadiths concerning it are well known and numerous. We mentioned in the previous section that it is recommended to separate the end of al-Fātiḥa and "Amin" with a brief pause of silence. *"Āmīn"* means, "O God, answer!" Other opinions are that it means, "And like this, let it be!"; "Make it so!"; "Of this, only You are capable!"; "Do not let down our hope!"; or "O God, entrust us with goodness!"

Other opinions proffer: It is God's seal on His worshipers and it repels disasters from them; it is a level in Paradise that one who says it deserves; it is one of the names of God Most High—but the accomplished authorities [*muḥaqqiqīn*] and the majority [of scholars] have rejected this—or it is a Hebrew word which has been Arabized. Abū Bakr al-Warrāq said that it is power endowed in the supplication which causes mercy to descend. And there are more opinions yet.

There are various pronunciations concerning *"Āmīn."* The opinions of the scholars are: the purest linguistically is *"Āmīn"* with elongation and lightening the *mim*. A second opinion is with the *alif* being short [*"Amīn"*]. These two opinions are well known. A third opinion is that *"Āmīn"* is with *imāla* [in which the *alif* is pronounced like the *yā*] with elongation between the two.[79] Al-Wāḥidī conveys this from Ḥamza and al-Kisā'ī. The fourth opinion posits that the *mīm* has a *shadda* with elongation [*"Āmmīn"*].

Al-Wāḥidī conveys this from al-Ḥasan and al-Ḥusayn ibn al-Faḍl. He said, "This is confirmed by what was related from Ja'far al-Ṣādiq (God be pleased with him) that he said, 'Its meaning is, "To You do we direct ourselves, and You are more generous than to turn back someone seeking You."'" These are al-Wāḥidī's words. This fourth opinion is very strange indeed, and most of the lexicographers consider it an error made by laymen. A group of our Shāfi'ī companions said, "Whoever says it in their Prayer [like this], his Prayer is invalid."

Arabic linguists said that proper Arabic usage demands that there be a full stop there [after the *nūn* in *Āmīn*] because it has the rank of a phoneme. If it is connected, the *nūn* gets a *fatḥa* because of the consecutiveness of two silent letters, just like it is given a *fatḥa* in [the words] *'ayn* and *kayf* [*'ayna, kayfa*], and it is not given a *kasra* since *kasra* is heavy after *ya*. This is a summary of what is associated with the pronunciation of "*Āmīn.*" I have expanded on this, providing the proofs and additional opinions, in [my] book *Tahdhīb al-Asmā' wa'l-Lughāt.*

The Ruling Concerning "Āmīn"

The scholars said that saying "*Āmīn*" in Prayer is recommended for the one leading the Prayer, his followers, and for individuals [praying alone]. The one leading the Prayer and the individual [praying alone] should audibly pronounce "*Āmīn*" in the audible Prayers. Scholars disagree, however, concerning the audibility of someone following an *imām*. The soundest [opinion] is that one should say "*Āmīn*" audible; the second is that he should not; and the third is that he should say it audible if [he prays with] a large congregation; otherwise he does not.

Its Utterance Being Simultaneous to the Īmām's

The follower saying "*Āmīn*" should say it simultaneously with the *imām*—not before nor after—because of the statement of the Prophet (God bless him and grant him peace) in the rigorously authenticated hadith: "If the *imām* says, *wa lā'ḍ-ḍāllīn* (Quran, 1:7), say, '*Āmīn,*' since whoever's '*Āmīn*' concurs with the

'*Āmīn*' of the angels, his previous sins are forgiven."[80] As for [the Prophet's (God bless him and grant him peace)] statement: "If the *imām* says '*Āmīn*' then say '*Āmīn*,'" this implies that [one should say *Āmīn*] when the *imām* is about to say "*Āmīn*." Our Shāfi'ī companions said that there is no occasion during Prayer in which it is recommended that the follower's utterance be simultaneous with the *imām*'s except in saying "*Āmīn*." All other utterances, [such as, "*Allāhu akbar*" that commences the Prayer and precedes the Prayer's various postures], are said after the *imām*'s utterance.

Prostration at the Recitation of Passages of the Quran

This topic is among the emphasized matters that one should give particular attention to. The scholars have consensus concerning the command to prostrate as occasioned by the recitation of [certain passages of] the Quran, but they disagreed whether this command indicates that it is recommended or obligatory. The majority of scholars said that it is not obligatory per se, but is recommended. This is the opinion of 'Umar ibn al-Khaṭṭāb, Ibn 'Abbās, Salmān al-Fārisī, 'Imrān ibn al-Ḥusayn, Mālik, al-Awzā'ī, al-Shāfi'ī, Aḥmad, Isḥāq, Abū Thawr, Dāwūd, and others (God be well pleased with them). Abū Ḥanīfa (God grant him mercy) said that [prostration] is obligatory. He justified it with the statement of God Most High, *Why do they not believe, and, when the Quran is recited to them, do they not prostrate?* (Quran, 84:20–21].[81] The majority of scholars justified [that prostration is not obligatory] by way of a rigorously authenticated account of 'Umar ibn al-Khaṭṭāb (God be pleased with him), that on one Friday he recited Sūrat al-Nahl (16) from the minbar, and when he reached the [verse occasioning the] prostration, he descended and prostrated, and the people prostrated with him. The next Friday he recited [the same passage] until he came to the verse of prostration and said, "O people! We have come upon a verse of prostration and whoever prostrated has indeed hit the mark, but there is no sin upon whoever did not prostrate." And 'Umar himself did not prostrate.[82] (Bukhārī related it.) This action and statement from

'Umar (God be pleased with him) in this gathering is clear evidence.

The response to the verse that Abū Ḥanīfa (God grant him mercy) cites as evidence [for his position that is obligatory] is obvious, for what is intended [by the verse] by censuring people for forsaking the prostration is declaring them to be liars, for God—Most High—said thereafter, *But the disbelievers deny it* (Quran, 84:22).

It has been established in the authentic books of Bukhārī and Muslim that Zayd ibn Thābit (God be pleased with him) recited Sūrat al-Najm (53) to the Prophet (God bless him and grant him peace) and he did not prostrate.[83] And it is also established in the rigorously authentic hadiths that he did prostrate in al-Najm.[84] So this indicates that it is not obligatory.

THE NUMBER OF VERSES OF PROSTRATION AND THEIR PLACES

As for their number, the preferred opinion of al-Shāfi'ī (God grant him mercy) and the majority of scholars is that there are fourteen verses of prostrations: Suras al-'Arāf (7); al-Ra'd (13); al-Naḥl (16); al-Isrā' (17); Maryam (19); two in al-Ḥajj (22); al-Furqān (25); al-Naml (27); al-Sajda (32); Fuṣṣilat (41); al-Najm (53); al-Inshiqāq (84); and al-'Alāq (96).

As for the prostration of Sūrat Ṣād (38), it is recommended [to prostrate]; it is not considered among the required prostrations. It is established in Bukhārī's *Ṣaḥīḥ* from Ibn 'Abbās (God be well pleased with them both) that he said, "Sūrat Ṣād is not among the required prostrations, and I have seen the Prophet (God bless him and grant him peace) prostrate in it."[85] This is the opinion of al-Shāfi'ī and those who have said something similar.

Abū Ḥanīfa said also that they are fourteen; however he omitted the second occurrence in al-Ḥajj (22) and affirmed the inclusion of the prostration of Ṣād (38) as among the required prostrations.[86]

There are two accounts from Aḥmad [ibn Ḥanbal]. The first is like what al-Shāfi'ī said. The second is that there are fifteen [occasions for prostration], adding Sūrat Ṣād [to the list of fourteen].

This is the opinion of Abū al-'Abbās ibn Surayj, and Abū Isḥāq al-Marwazī, one of al-Shāfi'ī's [later] companions.

There are two accounts from Mālik. The first is like what al-Shāfi'ī said. But the most well known of the two is that there are *eleven* [occasions of prostration] omitting al-Najm (53), al-Inshiqāq (84), and al-A'lāq (96). This is the old opinion of al-Shāfi'ī. The sound opinion is what we have previously mentioned. The rigorously authenticated hadith indicate it.

LOCATIONS OF THE VERSES OF PROSTRATION

The specific locations [of the prostration verses] are: al-'Araf, at its end *...but they praise Him and fall down in prostration before Him* [7:206]; al-Ra'd, immediately after God's statement, Mighty and Majestic is He, *...in the mornings and in the evenings* [13:15]; al-Naḥl, *...and they do all that they are commanded* [16:50]; al-Isrā', *...and it increases them in humility* [17:109]; Maryam, *they would fall down in prostration and tears* [19:58]; the first of al-Ḥajj's prostrations, *God does what He wills* [22:18] and the second, *...and do good, that you may succeed* [22:77]; al-Furqān, *And it increases them in aversion* [25:60]; al-Naml, *the Lord of the formidable Throne* [27:26]; al-Sajda, *and are not proud* [32:15]; Fuṣṣilat, *...and are never wearied* [41:38]; al-Najm, at its end, *...and worship Him* [53:62]; al-Inshiqāq, *do they not prostrate?* [84:21]; and al-'Alāq, at its end, *...and draw near [to God]* [96:19]. [See APPENDIX TWO listing the Quranic texts of these passages.]

DISAGREEMENT ABOUT SŪRAT FUṢṢILAT

There is no disagreement of any consideration as to their specific locations [in the suras], except for Fuṣṣilat (41), in which there is disagreement among the scholars. The opinion of al-Shāfi'ī and his companions is as we mentioned: it occurs immediately after God's statement, Most High is He, *...and are never wearied* (Quran, 41:38). This is the opinion of Sa'īd ibn al-Musayyib, Muḥammad ibn Sīrīn, Abū Wā'il Shaqīq ibn Salama, Sufyān al-Thawrī, Abū Ḥanīfa,[87] Aḥmad, and Isḥāq ibn Rāhūyah.

Others hold that it occurs immediately after God's statement, Most High is He, *...if you would worship Him* (Quran, 41:37).[88] Ibn Mundhir related this from 'Umar ibn al-Khaṭṭāb, al-Ḥasan al-Baṣrī, the companions of 'Abdallāh ibn Mas'ūd, Ibrāhīm al-Nakha'i, Abū Ṣāliḥ, Ṭalḥa ibn Muṣarrif, Zubayr ibn al-Ḥārith, Mālik ibn Anas, al-Layth ibn Sa'd. It is also an opinion of one or more of the companions of Imām al-Shāfi'ī. (Al-Baghawī related this in *al-Tahdhīb*.)

As for the statement of Abū al-Ḥasan 'Alī ibn Sa'd al-'Abdarī, one of our Shāfi'ī companions, in his book *al-Kifāya*, addressing the disagreement between the legists [*fuqahā'*] about the prostration of Sūrat al-Naml occuring at the saying of God Most High, *...and knows what you conceal and what you reveal* (Quran, 27:25),[89] he said, "This is the opinion of most of the legists. Mālik said that the prostration occurs at the statement of God Most High, *...Lord of the formidable Throne* (Quran, 27:26)." This quote of his, according to our opinion and the opinion of the majority of the legists, is not known or accepted. It is a manifest error. The books of our Shāfi'ī companions are explicit [that the verse of prostration] occurs at the statement of God Most High, *Lord of the formidable Throne* (Quran, 27:26).

And God knows best.

SPECIFIC RULINGS CONCERNING THE VERSES OF PROSTRATION

Prostration occasioned by the recitation of the Quran has the same general ruling as a supererogatory Prayer, in that its conditions are that one must be cleansed of impurity, free of filth, face the *qibla*, and his nakedness covered. So it is unlawful for anyone [to make the prostrations] while he has legally inexcusable filth on his body or clothes or has ritual impurity, unless he were to make dry ablution in a situation in which dry ablution is permissible. [Prostration] is also unlawful when turned toward a direction other than the *qibla*, except during a journey where supererogatory Prayers are permissible when one is turned toward a direction other than the *qibla*. All of this is agreed upon.

ABOUT SŪRAT ṢĀD

One who says that reciting [verse 24] of Sūrat Ṣād (38) requires prostration holds, moreover, that he should prostrate whether he reads it during Prayer or outside of it—treating it like all other verses of prostration. Al-Shāfiʿī and others who claim that it is not one [of the verses] requiring prostration say that when one recites it outside of Prayer, it is recommended to prostrate, since the Prophet (God bless him and grant him peace) prostrated at its recitation, as we have mentioned; but if one recites it during Prayer, he should not prostrate. If, however, one does prostrate out of ignorance or forgetting [that it is not required], it does not invalidate his Prayer, though he should make "prostration of forgetfulness." But if one knew of the sound [opinion] that his Prayer is rendered invalid [by such prostration] because he added something foreign to the Prayer, then [his Prayer] is invalid, the same way it would be invalid were he to make "prostration of thankfulness" within his Prayer; there is no disagreement about this [among the scholars]. The second [opinion] is that it is not invalidated since it has an association to the Prayer.

IF THE IMĀM PROSTRATES FOR [SŪRAT] ṢĀD

If the *imām* [leading a Prayer] were to prostrate for [verse 24] of Sūrat Ṣād (38) believing that it requires prostration, yet someone following him in [Prayer] does not hold this view, he should not follow the *imām*; instead he extricates himself altogether or he remains standing waiting for the *imām* [to complete the prostration]. And if one stands waiting for [the *imām*], must he perform a prostration of forgetfulness? There are two opinions, the preponderating one is that he does not.

FOR WHOM IT IS PROPER TO PROSTRATE

It is an established prophetic tradition [*sunna*] for someone reciting [a verse of prostration]—and who has ritual purity, by way of water or soil [when the latter is allowed]—[to make prostration] whether or not the recitation was made during Prayer or outside of it. This [holds true] for someone listening [to the recitation].

Moreover, this is established for someone who merely heard [the recitation] though he was not particularly listening [to it]. However, al-Shāfiʿī said, "I do not emphasize this for [the one who merely overheard it] as I emphasize it for the attentive listener." And this is the correct opinion. Imām al-Ḥaramayn, one of our Shāfiʿī companions, said that someone who [merely] heard [the recitation] does not prostrate. However, the well-known opinion is the first.

Whether or not the reciter was in or outside of Prayer, it is established, for the one who overheard [the recitation] and the attentive listener to prostrate; this holds true whether or not the one reciting actually prostrated himself. This is the well-known and correct opinion according to the companions of al-Shāfiʿī (God be well pleased with them). It is what Abū Ḥanīfa said as well.[90]

The author of *al-Bayān*,[91] one of al-Shāfiʿī's companions, said that a bystander listening to someone reciting [a verse of prostration] during Prayer does not prostrate. Al-Ṣaydalānī, one of al-Shāfiʿī's [later] companions, said that it is not established that he prostrate unless the one reciting prostrates. The correct opinion is the first.

There is no difference [in the rulings concerning the verses of prostration] if the one reciting is a Muslim, mature, in a state of ritual purity, and male or if [the reciter] is a non-Muslim, prepubescent, in a state of ritual impurity, or a woman. This is the sound opinion of our school, and it is the opinion of Abū Ḥanīfa. Some of our Shāfiʿī companions said that one does not prostrate if the reciter is a non-Muslim, prepubescent, in a state of ritual impurity, or intoxicated. A group of the scholars among the Righteous Forebears said that one does not prostrate at a woman's recitation. Ibn Mundhir conveyed it from Qatāda, Mālik, and Isḥāq. The correct opinion is what we previously mentioned.

PROSTRATING IN GENERAL

One recites one or two verses and then prostrates. Ibn Mundhir conveyed from al-Shaʿbī, al-Ḥasan al-Baṣrī, Muḥammad ibn Sīrīn, al-Nakhaʿi, Aḥmad, and Isḥāq that they disliked this. [He conveyed] from Abū Ḥanīfa, Muḥammad ibn al-ḥasan, and Abū Thawr that there is no harm in this, and this conforms to what our *madhhab* dictates.

PROSTRATION IN DETAIL

INDIVIDUALS: Someone praying individually should prostrate at his own recitation. If he omits the prostration for recitation and bows, and then wants to prostrate for the recitation, this is not permissible. And if he does so knowingly, his Prayer is invalid. If he descends to bow but does not reach the limit of what is customarily considered to be bowing [*rukūʿ*], it is permissible for him [to adjust and] prostrate for the recitation. If he descends for prostration and he realizes [he omitted the prostration of recitation] and returns to his standing position [to perform the prostration of recitation], this is permissible.

It is not permissible for someone praying individually to prostrate because of someone else's recitation, whether or not the [other] recitation is in a Prayer. If he knew this and still prostrated, his Prayer becomes invalid.

CONGREGATIONAL PRAYERS: If one is the *imām*, then his situation is like that of an individual. As for the follower of a Prayer: If the *imām* prostrates at his recitation, it is obligatory for the follower to prostrate with him, and the follower's Prayer is invalid if he fails to do so.

If the *imām* does not prostrate, it is not permissible for the follower to prostrate, and if the follower were to prostrate anyway, his Prayer is invalid. However, [in this case] it is recommended for him to prostrate when he finishes his Prayer, though this is not something emphasized.

If the *imām* prostrated and the follower did not know this until the *imām* raised his head from the prostration, his [momentary] departure from the *imām* is excused and it is not permissible to prostrate. But if the follower discovers this while the *imām* is still in the prostration, it is obligatory for him to prostrate. Yet if he descends to prostrate and the *imām* then rises [from his prostration] while the follower is in the process of bending down, the follower should then [adjust and] rise with the *imām*; it is not permissible for him to prostrate. It is the same for a weak person who bends down [to make prostration] with the *imām*, but the *imām* then rises before the weak person reaches prostration—because of the pace of the *imām* and the slowness of the follower—the weak person must rise back with *imām* and does not prostrate.

RECITATION OTHER THAN THE IMĀM'S

It is not permissible for someone following an *imām* to prostrate at his own recitation [in a silent Prayer] nor the recitation of anyone except the *imām*. If he prostrates, his Prayer is invalidated. It is offensive for him to recite a [verse containing a] prostration, and it is offensive for him to listen to any recitation other than the *imām*'s.

THE TIMING OF PROSTRATION

The scholars said one's prostration should occur immediately after reading or hearing the verse containing the prostration. If he delays and the separation is not long, he still may prostrate. If [the span of time] is long, then he has missed the prostration altogether and does not need to make up according to the well known and sound opinion [just as one does not make up the Prayer of the eclipse]. Some of our Shāfi'ī companions said that there is a weak opinion that one should make it up [the prostration], as one would make up *sunna* Prayers that precede or follow the obligatory Prayers, such as the *sunna*s of the Morning, Noon, and other Prayers.

RITUAL IMPURITY

If the reciter or the listener is in a state of ritual impurity when the verse of prostration is recited and he makes ritual purity soon thereafter, he should then prostrate. If he delays [ablution] to the point that the separation in time becomes long, he does not prostrate, which is the correct and preferred opinion of which the majority of scholars are certain. Another opinion, however, holds that he still should prostrate—and it is the choice of al-Baghawī, one of our Shāfiʿī companions. This is analogous to one responding to the Call to Prayer [*ādhān*] after finishing his Prayer [that he was engaged in while the *ādhān* was called]. Custom [*ʿurf*] is considered for determining the length of time [for the separation being short of long], according to the preferred opinion.

And God knows best.

MULTIPLE PROSTRATIONS

If one reads some or all of the verses of prostration in a single sitting, he prostrates for each of them; there is no disagreement on this. If he repeats a single verse of prostration in several sittings, he prostrates for each occurrence; there is no disagreement on this. If he repeats a single verse of prostration in a one sitting, he examines the following: First, if he did not prostrate for the first occurrence, a single prostration suffices him for them all. Second, if he prostrated for the first occurrence, there are three opinions: [First,] he should prostrate for each occurrence, since the cause is renewed after fulfilling the ruling of the first—which is the soundest opinion. [Second,] the first prostration suffices him for them all. It is the opinion of Ibn Surayj, and it is the opinion of Abū Ḥanīfa (God grant him mercy).[92] The author of *al-ʿUdda*,[93] one of our Shāfiʿī companions, said that religious verdict accords with this. This is the preference of Shaykh Naṣr al-Maqdisī, the ascetic and one of our Shāfiʿī companions. [Third,] if the separation [between occurrences] is long he prostrates [for each], otherwise the first prostration suffices [for them all]. When he repeats a single verse of prostration during Prayer in one *rakʿa*, it is analogous to [repeating it] in a single sitting and thus has the same three opinions. If he repeats it during two *rakʿa*s, it is like two sittings, so he repeats the prostration without any disagreement.

WHILE RIDING

If one recites a verse of prostration while riding an animal during a journey, he prostrates by way of gesture. This is our opinion, and the opinion of Mālik, Abū Ḥanīfa, Abū Yūsuf, Muḥammad, Aḥmad, Zufar, Dāwūd, and others. Some of Abū Ḥanīfa's companions said that he does not prostrate.[94] The opinion of the majority is correct. As for someone riding an animal but not traveling, it is not permissible for him to prostrate by way of gesture.

READING A VERSE OF PROSTRATION BEFORE AL-FĀTIḤA

If one recites a verse of prostration during Prayer before reciting Sūrat al-Fātiḥa, [in the opening invocation,] he prostrates. This is different than had he recited while bowing or prostrating, since it is not permissible to recite [in those postures] because standing [in Prayer] is the place of recitation. If one recited a verse of prostration, descended to prostrate, and doubted that had he read al-Fātiḥa, he then prostrates for the recitation, returns to standing, and recites al-Fātiḥa, since prostration for recitation should not be delayed.

READING A VERSE OF PROSTRATION IN PERSIAN OR AS AN EXPLICATION

If one recites a verse of prostration in Persian,[95] it is our opinion that he not prostrate. It is the same if he were to explicate a verse of prostration.

Abū Ḥanīfa, however, said that one does prostrate.[96]

LISTENERS PROSTRATING WITH A RECITER

One listening [to the recitation] may prostrate with the reciter, but is not bound to the reciter and should not intend to be led by him, and so he may rise from the prostration before [the reciter does].

THE RULING CONCERNING AN IMĀM RECITING A VERSE OF PROSTRATION

In our *madhhab*, it is not offensive for the *imām* to read a verse of prostration whether the Prayer is silent or audible. One prostrates whenever he recites [a verse of prostration]. Mālik said that is categorically offensive. Abū Ḥanīfa said that it is offensive in the silent, but not the audible.[97]

PROSTRATION AT TIMES WHEN PRAYER IS PROHIBITED

In our *madhhab*, the prostration for Quranic recitation is not offensive during the times in which Prayer itself is prohibited [e.g., the exact moment of sunrise or sunset]. This is the opinion of al-Shu'bī, al-Ḥasan al-Baṣrī, Sālim ibn 'Abdallāh, al-Qāsim, 'Aṭā', 'Ikrima, Abū Ḥanīfa, the people of juristic opinion, and Mālik according to one of two accounts. A group of scholars, though, disliked it. They include 'Abdallāh ibn 'Umar (God be pleased with him), Sa'īd ibn al-Muṣayyib, Mālik in the other account, Isḥāq ibn Rāhūyah, and Abū Thawr.

BOWING INSTEAD OF PROSTRATING

Bowing [*rukū'*] does not take the place of prostration for Quranic recitation, when it is optional. This is our opinion, and the opinion of the majority of the scholars of the early generations [the *Salaf* and *Khalaf*]. Abū Ḥanīfa (God grant him mercy) said that the bowing may take its place.[98] The evidence of the majority, however, is that [prostration for Quran recitation] is analogous to prostration in the Prayer [which cannot be replaced by bowing]. Someone incapable of prostrating may gesture, just as he gestures for prostrating in Prayer.

THE DESCRIPTION OF THE PROSTRATION

Know that someone prostrating for Quranic recitation [is in either] two states: outside of Prayer, or during it. If it is outside of Prayer and one wants to prostrate, he does the following: (1) He makes his intention for the prostration of recitation; (2) says the opening *"Allāhu akbar"* [*takbīrat al-iḥrām*], raising his hands parallel to his shoulders, just as he does for the opening *"Allāhu akbar"* of any Prayer; (3) he then says a second *"Allāhu akbar"* as he moves toward the prostration, but does not raise his hands during it. Saying *"Allāhu akbar"* a second time is recommended and is not a condition [for validity], just as the saying of *"Allāhu akbar"* for prostration during a Prayer.

Our Shāfi'ī companions have three opinions concerning the opening *"Allāhu akbar."* (1) It is an integral part [*rukn*] and the prostration is not valid without it, according to the most obvious opinion, which is the opinion of the majority. (2) It is *recommended*, and if one omits it, the prostration would still be valid, and this is the opinion of al-Shaykh Abū Muḥammad al-Juwaynī. (3) It is not even recommended.

And God knows best.

STANDING OR SITTING

If the one intending to make the prostration of reciation is standing, he says the opening *"Allāhu akbar"* while standing, and then says *"Allāhu akbar"* again for his actual prostration while descending therein. If one is sitting, a group of our Shāfi'ī companions have said that it is desirable for him to stand and say the opening *"Allāhu akbar"* while standing, and then descend down to the prostration, just as if he were standing to begin with. The evidence for this is it that this [practice] is analogous to the opening *"Allāhu akbar"* and prostration during Prayer. Our *imāms* who unequivocally hold this include Shaykh Abū Muḥammad al-Juwaynī, al-Qāḍī Ḥusayn and his companions (the author of *al-Tatimmah*[99] and *al-Tahdhīb*[100]) and the *imām* and masterfully skillful Abū al-Qāsim al-Rāfi'ī. Imām al-Ḥaramayn [al-Juwaynī] related it from his father, al-Shaykh Abū Muḥammad, and then rejected it saying, "I do not see any source or mention for this." Imām al-Ḥaramayn's statement is obvious, since nothing concerning this is established from the Prophet (God bless him and grant him peace), nor from any of the exemplary Righteous Forebears. Also the majority of our Shāfi'ī companions did not address the topic.

And God knows best.

ETIQUETTE AND MANNER

When one prostrates, he should observe the etiquette of prostration concerning the invocations [*tasbīḥ*] one makes. The manner is as follows: (1) he places his hands on the ground parallel to his shoulders; (2) places his fingers together and points them towards the direction of the *qibla*; (3) takes [his hands] out of his sleeves and directly places them on the Prayer surface; (4) spreads his elbows out from his sides and raises his stomach from his thighs if he is a male (a female or a hermaphrodite does not spread them out);[101] (5) he raises his posterior higher than his head, firmly placing his forehead and nose on the Prayer surface, (6) and comes to rest during his prostration.

As for making invocations [*tasbīḥ*] during the prostration, our Shāfiʿī companions said that he makes invocations using the invocations he makes normally in his prostration during Prayer. So he says three times *"Subḥāna rabbi al-aʿlā"* ["My Lord Most Great is exalted above all imperfection"], then he may say: *"Allāhumma laka sajadtu wa bika āmantu wa laka aslamtu, sajada wajhī lilladhī khalaqahu wa ṣawwarahu wa shaqqa samʿahu wa baṣarahu bi ḥawlihi wa quwwatihi, tabāraka Allāhu aḥsanu al-khāliqīn"* ["O God, I prostrate myself to You, believe in You, and surrender to You. My face prostrates to Him who created it and gave it form, who opened its hearing and vision by His power and strength. God is exalted in perfection, the Best of Creators"]. And he says, *"subbūḥun quddūsun rabbu al-malā'ikati wa al-rūḥ"* ["Most Exalted and Holy: Lord of all angels and souls"]. All of this is from what someone says in his prostration during Prayer.

They said that it is recommended to say: *"Allāhumma uktub li bihā ʿindika ajran, wa ijʿalhā lā ʿindika dhākhran, wa ḍaʿ ʿannī bihā wizran, wa-qbalhā minnī kamā qabalatuhā min ʿabdika Dāwūd* (God bless him and grant him peace)"[102] ["O God, write for me a reward because of [this prostration] and keep it with You, and remove a sin from me because of it. Accept it from me just as You accepted it from Your servant Dāwūd (God bless him and grant him peace)"]. This supplication is particular for this prostration, so he should be mindful of it.

The theologian Ismāʿīl al-Ḍarīr mentioned in his book *Al-Tafsīr* that al-Shāfiʿī's choice supplication during the prostration for recitation was, *"Subḥānna rabbinā in kāna waʿdu rabbinā lamafʿūlā"* [*"Transcendant is our Lord! Indeed our Lord's promise is ever done!"*] (Quran, 17:108). This attribution to al-Shāfiʿī is quite strange, but it is nonetheless fine since what [this verse of] the Quran implies is praise for the one saying it during prostration.

It is recommended to combine all of these litanies, and to supplicate for whatever one wishes among matters of the Hereafter and this life. If one limits himself to [just] some of them, he achieves the foundation of the invocation. If he were not to make invocations at all, the prostration then will have occurred like the prostration of Prayer.

RAISING THE HEAD AND SAYING THE CLOSING SALUTATION

When one finishes saying the *tasbīḥ* and the supplications [in prostration], he raises his head saying *"Allāhu akbar."* But is it necessary to say [the salutation] *"al-salāmu 'alaykum"*? There are two well-known opinions recorded from al-Shāfi'ī. The stronger, according to the majority of our companions, is that indeed [the salutation] is required because it requires the opening *takbīr*; like the Funeral Prayer. This is supported by what Abū Dāwūd related with his rigorously authenticated chain of narrators that Ibn Mas'ūd (God be pleased with him) said, "When he recited a verse of prostration, he would prostrate and than say *'al-salāmu 'alaykum...'*." The second opinion is that [salutation] is not required, like the prostration for Quranic recital during Prayer, for this is not related from the Prophet (God bless him and grant him peace).

Following the first opinion, does [prostration for recitation] need the *tashahud* ["O God, send blessings upon Muḥammad as you have sent them upon Ibrāhīm..."]? There are two opinions concerning this. The stronger opinion is that it does not need it, just as [prostration for recitation] does not need standing.

Some of our Shāfi'ī companions join the two issues. Concerning the *tashahud* and the salutation, there are three opinions: The strongest is that there is no avoiding the salutation, but this is not the case with the *tashahud.* The second is that there is no need of either one of them. The third is that there is no avoiding either. Among the Righteous Forebears who said that one should make the salutation are Muḥammad ibn Sīrīn, Abū 'Abd al-Raḥmān al-Sulamī, Abū ʿAbd al-Raḥmān Abū al-Aḥwaṣ, Abū Qilāba and Isḥāq ibn Rāhūyah. Those who said that one does not make the salutation include al-Ḥasan al-Baṣrī, Saʿīd ibn Jubayr, Ibrāhīm al-Nakhaʿī, Yaḥyā ibn Waththab, and Aḥmad.

All of the foregoing concern the first situation, that is, prostrating outside of the Prayer.

PROSTRATION OF RECITATION DURING PRAYER

The second situation is prostration of recitation during the Prayer. One does not say "*Allāhu akbar*" in the opening. But it is recommended to say "*Allāhu akbar*" upon prostration, but one does not raise his hands. One also says "*Allāhu akbar*" upon rising from the prostration. This is the sound, well known opinion that the majority holds. Abū ʿAlī ibn Abī Hurayra, one of our Shāfiʿī companions, said that one does not say "*Allāhu akbar*" upon prostration nor upon rising from it. But the first [opinion] is well known.

THE PROSTRATION AND INVOCATION

The etiquette concerning the manner of prostration and invocation [*tasbīḥ*] is as we previously mentioned with regard to prostration outside of Prayer. However, if the one prostrating is leading others in Prayer then he should not lengthen the invocation unless he knows that they prefer it being lengthy.

RISING FROM PROSTRATION

When one rises from the prostration, he stands and does not briefly rest by sitting [as one does between *rakʿa*s of Prayer]. There is no disagreement about this. This issue is seldom mentioned, and there are few who have advocated it. Among those who did are al-Qāḍī Ḥusayn, al-Baghawī, and al-Rāfiʿī.

This is different than the prostration of Prayer, since the sound and unequivocally preferred opinion of al-Shāfiʿī—for which there are rigorously authenticated hadiths in Bukhārī and other compilations—is that it is recommended in all Prayers to briefly rest by sitting immediately after the second prostration in the first *rakʿa*, and from the third in four-part Prayers.[103]

STANDING ERECT

When one rises from the prostration for recital, he must stand fully erect. When he stands upright fully, it is recommended to recite something [additional of the Quran] and then bow [as he normally would in Prayer], though it is permissible if he stands upright and then bows immediately without [additional] recitation. [This marks the end of the discussion on prostration.]

Optimal Times for Recitation

Know that the best recitation is during Prayer. The opinion of al-Shāfiʿī and others is that lengthening one's standing during Prayer is better than lengthening the prostration. When outside of Prayer, it is best to recite at night—the last half of the night being better than the first. And reciting between the sunset and nightfall Prayers is also beloved. When reciting during the day, the best time is after the Morning Prayer.

There is nothing offensive in reciting any time because of something inherent to that time. What Ibn Abī Dāwūd related from Muʿādh ibn Rifāʿa from his shaykh—that they disliked reciting Quran after the Mid-Afternoon Prayer, saying that it is the time of study for the Jews—is rejected and is baseless.

The especially preferred days [to recite] are Friday, Monday, Thursday, and the Day of ʿArafa. The [preferred] ten [contiguous days] are the last ten of Ramadan, the first ten of Dhū'l-ḥijja. The [preferred] month is Ramadan.

Losing One's Place During the Recitation

If the reciter becomes tongue-tied and does not know what follows what he stopped at and asks someone else, he should follow the etiquette as related from ʿAbdallāh ibn Masʿūd, Ibrāhīm al-Nakhaʿī, and Bashīr ibn Abī Masʿūd (God be pleased with them). They said, "If one of you asks his brother about a verse, he should read what comes before it and then remain silent. He should not ask unnecessary questions.[104]

Quoting the Quran

If someone wishes to use a verse as proof [for his argument] he may say: "God Most High *said* such-and-such," or, "God Most High *says* such-and-such." Neither one of them is offensive. This is the sound, preferred opinion which follows the action of the early generations.

Ibn Abī Dāwūd related that Muṭarrif ibn 'Abdallāh ibn al-Shikhkhīr, the well-known Successor, said, "Do not say, 'God Most High *says*.' Instead say, 'God Most High *said*.'" What Muṭarrif (God grant him mercy) rejected, however, is contrary to what the Quran and *Sunna* brought, and what the Companions and those after them did [God be well pleased with them], since God Most High Himself has said, *And God says the truth and He guides to the path* (Quran, 33:4).

In Muslim's *Ṣaḥīḥ,* Abū Dharr (God be pleased with him) relates that the Messenger of God (God bless him and grant him peace) said, "God Sublime and Most High says, *Whoever brings a good deed will receive tenfold the like of it...*" (Quran, 6:160).[105]

In Bukhārī's *Ṣaḥīḥ*, in the chapter on the commentary of the verse, *You will not attain to righteousness until you spend of what you love* (Quran, 3:92), Abū Ṭalḥa (God be pleased with him) said, "O Messenger of God! God Most High says, *You will not attain to righteousness until you spend of what you love*." These are the words of Abū Ṭalḥa in the presence of the Prophet (God bless him and grant him peace).[106]

Masrūq (God grant him mercy), in a rigorously authenticated hadith, said:

> I said to 'Ā'isha (God be pleased with her), "Did not God Most High say, *He saw him [Gabriel] on the clear horizon* (Quran, 81:23)." She said, "Did you not hear that God Most High says, *Vision comprehends Him not, but He comprehends all vision?* (Quran, 6:103)? And did you not hear that God Most High says, *And it is not given to any human being that God should speak to him unless it be by revelation or from behind a veil* (Quran, 42:51)." And then she said in this hadith, "And God Most High

> says, *O Messenger! Make known that which has been sent down to you from your Lord* (Quran, 5:67)." And then she said, "And God Most High says, *Say: None in the heavens and the earth knows the unseen save God...* (Quran, 27:65)."[107]

Comparable accounts from the early generations are innumerable.

And God knows best.

The Etiquette of Completing the Quran

There are several issues concerning completing the recitation of the Quran [*khatma*].

1. WHEN TO COMPLETE: The first etiquette concerns its timing. As previously mentioned, it is preferable for someone reciting the Quran on his own that [he complete it] during Prayer. Another opinion is that it is preferable for it to occur in the two *rak'a* of the obligatory Morning Prayer, and in the two sunna *rak'a*s of the Sunset Prayer, and the two *rak'a*s of the Morning Prayer is better. In another opinion, it is preferable for the completion [*khatma*] in the beginning of the day for one turn [of recitation], and at the end of the day for next turn.

When someone completes the recitation outside of Prayer or a group completes while assembled together, it is recommended that it be at the beginning of the day or in the beginning of the night, as we previously mentioned. According to some scholars, though, the beginning of the day is better.

2. FASTING THE DAY OF THE KHATMA: It is recommended to fast the very day of the *khatma* unless it falls on a day in which it is forbidden to fast according to the *Sharī'a*. Ibn Abī Dāwūd related with his rigorously authenticated chain of narrators that Ṭalḥa ibn Muṣarrif, Ḥabīb ibn Abī Thābit, and al-Musayib ibn Rāfi'ī—all well known Kūfan Successors [God be well pleased with them]—would awaken fasting on the mornings in which they would complete the Quran.

3. ATTENDING THE KHATMA: It is emphatically recommended to attend gatherings in which the *khatma* takes place. It has been established in the rigorously authenticated hadiths of Bukhārī and

Muslim that the Messenger of God (God bless him and grant him peace) ordered women during their menses to go out on Eid to participate in the goodness and the supplications of the Muslims.[108]

Dārimī and Ibn Abī Dāwūd related with their chains of narration that Ibn 'Abbās (God be pleased with them both) would make a person watch over someone finishing the Quran, and when he wanted to finish he would inform Ibn 'Abbās so he could participate in it.[109]

Ibn Abī Dāwūd related with two rigorously authenticated chains of narration that Qatāda, the illustrious Successor and companion of Anas (God be pleased with him), said, "When Anas ibn Mālik (God be pleased with him) would complete [the Quran], he would gather his family and supplicate [to God]."

He [also] related with his rigorously authenticated chain of narration that al-Ḥakam ibn 'Utaybah, the illustrious Successor, said, "Mujāhid and 'Abdata ibn Lubāba sent for me and said, 'We sent for you because we want to finish the Quran, and supplication when finishing the Quran is answered.'" In some of the authenticate narrations he would say, "Indeed, mercy descends when completing the Quran." [And] he related with his rigorously authenticated chain of narration from Mujāhid that he said, "They would gather when completing the Quran, saying that the Mercy now descends."

4. THE SUPPLICATION: It is emphatically desirable to supplicate immediately after a *khatma* because of what we have just mentioned in the previous issue. Dārimī related with his chain of transmitters that Ḥumayd al-A'raj said, "Whoever recites the Quran and then supplicates, four thousand angels say *"Amīn!"* to his supplication."[110]

One should be persistent in his supplication and ask for important matters. He should [supplicate] much for the well-being of the Muslims, their leadership, and all others who attend to their affairs. Al-Ḥakim Abū 'Abdallāh al-Nīsābūrī has related with his chain of narration that when 'Abdallāh ibn al-Mubārak (God be pleased with him) would finish the Quran, he would make a great deal of his supplication for the Muslims and believers, male and female." Others have said similar to this.

The one supplicating should choose all-encompassing supplications, such as the following:

> O God! Mend our hearts, remove our faults, assign us the best of outcomes, adorn us with Godfearingness, join for us the best of the first and last, and sustain us with obeying You as long as You make us remain.
>
> O God! Make easy what is easy for us, avert us from what is difficult; protect us from the torture of Hellfire and the torture of the grave, and the trials of life and death, and the trials of the false messiah.
>
> O God! We ask You for guidance, protection, virtue, and affluence.
>
> O God! We entrust You with our religion and bodies, with the finality of our deeds and lives—our families, our loved ones, and all of the Muslims—and all matters of the next life and this one that You bestowed upon us and upon them.
>
> O God! We ask You for pardon and well-being, in religion, and in this life and the next. And to unite us together with our loved ones in the abode of Your generosity with Your favor and mercy.
>
> O God! Mend those who oversee the Muslims, give them success in justice concerning their charges, being benevolent to them, sympathetic to them, being kind with them, and being attentive to their welfare. Make them love their charges, and make their charges love them. Make them successful for Your straight path and for the assignments of Your solid, true religion.
>
> O God! Be gentle with Your servant our leader, and make him successful in the welfare of this life and the next, and make him beloved to the charges and make the charges beloved to him.

The reciter says the rest of the mentioned supplications which concern those who oversee [the affairs of Muslims] and adds:

> O God! Protect his life and his land, safeguard his followers and his armies. Give him victory over the enemies of the religion and all other opponents. Give him success in removing the reprehensible and making manifest the benevolent and all kinds of goodness. Through him make Islam more manifest, and make him and his charges mighty and magnificent.
>
> O God! Mend the conditions of the Muslims, reduce the cost of living, and give them safety in their lands. Settle their loans, heal their sick, and give victory to their armies. Bring forth their missing persons, and release their prisoners of war. Heal their breasts, remove rage from their hearts, and unite them. Put belief and wisdom in their hearts and make them firm on the creed of Your Messenger (God bless him and grant him peace). Inspire them to fulfill Your covenant that You made with them. Give them victory over Your enemies and their enemies, O God of Truth. Make us among them.
>
> O God! Make them to enjoin what is right and act according to it, and to prohibit the reprehensible and avoid it, mindful of Your limits, and perpetually in Your obedience, demanding justice, and following council.
>
> O God! Safeguard them in their words and deeds, and bless them in all of their states.

He begins and ends his supplication by saying:

> All praise is for God, Lord of the worlds: a praise reaching His bounties and matching His provision. O God! Pray upon and give peace to Muḥammad and his followers of Muḥammad, just like you prayed on Ibrāhīm and the followers of Ibrāhīm. And bless Muḥammad and the followers of Muḥammad, just like you blessed Ibrāhīm and the followers of Ibrāhīm; in all of the worlds, indeed You are the praiseworthy and illustrious.

[The Arabic text and English transliteration of these supplications are collected in APPENDIX ONE.]

5. STARTING AGAIN: When he finishes the *khatma*, it is recommended for him to begin the next [round of recitation] immediately after it. The [righteous among] the early generations recommended this. They justified their position by way of a hadith of Anas (God be well please with him) that the Messenger of God (God bless him and grant him peace) said, "The best of works are *al-ḥall* and *al-riḥlat*." It was asked, "What are they?" He said, "Beginning the Quran and completing it."[111]

7

THE ETIQUETTE OF ALL PEOPLE WITH THE QURAN

It is established in Muslim's *Ṣaḥīḥ* that Tamīm al-Dārī (God be pleased with him) stated, "The Messenger of God (God bless him and grant him peace) said, 'Religion is sincerity.' We said, 'To whom?' He said, 'To God, His Book, His Messenger, the leaders of the Muslims, and their common folk.'" The scholars (God grant them mercy) said that having sincerity regarding the Book of God is believing that it is the speech of God Most High and His revelation; that it does not resemble anything from the words of people; and that people are incapable of anything like it even if they all joined together [to attempt it]. [Sincerity is] to extol its glory; recite it and give its recitation its just due—beautifying it, being humble while doing so, and correctly pronouncing its letters. [Sincerity is] defending it from the misinterpretations of the deviators and the opposition of the tyrants; believing in everything that it contains; not exceeding its boundaries; and understanding its knowledge and examples. [It is] paying attention to its exhortations; pondering its amazing wonders; acting according to what has unequivocal meaning; submitting to what is open to interpretation; searching out its universal and restricted [rulings]; its abrogating and abrogated [passages]; and propagating its sciences; and calling others to them and to all the sincere counsel that we have mentioned.

What Muslims Must Believe Concerning the Quran

The Muslims have consensus that it is obligatory to extol the glory of the Mighty Quran without exception, to declare it beyond any imperfection, and to safeguard it. They have consensus that whoever intentionally rejects a single letter over which there is consensus, or intentionally adds a single letter that no one recited, commits an act of disbelief. The Imām and hadith master Abū al-Faḍl al-Qāḍī 'Iyāḍ (God grant him mercy) said:

> Know that anyone who knowingly belittles the Quran, the text itself [*muṣḥaf*], or anything from it; abuses it; rejects one of its letters; disbelieves something about which it is explicit, whether a ruling or an account; affirms what it negates, or negates what it affirms—is a disbeliever according to the consensus of the Muslims. It is the same if he were to reject the Torah, the Evangel, or the revealed books of God. If he were to disbelieve in them, abuse them, or belittle them, he is a disbeliever.
>
> Muslims have consensus that the Quran recited in all the lands and written in the *muṣḥaf* which is in the hands of the Muslims—gathered between two covers, from the beginning of *Praise be to God, the Lord of the Worlds* (Quran, 1:2)[1] until ... *of Jinn and Men* (Quran, 114:6)[2]—is the word of God and His revelation revealed to His Prophet Muḥammad (God bless him and grant him peace), and that all that it contains is the truth. Anyone who deliberately removes a single letter from it, changes one of its letters by putting another in its place, or adds a single letter to it that is not included in the *muṣḥaf*, over which the consensus has occurred and there is consensus that it is not from the Quran—one doing any of this intentionally—is a disbeliever.
>
> Abū 'Uthmān ibn al-Ḥaddād said, "Everyone ascribing to Islam agrees that rejecting one letter from the Quran is disbelief. The legists [*fuqahā'*] of Baghdad agreed with Ibn Shanbūdh al-Muqri', one of the foremost reciters, demanding that Ibn Mujāhid make repentance for his reciting and teaching anomalous dialects [*ḥurūf*] which are not in the muṣḥaf, and they made a contract with him to cease [such recitation] and to duly repent. They wrote up a disposition about him testifying against him-

> self, in the assembly of the vizier Abū ʿAlī ibn Muqla, in the year of 323 [AH]."
>
> Abū Muḥammad ibn Abī Zayd announced a legal verdict concerning someone who says to a youth, "May God curse your teacher and what he taught!" but says, "I only meant by it bad etiquette and I did not mean the Quran." Abū Muḥammad said, "The one who said this should be disciplined." And he said, "As for someone who abuses the *muṣḥaf*, he should meet his demise."

This is the end of the words of al-Qāḍī ʿIyāḍ.

Explicating the Quran

It is unlawful for someone to explicate the Quran without knowledge and the qualification to speak about its meanings. The hadiths concerning this are many, and there is consensus on this. It is permissible and fitting that only scholars explicate [the Quran]; there is consensus concerning this as well. When someone is qualified to explicate the Quran—one who gathers all the tools through which [the Quran's] meanings are known and the intended meaning is particularly apparent to him—he may indeed explicate it, if it is something attained through independent intellectual reasoning [*ijtihād*]. Such matters include the [Book's] meanings and rulings—the hidden and apparent—what is universal and what is restricted, grammatical inflections, and more. But if it is something not attained through independent intellectual reasoning, but by transmitting [the thoughts of others][3] and explicating linguistic phrases, it is not permissible for one to communicate this except through rigorously authenticated transmissions of qualified experts. As for one who is not qualified [to offer original explications] because of not having attained the scholarly tools, it is forbidden for him to offer explication. But he may transmit explications from qualified experts.

Using Uninformed Opinion

Explicators who proffer their opinions without valid evidence may be categorized as follows: (1) One who uses a verse to justify the validity of his particular *madhhab* [legal approach] and to strengthen his thoughts, even though what is intended by the verse may not be preponderate in his mind as [proof of his opinion], but he nonetheless seeks only to triumph over his opponent; (2) one who intends to call to what is good, but uses a verse to justify his position without [the verse's] indication really being apparent to him; and (3) one who explicates [the Quran's] Arabic phrases without being familiar with their meanings as proffered by qualified scholars, while the phrases are something that can only be taken by way of qualified scholars of Arabic and explication. This includes elucidating the meaning of a phrase and its grammatical inflections, what it contains in terms of ellipses, abridgment, interpolations, literal and metaphorical meanings, universal and restricted [significance], ambiguous and detailed [aspects], matters of transposition [*muqaddamahu wa mu'akhkharahu*], and other things that are not so obvious.

Knowledge of Arabic Is Not Sufficient

It is not sufficient to simply know Arabic. Rather, one must also know all that qualified scholars of explication have said about [a given passage of the Quran], for they may have consensus that the apparent [meaning of a verse, for example,] is something to be disregarded and that what is intended is a specific or implied meaning, or something else contrary to the obvious. Likewise, if a phrase has different meanings and it is known that one of those meanings is intended, one then explicates each occurrence [of the phrase] that comes [separately].

All of the foregoing [depicts] the offering of explication by way of [uninformed] opinion, and this is unlawful.

And God knows best.

Arguing and Debating Without Justification

It is unlawful to argue and debate about the Quran without justification, as in the case of a person to whom it becomes apparent that there is a preponderating likelihood that a verse runs contrary to his opinion and carries a weak possibility of concurring, but still he applies it to his opinion. In fact, he [persists in] debating it even though it is apparent to him that it runs contrary to his view. (But if this not apparent to him, then he is excused.)

It is rigorously authenticated that the Messenger (God bless him and grant him peace) said, "Arguing about the Quran is disbelief."[4] Al-Khaṭṭābī said, "What is meant by 'arguing' here is 'doubt.' Other opinions state that it is 'debating' in itself that is questionable or the 'debate' of capricious people concerning the verses that speak of destiny and the like."

Asking About the Wisdom of a Verse

Someone who wishes to ask a question—why, for example, one verse precedes another or the appropriateness of a verse in a specific context—should say, "What is the wisdom in this?"

Saying "I was caused to forget" Instead of "I forgot"

It is offensive to say, "I *forgot* such-and-such verse." Instead one should say, "I was *caused to forget* it" or "I was *caused to neglect* it," for it is established in the *Ṣaḥīḥayn* [of Bukhārī and Muslim] that 'Abdallāh ibn Mas'ūd (God be pleased with him) stated that the Messenger of God (God bless him and grant him peace) said, "Let none of you say 'I *forgot* such-and-such verse,' rather it is something he was caused to forget." Also in a narration in the *Ṣaḥīḥayn*: "Let none of you say, 'I forgot such-and-such verse'; indeed, he was *caused* to forget."[5]

It is also established in the *Ṣaḥīḥayn* that 'Ā'isha (God be well pleased with her and her father) said that the Prophet (God bless him and grant him peace) heard a man reciting and said, "God grant him mercy! He has reminded me of a verse that I was caused to omit." And in another narration in [Bukhārī]:[6] "I was caused to forget it."

What Ibn Abī Dāwūd related—that Abū 'Abd al-Raḥmān al-Sulamī, the illustrious Successor, said, "Do not say, 'I omitted the verse,' rather say, 'I neglected [it]"'—is contrary to what is established in the rigorously authenticated hadith. What should be relied upon is the hadith which allows for the permissibility of saying, "I omitted [it]," without it being offensive.

Referring to Suras

It is permissible to say: "Sūrat al-Baqara," "Sūrat Āl 'Imrān," "Sūrat al-Nisā'," "Sūrat al-Mā'ida," and likewise for all the suras, without there being any offensiveness in [saying *sūra*]. Some scholars of the early generations disliked this. Their opinion is that what should be said is, "The sura in which *the cow* [*al-baqara*] is mentioned," "the sura in which the *Family of 'Imrān* is mentioned," "the sura in which *women* are mentioned," and so on.

The correct opinion is the first, since in the *Ṣaḥīḥayn* it is established that the Messenger of God (God bless him and grant him peace) himself said, "Sūrat al-Baqara," "Sūrat al-Kahf," and many other instances. The same thing is related from the Companions (God be well pleased with them). 'Abdallāh ibn Mas'ūd said, "This is the very place in which Sūrat al-Baqara was revealed." And it was related from ['Abdallāh ibn Mas'ūd] in the *Ṣaḥīḥayn*, "I recited Sūrat al-Nisā' to the Messenger of God (God bless him and grant him peace)." The hadiths and statements of the Righteous Forebears concerning this are innumerable.

Pronunciations of the Word "Sūra"

There are two pronunciations concerning the word "*sūra*": [mentioning] the *hamza* and omitting it. Omitting it is purer linguistically, and it is what is in the Quran. Among those who mentioned the two pronunciations is Ibn Qutayba in [the book] *Gharīb al-Ḥadīth*.

Saying "The recitation of" So-and-So

It is not offensive to say, "This is the recitation of Abū 'Amr," "the recitation of Nāfi'," "Ḥamza," "al-Kisā'ī," or someone else. This is the preferred opinion that conforms to the action of the early generations without objection. However, Ibn Abī Dāwūd related that Ibrāhīm al-Nakha'ī said, "They disliked it when it was said, 'the *sunna* of so-and-so' and 'the recitation of so-and-so.'" The sound opinion is what we have just mentioned.

The Quran and Non-Muslims

A non-Muslim should not be prevented from listening to the Quran; this is based on the statement of God Most High, *And if one of the idolaters seeks refuge from you, then grant him refuge until he hears the words of God* (Quran, 9:6). But he is prevented from touching the *muṣḥaf*.[7] Is it permissible to teach him Quran? Our Shāfiʿī companions said that if his entering Islam is not expected, teaching him is impermissible; and if his entering Islam is expected, there are two opinions: the sounder is that it is permissible out of hope for his entering Islam, and the second is that it is not permissible, just like it is not permissible to sell him a *muṣḥaf*, even if it is expected that he will enter Islam.[8] If we were to see [an idolater] learning [the Quran], do we prevent him? There are two opinions.[9]

The Quran as Medicine

The scholars disagreed about the practice of writing the Quran [then placing it] into a vessel and then washing and giving it to someone sick to drink. Al-Ḥasan al-Baṣrī, Mujāhid, Abū Qilāba, and al-Awzāʿī said there is no harm in it. Al-Nakhaʿī disliked it. Al-Qāḍī Ḥusayn, al-Baghawī, and others of our Shāfiʿī companions said that if one wrote the Quran on something edible, like pastry, there is no harm in eating it. Al-Qāḍī [Ḥusayn] said that if he wrote it on wood it is offensive to burn it.

The Quran as Decoration

Our school holds that it is offensive to pattern walls and clothes with the Quran and the names of God Most High. 'Aṭā' said that there is no harm in writing Quran on the *qibla* of a mosque. As for writing the letters of the Quran, Mālik said that there is no harm if it was on a reed or skin, if it is sewn over. Some of our Shāfiʿī companions said that it is not unlawful if the Quran was written on a small amulet along with something else. But it is better not to do so since it will be carried while in the state of ritual impurity [that one inevitably attains]. If it is written, it should be protected, as Imām Mālik (God Most High grant him mercy) had said. Abū ʿAmr ibn al-Salām ibn Ṣalāḥ (God grant him mercy) gave a religious verdict with this [last opinion].

Puffing the Words of the Quran for Protective Purposes

Ibn Abī Dāwūd related from Abū Juḥayfa, the Companion (God be pleased with him)—his name is Wahb ibn ʿAbdallāh, according to one opinion—and from al-Ḥasan al-Baṣrī and Ibrāhīm al-Nakhaʿī that they disliked this.[10]

The preferred opinion is that this is not offensive. Rather, it is a recommended sunna since it is established that ʿĀ'isha (God be well pleased with her and her father) said, "Each night when the Prophet (God bless him and grant him peace) retired to his bed he would gather his hands together, puff in them, and then recite in them [Sūrat al-Ikhlāṣ, Sūrat al-Falaq, and Sūrat al-Nās] and then wipe over with his hands whatever he could of his body, beginning with his head and face and the front of his body. He would do this three times." (Bukhārī and Muslim related it in their books.)

ʿĀ'isha (God be pleased with her) said, "When he became exhausted I would puff for him [with Sūrat al-Falaq and Sūrat al-Nās], and wipe with his own hand for its blessings [*baraka*]." And in some narrations: "When he became sick he would read over himself [Sūrat al-Ikhlāṣ, Sūrat al-Falaq and Sūrat al-Nās] and then puffed."[11] The linguists said that "puffing" [*al-nafath*] is a light breath without saliva.

And God knows best.

8

RECOMMENDED TIMES AND CIRCUMSTANCES FOR RECITATION

Know that this topic is vast, and it is impossible to encompass it all because of the sheer number of aspects that have been spoken about it. Nonetheless, we will touch upon most—or actually much—of this employing concise expressions, since most of what we will mention is known to both the elite and the layman. For this reason, I will not provide the textual proofs for most [of the following].

Specific Months and Specific Suras

There is much in the normative practice of the Prophet (God bless him and grant him peace) [*sunna*] about paying close attention to reciting the Quran during the month of Ramadan, and more so during its last ten days, with its odd nights being specially emphasized. Also included are the first ten days of [the month of] Dhū'l-Ḥijja, the Day of ʿArafa, Friday, after dawn, and during the night.

Suras Yā Sīn, al-Wāqiʿa, and al-Mulk

One should be especially observant in reciting Sūrat Yā Sīn (36), Sūrat al-Wāqiʿa (56), and Sūrat al-Mulk (67).

Friday and Eid Prayers

It is *sunna* to recite—after Sūrat al-Fātiḥa—all of Sūrat al-Sajda (32) in the first *rakʿa* and all of Sūrat al-Insān (76) in the second. One should not do what many *imāms* of mosques do, namely, confine [the recitation] to a few verses from each [*sura*] and then draw out the recitation. Instead, one should read them both completely, and make his recitation distinct, prompt, and without interruption.

It is *sunna* in the Friday congregational Prayer to recite all of Sūrat al-Jumu'a (62) in the first *rak'a* and all of Sūrat al-Munāfiqīn(63) in the second. If one wishes [he may recite] Sūrat al-A'lā (87) [in the first *rak'a*] and Sūrat al-Ghāshiya (88) in the second, since both practices are rigorously authenticated from the actions of the Messenger of God (God bless him and grant him peace).[1] One should not confine [the recitation] to part of the suras, but should do as we have just said. The *sunna* in the Eid Prayer is [to recite] all of Sūrat Qāf (50) in the first *rak'a* and all of Sūrat al-Qamr (54) in the second. If one wishes, [he may recite] Sūrat al-A'lā and Sūrat al-Ghāshiya since both practices are rigorously authenticated from the Messenger of God (God bless him and grant him peace). One should not confine [the recitation] to part of the suras.

Daily Prayers

One should recite in the *rak'a*s of the *sunna* [Prayer before] the Morning Prayer—after Sūrat al-Fātiḥa— Sūrat al-Kāfirūn (109) in the first *rak'a* and Sūrat al-Ikhlāṣ (112) in the second. If one wishes, he may recite verse 126 [of al-Baqara] in the first and verse 64 [of Āl 'Imrān] in the second. [This is] because both of them are rigorously authenticated from the action of the Messenger of God (God bless him and grant him peace).[2]

In the first *rak'a* of the Sunset's *sunna* Prayer one should recite Sūrat al-Kāfirūn and in the second Sūrat al-Ikhlāṣ. He also should recite these two in the two *rak'a*s of *Ṭawwāf* [circumambulating around the Ka'ba] and the two *rak'a*s of *Istikhāra* [the Prayer of seeking guidance]. Someone praying *Witr* with three *rak'a*s should recite in the first [*rak'a*] Sūrat al-A'lā (87); Sūrat al-Kāfirūn in the second (109); and, in the third, Sūrat al-Ikhlāṣ (112), Sūrat al-Falaq (113), and Sūrat al-Nās (114).

Recommended Recitations on Friday

It is recommended to recite Sūrat al-Kahf (18) on Friday because of the [well-known] hadith of Abū Sa'īd al-Khudrī (God be pleased with him) and others concerning this. In [his book] *Al-Umm*, Imām al-Shāfi'ī said that it is also recommended to read [Sūrat al-Kahf] Friday night. The evidence for this is in what Abū Muḥammad al-Dārimī related with his chain of narration that Abū Sa'īd al-Khudrī (God be pleased with him) said, "Whoever reads Sūrat al-Kahf Friday night is illuminated by a light extending between him and the Ancient House [the Ka'ba]."[3]

Dārimī mentioned a hadith[4] that it is recommended to recite Sūrat Hūd (11) on Friday. And he relates from Makḥūl, the illustrious Successor, that it is recommended to recite Sūrat Āl 'Imrān (3) on Friday.

Frequently Reciting Ayat al-Kursī and the Mu'awidhatayn

It is recommended to make frequent recitation of Ayat al-Kursī (Quran, 2:255) in all places, and to recite it each night when one retires to his bed. It is recommended to recite Sūrat al-Falaq (113) and Sūrat al-Nās (114) immediately after each Prayer, since it is rigorously authenticated that 'Uqba ibn 'Āmir (God be pleased with him) said, "The Messenger of God (God bless him and grant him peace) ordered me to recite the *Mu'awidhatayn* [Sūrat al-Falaq and Sūrat al-Nās] after the end of every Prayer."[5] (Abū Dāwūd, Tirmidhī, and Nasā'ī related it. Tirmidhī said it is a well-rigorously authenticated hadith.)

Reciting at Bedtime

When going to sleep, it is recommended to recite Ayat al-Kursī, Sūrat al-Ikhlāṣ, Sūrat al-Falaq, Sūrat al-Nās, and the end of al-Baqara (Quran, 2:284–86). This is something to give particular attention to and is emphasized to heed, since rigorously authenticated hadiths concerning this have been established.

Abū Mas'ūd al-Badrī (God be pleased with him) relates that the Messenger of God (God bless him and grant him peace) said, "The two verses at the end of al-Baqara are sufficient [in their blessings] for anyone who reads them in one night."[6] A group from the people of knowledge said that they suffice him from praying at night; and others said that they suffice him from what is offensive during his night.

'Ā'isha (God be pleased with her) said, "The Prophet (God bless him and grant him peace) each night would recite Sūrat al-Ikhlāṣ, Sūrat al-Falaq, and Sūrat al-Nās." (We have already mentioned this in the section of "puffing" with the [words of the] Quran.)

Ibn Abī Dāwūd related with his chain of transmitters that 'Alī [ibn Abī Ṭālib] (God be pleased with him) said, "I have not seen any rational person who has entered Islam sleep until he had recited Ayat al-Kursī (Quran, 2:255)." 'Alī (God be pleased with him) also said, "I have not seen any rational person sleep before reciting the last three verses of [Sūrat] al-Baqara."[7] Its chain is rigorously authenticated according to the criteria of Bukhārī and Muslim. 'Uqba ibn 'Āmir (God be pleased with him) said, "The Messenger of God (God bless him and grant him peace) said to me, 'Do not let a night pass you unless you recite therein al-Ikhlāṣ, al-Falaq, and al-Nās.' Thereafter, not a night passed me unless I recited them."[8]

Ibrāhīm al-Nakha'ī said, "[The Righteous Forebears] recommended reciting these chapters every night three times: al-Ikhlāṣ, al-Falaq, al-Nās," with a rigorously authenticated chain of transmission that meets the criteria of Muslim. Ibrāhīm also said, "They would teach them that when they retire to their beds they should recite al-Falaq and al-Nās." 'Ā'isha (God be pleased with her) said, "The Prophet (God bless him and grant him peace) did not sleep until reciting Sūrat al-Zumar (39) and Sūrat Banī Isrā'īl (17).[9] (Tirmidhī related it and said it is well authenticated.)

Upon Waking Up

When one wakes up from his sleep each night, it is recommended to recite the closing [verses] of Āl 'Imrān (3), beginning with the statement of God Most High: "*Inna fī khalqi's-samāwāti wa'l-arḍ*" to its end (Quran, 3:190–200), for it has been established in the *Ṣaḥīḥayn* that the Messenger of God (God bless him and grant him peace) would recite the final verses of Āl ʿImrān when he woke up."[10]

Reciting Quran in the Presence of Someone Ill

It is recommended to recite Sūrat al-Fātiḥa in the presence of someone ill, based on the rigorously authenticated hadith that the Prophet (God bless him and grant him peace) said [to his Companions], "What made you realize that [al-Fātiḥa] is protective words [*ruqya*]?"[11]

Also, it is recommended to recite in the presence of someone ill al-Ikhlāṣ, al-Falaq, and al-Nās applying the "puffing" in the hands, since this has been established in the *Ṣaḥīḥayn* that it was the practice of the Messenger of God (God bless him and grant him peace). (This discussion came in the section of "puffing" at the end of the proceeding chapter.)

Ṭalḥa ibn Muṣarrif stated, "It is said that when the Quran is recited in the presence of an ill person, he finds a lightness because of it. I entered upon Khaythama while he was sick and I said, 'I see you are well today.' He said, 'The Quran was recited over me.'"

Al-Khaṭīb Abū Bakr al-Baghdādī (God grant him mercy) related with his chain of narration that when al-Ramādī (God be pleased with him) complained from something he would say, "Bring me the people of hadith." When they came he would say, "Read hadith to me."[12] This is with hadith, so it is even better with the Quran.

Reciting Quran in the Presence of Someone on the Brink of Death

The scholars, including our Shāfiʿī companions and others, said that it is recommended to recite Sūrat Yā Sīn (36) in the presence of someone on the brink of death,[13] based on the hadith of Maʿqil ibn Yasār (God be pleased with him) relating that the Prophet (God bless him and grant him peace) said, "Recite Yā Sīn to those on the brink of death."[14] (Abū Dāwūd related this hadith, as did Nasā'ī in *'Amal al-Yawm wa al-Layla*, as well as Ibn Mājah with a weak chain of narrators.)

Mujālid related from al-Sha'bī that he said, "When the Anṣār gathered by someone on the brink of death they would read Sūrat al-Baqara (2)." (Mujālid is weak [in narration].)

And God knows best.

9

WRITING THE QURAN AND RESPECTING THE MUṢḤAF

Know that the Mighty Quran was compiled during the lifetime of the Prophet (God bless him and grant him peace), corresponding to what is in the *maṣāḥif* [pl. of *muṣḥaf*, a compiled volume of the entire Quran] today. But it was not gathered as a *muṣḥaf*; rather, it was preserved in the hearts of men. There were groups of the Companions (God be well pleased with them) who had memorized its entirety, and others who had memorized its parts.

After the Prophet (God *bless him and grant him peace)*

During the caliphate of Abū Bakr al-Ṣiddīq (God be pleased with him) many of the bearers of the Quran were killed. He was alarmed at their deaths—that people after them would disagree about [the content of the Quran]. Therefore, he sought counsel from the Companions (God be pleased with them) regarding gathering of the Quran into a *muṣḥaf*. This was, in fact, their counsel; so he had [the Quran] written down in a *muṣḥaf* and placed it in the house of Ḥafṣa, Mother of the Faithful (God be pleased with her).

Islam spread during the caliphate of 'Uthmān (God be pleased with him). 'Uthmān feared that any discord [over the Quran] would lead to abandoning something of the Quran or adding something to it, so he had many copies made based on the *muṣḥaf* kept with Ḥafṣa, which the Companions had universally agreed upon. He then had them dispatched to the various regions, and ordered the destruction of [any versions] that varied from it.[1] His action was based on the agreement concluded between himself,

'Alī ibn Abī Ṭālib, the rest of the Companions, and the others [*tābi'īn*] (God be well pleased with them all).

Why the Quran Was Not Completely Written Down Beforehand

It was only because of the coming of new revelation and the abrogation of the revelation already recited that the Prophet (God bless him and grant him peace) did not gather [the Quran] into a single *muṣḥaf*; this [possibility] did not cease until his death (God bless him and grant him peace). So when Abū Bakr and the rest of his Companions were safe from this occurring and the public good called that it indeed be gathered, they therefore did so (God be well pleased with them).

The Number of Maṣāḥif 'Uthmān (God be pleased with him) Dispatched

There is disagreement over the number of *maṣāḥif* that 'Uthmān (God be pleased with him) sent. Imām Abū 'Amr al-Dānī said that the majority of the scholars are of the opinion that 'Uthmān (God be pleased with him) had four *maṣāḥif* written and sent one copy to each of the regions of Baṣra, Kūfa, Greater Syria, and the last one he kept with himself.

Abū Ḥātim al-Sajistānī said that 'Uthmān wrote seven *maṣāḥif* and sent one copy to each of the regions of Makkah, Greater Syria, Yemen, Baḥrayn, Baṣra, and Kūfa, and he kept one in Madinah.

This is a synopsis of what is associated with the beginning of the Quran's compilation as a *muṣḥaf*. There are many rigorously authenticated hadith concerning this.

Pronunciations of the Word "Muṣḥaf"

There are three pronunciations of the word "*muṣḥaf*": *muṣḥaf*, *miṣḥaf*, and *maṣḥaf*. The first and second are well known. Abū Ja'far al-Naḥḥās and others mentioned the third.

Writing the Muṣḥaf is a Recommended Innovation

The scholars agree that it is recommended to write down the Quran in a *muṣḥaf*; to beautify and make clear its writing; and to be precise in its calligraphy without writing the letters in an elongated or oblique manner.

Scholars have recommended to include the dots [on the letters] and vowelize [the words of the Quran], since this guards against errors and alterations.

As for al-Sha'bī and al-Nakha'ī disliking dotting [the letters], they did so at the time only out of fear that some alterations would occur. But this is no longer feared today; so there is nothing to disallow [such dotting], for it cannot be disallowed based on it being some kind of innovation, since it is considered a *good* innovation. And this is true with other similar matters, such as recording knowledge, building schools and Sufi lodges, and the like.

And God knows best.

How and Where Quran Is Written

It is not permissible to write down the Quran with something filthy. The Shāfi'īs opine that it is offensive to write the Quran on the wall. With regard to this matter, we previously mentioned the opinion of 'Aṭā'. We also mentioned that if [a passage of the Quran] is written on something edible then there is no harm in eating it, but if it is written on wood, it is offensive to burn it.

Safeguarding and Respecting the Muṣḥaf

Muslims have consensus that it is obligatory to protect and respect the *muṣḥaf*. Our Shāfi'ī companions and others have said that if a Muslim places [a *muṣḥaf*]—God Most High is our refuge—in a garbage receptacle, he becomes a disbeliever. They said that it is unlawful to use the *muṣḥaf* as a headrest; indeed, it is unlawful to use any book of knowledge as a headrest.

If someone is presented with a *muṣḥaf*, it is recommended that he stand. Since it is recommended to stand for the meritorious scholars and elite, it is even more appropriate with regard to the

Quran. (I presented evidence that it is recommended to stand in a monograph I composed on this topic.)

We related in the *Musnad* of Dārimī with a rigorously authenticated chain of narrators that Ibn Abī Mulayka said that ʿIkrima ibn Abī Jahl (God be pleased with him) would place the *muṣḥaf* on his face and say, "My Lord's Book! My Lord's Book!"[2]

The Muṣḥaf and Non-Muslims

It is unlawful to journey to hostile lands with the *muṣḥaf* if it is feared that it will fall into their possession, based on the well-known hadith in the *Ṣaḥīḥayn* that the Messenger of God (God bless him and grant him peace) prohibited that [Muslims] journey with the Quran to hostile lands.[3]

Selling the Muṣḥaf to Non-Muslims

It is unlawful to sell a *muṣḥaf* to a non-Muslim resident of the Islamic state. Imām al-Shāfiʿī has two opinions concerning the validity of the sale. The most sound is that it is invalid; the second is that [the sales transaction in itself] is valid but [because it is unlawful that a *muṣḥaf* be sold to non-Muslims] he is immediately ordered to remove it from his possession.

The Insane and the Young

Someone insane or a youth who has not reached the age of discernment is forbidden from carrying the *muṣḥaf* out of fear of violating its sacrosanct nature [out of ignorance]. It is an obligation that the guardian, or someone else responsible, prevent this when he sees such a person about to carry [a *muṣḥaf*].

Ritual Impurity

It is unlawful for someone in a state of minor ritual impurity to touch or carry the *muṣḥaf*; it is the same whether [one] carries it by its strap or something else—whether touching the Book itself, the margin, or the cover. It is unlawful to touch the bag, cover, or box in which the *muṣḥaf* is contained. This is the preferred opinion. There is an opinion that these [latter] three are not unlawful, but it is weak. If [verses of the] Quran is written on a board, the board then assumes the ruling of a *muṣḥaf*, whether the amount written is little or much. It is unlawful to touch the board [when one has minor ritual impurity] even if it is part of a verse written for the sake of study.

Major Ritual Impurity

Our Shāfiʿī companions have two opinions regarding someone in the state of minor or major ritual impurity or menstruation touching the pages of the *muṣḥaf* with a stick or something like it. The most obvious opinion is that it is permissible, and our Iraqi companions were certain of it, since this does not constitute actual *touching or carrying*. The second opinion is that it is unlawful, since it is regarded as holding one of the pages, and a page is like the entirety [of the Quran].

If one wraps his sleeve over his hand and turns the pages [of the *muṣḥaf*], it is still unlawful without any disagreement. Some of our Shāfiʿī companions were mistaken by conveying two opinions about this. The correct opinion is certain of its unlawfulness, since turning pages takes place by the hand, not the sleeve per se.

Writing the Quran While One Is Ritually Impure

It is unlawful for someone who writes a *muṣḥaf* while in the state of major or minor ritual impurity to actually carry the pages or to touch them while writing. If he does not carry them and does not touch them, there are three opinions: (1) Writing is permissible (and this is the sound opinion); (2) it is unlawful; and (3) it is permissible when in the state of minor ritual impurity but unlawful when in the state of major ritual impurity.

Touching Books Containing the Quran

The sound opinion is that it is permissible for someone in the state of minor or major ritual impurity or menstruation to touch or carry the following since they are not considered to be a *muṣḥaf*: (1) a book of *fiqh* or some other field of knowledge that contains verses from the Quran; (2) a garment embroidered with Quran;

(3) a gold or silver coin which has been engraved with [Quran]; (4) luggage whose contents include a *muṣḥaf*; and (5) a wall, pastry, or bread engraved with it. There is also an opinion that this is unlawful.

Garments Embroidered with the Quran

The chief judge Abū al-Ḥasan al-Māwardī said in his book *Al-Ḥāwī*: "It is permissible to touch garments embroidered with the Quran, but it is not permissible to wear them—without any disagreement—since what is intended by wearing them is obtaining blessing through the Quran."

This statement of his is weak. No one agreed with him about this from what I have seen. Indeed, Shaykh Abū Muḥammad al-Juwaynī and others were explicit that it is permissible to wear [such clothing], and this is the correct opinion.

And God knows best.

Commentary of the Quran

It is unlawful [while ritually impure] to touch and carry a book of commentary of the Quran [*tafsīr*] if the amount of the actual Quran exceeds that of the commentary itself. If the commentary is more, which is the majority [of *tafsīr* literature], there are three opinions concerning this: (1) Touching it is not unlawful, and it is the soundest opinion; (2) it is unlawful; and (3) if the Quran is in a distinctive calligraphy—by being thick, red, or the like—it is unlawful, and if it is not distinctive it is not unlawful. If [the amount of commentary and Quran are equal], I say that it is unlawful to touch it. The author of *al-Tatimma*,[4] one of our Shāfiʿī companions, said, "If we say that it is not unlawful, then it is offensive [at least]."

Books of Hadith

It is not unlawful to touch books of hadith from the Messenger of God (God bless him and grant him peace) if they do not contain verses from the Quran, but it is better not to touch [such books] except while in the state of ritual purity. If they contain verses from the Quran, it is *not* unlawful according to the Shāfiʿīs, though it is considered offensive. According to the Shāfiʿīs, there is an opinion that it is unlawful, and this is found in some books of *fiqh*.

Something Whose Recitation Has Been Abrogated

It is *not* unlawful to touch or carry something whose recitation has been abrogated, such as, "When a married man or a married woman commits adultery, their punishment shall be stoning as a retribution" and others. Our Shāfiʿī companions said that this ruling applies the same regarding the Torah and the Evangel.

Touching While Having Inexcusable Filth

It is unlawful—without disagreement—for someone with ritual purity but who has a spot of filth on his body, which is not legally excused, [such as drops of blood,] to bring the *muṣḥaf* into contact with that spot of filth. But it is not unlawful with another part, according to the sound, well-known opinion that the majority of our Shāfiʿī companions and other scholars have held.

Abū al-Qāsim al-Ṣaymarī, one of our Shāfiʿī companions, said that it is unlawful [to carry the *muṣḥaf*]. Our Shāfiʿī companions declared him mistaken concerning this, and al-Qāḍī Abū al-Ṭayyib said that this statement of his is unanimously rejected.

So in keeping with the well-known opinion, some of our Shāfiʿī companions said that it is offensive, but the preferred [opinion] is that it is not.

In the Absence of Water or Earth

If a person [with ritual impurity] does not find water and it is permissible for him to make dry ablution [*tayammum*]—whether his dry ablution was [in preparation] for Prayer or something else—it is permissible for him to touch the *muṣḥaf*. Someone who finds neither water nor earth [for ablution] may pray in whatever state he is in, but it is not permissible for him to touch the *muṣḥaf* because of his ritual impurity. We hold that it is permissible for him to pray only out of the necessity [of Prayer when time is running out].

If one had in his possession a *muṣḥaf* with him and does not find someone to give it to for safekeeping and he is incapable of making ablution, it is permissible for him to carry it because of the necessity of safeguarding the *muṣḥaf*.

Al-Qāḍī Abū al-Ṭayyib said that it is not essential for him to make dry ablution [for the purpose of immediately safekeeping the Quran]. But what he said is questionable, and one should be required to make dry ablution.

When Fearing Its Destruction

If one fears that a *muṣḥaf* will be burned, submerged in water, fall into filth, or land in the hands of a disbeliever, then he may take possession of it, even while in the state of ritual impurity, out of necessity.

The Guardian's Responsibilities

Is it obligatory for the teacher and the guardian of a youth who has reached the age of discernment to require him to have ritual purity in order for him to carry the *muṣḥaf* and the study tablet from which he recites? Our Shāfiʿī companions have two well-known opinions. The sounder opinion in their eyes is that it is not obligatory because of the ensuing hardship.

Commercial Transactions

It is valid to buy and sell the *muṣḥaf*. There is no offense in buying the *muṣḥaf*. Our Shāfiʿī companions, however, have two opinions concerning its sale. The sounder is that it is offensive, and it is the explicit opinion of al-Shāfiʿī. Those who consider neither buying nor selling the Quran offensive include al-Ḥasan al-Baṣrī, ʿIkrima, and al-Ḥakam ibn ʿUtayba; and this is related from Ibn ʿAbbās (God be pleased with him). A group of scholars considered it offensive to buy and sell [the Quran]. Ibn al-Mundhir conveyed this from ʿAlqama, Ibn Sīrīn, al-Nakhaʿī, Shurayḥ, Masrūq, and ʿAbdallāh ibn Yazīd.

Strong aversion to selling [the Quran] is attributed to Ibn ʿUmar and Abū Mūsā al-Ashʿarī (God be pleased with him). A group of scholars considered buying [the Quran] to be a legal dispensation, while selling it is offensive. Ibn Mundhir conveyed this from Ibn ʿAbbās, Saʿīd ibn Jubayr, Aḥmad ibn Ḥanbal, and Isḥāq ibn Rāhūyah (God be pleased with them all).

And God knows best.

10

IMĀM AL-NAWAWĪ'S LEXICON

[What follows] is a list of precise renditions of the names and terms mentioned in this book, arranged in order of their appearance. Instances of this are many. To completely vowelize each, clarify them, and explain them all would make this volume quite thick. However, I will touch upon them in the most concise fashion, and will point them out as briefly as possible. The first of them is in the introduction.

al-Ḥamd: Praising with pleasing attributes.

al-Karīm: Noble in the attributes of God Most High. It is said to mean: the *superior* or other such things.

al-Mannān: We relate from 'Alī ibn Abī Ṭālib (God be pleased with him) that it means: the one who gives before being asked.

al-Ṭuwl: Free of need and completely powerful.

al-Hidāyā': Success and benevolence. The following are said: He guided us *to* [*li*] belief, He guided us *with* [*bi*] belief, and He guided us *unto* [*ilā*] belief.

Sā'ir: Meaning *the rest.*

Laday: Unto Him.

Our Prophet (God bless him and grant him peace) was named "Muḥammad" because of his many praiseworthy qualities (Ibn Fāris and others said this), meaning, God Most High inspired his family to name him this because of what He knew of his pleasing qualities and noble characteristics. May God increase his honor and nobility.

Taḥaddā: To challenge and withstand.

Bi'ajma'ihim: With a *ḍamma* or a *fatḥa* on the *mīm* [*ajmu'ihim*, *ajma'ihim*] (both well-known dialects), meaning, in their entirety.

Wa afḥama: To silence and overwhelm.

Lā yakhluq: Its magnificence and sweetness never ceasing.

Istaẓharahu: To memorize.

al-Wildān: Youths.

al-Ḥadathān: With a *fatḥa* on the *ḥa* and the *dāl*. *Al-Ḥadath*, *al-ḥaditha*, and *al-ḥudtha* are synonymous. It is the occurrence of something that did not previously exist.

al-Malawān: Night and day.

al-Riḍwān: With a *kasra* or *ḍamma* on the *rā'* [*riḍwān*, *ruḍwān*].

al-Anām: This means people, according to the preferred opinion. *Al-Anaym* is also said.

al-Dāmighāt: Cogent, irrefutable arguments.

al-Ṭaghām: With a *fatḥa* on the dot-less *ṭā'* and on the dotted *ghayn*. They are ignoble people.

al-Amāthil: The exemplary; its singular is *amthal*.

al-A'lām: The plural of *'alam*. It is what is used to indicate the path, such as a mountain or something else. A scholar is called this because he guides others.

al-Nuhā: Intellects; the singular is *al-nuhya* with a *ḍamma* on the *nūn*. This is because it holds its possessor back from disgusting acts.

Dimashq: With a *kasra* on the *dāl* and a *fatḥa* on the *mīm*, according to the well-known opinion. The author of *Maṭāli' al-Anwār* also relates a *kasra* on the *mīm* [*Dimishq*].

Mukhtaṣr: Something with few phrases yet has many meanings.

al-'Atīda: Present and prepared.

Abtahal: To be humble.

al-Tawfīq: Creating the ability to worship.

Ḥasbunā Allāh: Meaning, *[He is] our sufficiency.*

al-Wakīl: The one made an agent. It is also said, the one who is given the agency of managing His creation, or the one sustaining the general welfare of His creation, or the Sustainer.

al-Infāq: Spending which is praiseworthy according to Sacred Law is extracting wealth in worshiping God Most High.

Tijāra lan tabūr: Meaning, it will not be consumed or spoiled.

al-Barara: The plural of *bārr*, meaning obedient [*muṭī'*].

al-Safara: The recording angels.

Yatata'tā': Meaning, to be severe and to be difficult.

Abū Mūsā al-Ash'arī: 'Abdallāh ibn Qays, ascribed to al-Ash'ar, the grandfather of the tribe.

al-Utrujja: With a *ḍamma* on the hamza and *rā'*. This is a well known [fruit, the citron]. Al-Jawharī stated that Abū Zayd said that it is called *tarnaja* in Bukhārī's *Ṣaḥīḥ*, in the book of food. In this hadith: "The example of *al-utrunja*."

Al-Ḥasad: [Envy] is hoping for the removal of someone else's blessing. *Ghibṭ* is similar to it but without wanting the blessing to be removed. Envy is unlawful but *ghibṭ* in good things is praiseworthy and desirable. What is intended by his saying (God bless him and grant him peace): "There is no envy except in two" is: "there is no praiseworthy *ghibṭ* whose importance is emphasized except in two."

Anā' al-layl: The hours of the night. There are four dialects the singular: *inān, anān* with a *kasra* or *fatḥa* on the *hamza*, and *iniy* and *inwun* with a *yā'* and *waw*, and the *hamza* has a *kasra* in both of them.

al-Alā' is identical to [the above in its morphology], and it means "bounty." There are four dialects concerning the singular: *ila*, *ala*, *iliy*, *ilwu*. Al-Wāqidī conveyed all of this.

al-Tirmadhī: Ascribed to Tirmidh. Abū Sa'd al-Sam'ānī said that it is an ancient land on the bank of the Balkh, which is called Jayhun. When using it as an attribute, it is said, Tirmidhī with a *kasra* on the tā' and *mīm*, and with a *ḍamma* on them both [*turmudhī*], and with a *fatḥa* on the *tā'* and a *kasra* on the *mīm* [*tarmadhī*]—three variations that al-Sam'ānī conveyed.

Abū Sa'īd al-Khudrī: His name is Sa'd ibn Mālik, ascribed to Banī Khudra.

Abū Dāwūd al-Sajistānī: His name is Sulaymān ibn al-Ash'ath.

al-Nasā'ī: He is Abū 'Abd al-Raḥmān Aḥmad ibn Shu'ayb.

al-Dārimī: He is Abū Muḥammad 'Abdallāh ibn 'Abd al-Raḥmān. Ascribed to Dārim, the grandfather of the tribe.

Abū Mas'ūd al-Badrī: His name is 'Uqba ibn 'Amr. The majority of the scholars said that he lived at the time of Badr and did not participate in the battle. Al-Zuhrī, Bukhārī, and others said that he participated in it with the Messenger of God (God bless him and give him peace).

Sha'ā'ir'-Allāh tā'ala: The outward signs [rites] of His religion; one of them is *sha'īra*. Al-Jawharī said, the singular is said *shi'ara*.

al-Bazzār: The author of *al-Musnad*, with a *rā'* at the end.

Laḥd al-qabr: With a *fatḥa* or *ḍamma* on the *lām* [*laḥd, luḥd*]—two well-known dialects, and the *fatḥa* is linguistically purer. It is a niche in the side of the grave closest to the *qibla* which the deceased is lowered into. One says: *laḥadtu al-mayit* and *alḥadtuhu.*

Abū Hurayra: His name is 'Abd al-Raḥmān ibn Ṣakhr, according to the strongest of among approximately thirty opinions. He was given his agnomen because of a cat he had when he was small. He is the first to have this agnomen.

Adhanani bi'l-ḥarb: Made it known to me. It means, *declaring war against me.*

Abū Ḥanīfa: His name is al-Nu'mān ibn Thābit ibn Zūṭā.

al-Imām al-Shāfi'ī: Abū 'Abdallāh Muḥammad ibn Idrīs ibn al-'Abbās ibn 'Uthmān ibn Shāfi' ibn al-Sā'ib ibn 'Ubayd ibn 'Abd Yazīd ibn Hāshim ibn al-Muṭṭalib ibn 'Abd Manāf ibn Qasiy.

al-Thalb: With a *fatḥa* on the *thā'* with three-dots and a *sukūn* on the *lām*. It is a defect.

Ḥunafā': The plural of *ḥanīf*. It is that which is straight, or the one leaning towards the truth and averting falsehood.

al-Mar'ashī: With a *fatḥa* on the *mīm* and a *sakun* on the *rā'*, and *fatḥa* on the dot-less *'ayn*, and a dotted *shīn*.

al-Tustarī: With a *ḍamma* on the first *tā'*, a *fatḥa* on the second, the dot-less *sīn* having *sukūn* between them. An ascription to Tustar, the well-known city.

al-Muḥāsibī: With a *ḍamma* on the *mīm*. Al-Sam'ānī said that this was said about him because he would take himself to account [*yuhasib nafsahu*], and he was among those who joined the outward and inward disciplines.

'Arf al-Janna: With a *fatḥa* on the *'ayn* and *sukūn* on the *rā'* and *fā'*. The scent of Paradise.

Fa-l-yatabawwa' maq'adahu min al-nār: Meaning, *he descends to it*, or *he occupies it*. Some say that it is a supplication [May God descend him into...], and others that it is a declaration [God has lowered him...].

Dalāla: With a *fatḥa* or *kasra* on the *dāl* [*dalāla*, *dilāla*]. *Dulūla* with a *ḍamma* on the *dāl* and *lām* is said.

Ṭawiyya: With *fatḥa* on the *ṭā* and a *kasra* on the *waw*. The lexicographers said that it is conscience.

Ṭarāqī: The plural of *ṭarquwa*. It is the bone between the nape of the neck and the shoulder.

Yajlisūna ḥilaqā: It is said with a *fatḥa* or *kasra* in the *ḥa* [*ḥalaqā*, *ḥilaqā*], two dialects.

Ibn Mājah: He is Abū 'Abdallāh Muḥammad ibn Yazīd.

Abū al-Dardā': His name is 'Uwaymir or 'Āmir.

Yaḥnu 'alā al-ṭālib: Meaning, to be kind to him, to feel compassion for him.

Ayyūb al-Sakhtiyānī: With a *fatḥa* on the *sīn* and a *kasra* on the *tā'*. Abū 'Umar ibn 'Abd al-Barr said, Ayyūb tanned skins in Basra, and because of this he was called "al-Sakhtiyānī."

Barra'a: With a *fatḥa* on the bā'. The gerund of *barā'a al-rajl wa baru'a*, with a *fatḥa* or *ḍamma* on the *rā'* [*barra'a*, *barru'a*], if he surpassed his companions.

Ḥalqa al-'ilm and their likes: With a *sukūn* on the lām—this is the pure, well-known dialect. It is rarely said with a *fatḥa* [*ḥalaqa*] in one dialect. Tha'lab, al-Jawharī, and others conveyed it.

al-Rufqa: With a *ḍamma* or *kasra* on the *rā'* [*rufqa*, *rifqa*], two dialects.

Qi'dat al-muta'llimīn: With a *kasra* on the *qāf*.

Ma'shar: A group with a common cause.

Yunfidhūnaha bi-l-nahār: Meaning, performing what it contains.

Abū Sulaymān al-Khaṭṭābī: He is ascribed to one of his grandfathers named al-Khaṭṭāb. Abū Sulaymān's name is Ḥamd ibn Muḥammad ibn Ibrāhīm ibn al-Khaṭṭāb. And it is said that his name is Aḥmad.

al-Zuhrī: He is Abū Bakr Muḥammad ibn Muslim ibn 'Ubaydullāh ibn 'Abdallāh ibn Shihāb ibn 'Abdallāh ibn al-Ḥārith ibn Zuhra ibn Kilāb ibn Murra ibn Ka'b, al-Baṣrī, with a *fatḥa* or *kasra* on the *bā'* [*Baṣrī*, *Biṣrī*].

al-Sha'bī: With a *fatḥa* on the *shīn*: his name is 'Āmir ibn Sharāḥīl, with a *fatḥa* on the *sīn*.

Tamīm al-Dārī: Ascribed to a grandfather he has who is named al-Dār. Other opinions include: he is ascribed to Dārayn, a place in the plains; or: "Tamīm al-Dayrī" ascribed to a cloister that he would worship in; and there are others. I have clarified the disagreement in the beginning of *Sharḥ Ṣaḥīḥ Muslim.*

Sulaym ibn 'Itr: With a *kasra* on the dot-less *'ayn*, *sukūn* on the twice-dotted-above *tā'*.

Aḥmad al-Dawraqī: With a dot-less *dāl* with a *fatḥa*, then a *qāf*, then *yā'* of ascription. It is said that it is an ascription to the long caps that are called *al-dawraqiyya*. Other opinions are that his father was a hermit, and at that time they called hermits *dawriqī*; or that it is an ascription to Dawraq, a land in Persia or elsewhere.

Manṣūr ibn Zādhān: With a *zay* and dot-less *dhāl*.

Yaḥtabī: Raising ones shins and then encircling the shins and the thighs with the arms or a garment.

al-Ḥubwa: With a *ḍamma* or *kasra* on the *ḥā'* [*ḥubwa*, *ḥibwa*] are two dialects. It is doing the action [of the previous note].

al-Hadhrama: With a single-dotted *dhāl*: quick quiet talk.

al-Ghazālī: He is Muḥammad ibn Muḥammad ibn Muḥammad ibn Aḥmad. This is how it is said, with a *shadda* on the *zay* [*ghazzālī*]. It was related that he denied this and said, "I am al-Ghazālī with a light [single] *zay* ascribed to one of the villages in Ṭūs which is called "Ghazāla."

Ṭalḥa ibn Muṣarrif: With a *ḍamma* on the *mīm*, a *fatḥa* on the *ṣād*, and*kasra* on the *rā'*. It is said that it is permissible to put a *fatḥa* on the *rā'* [Muṣarraf], but this opinion is baseless.

Abū al-Aḥwaṣ: With a *ḥa* and *ṣād* without dots. His name is 'Awf ibn Mālik al-Jushamī, with a *ḍamma* on the *jīm* and a *fatḥa* on the dotted *shīn*. Ascribed to Jusham, the grandfather of the tribe.

al-Fusṭāṭ: It has six dialects: *fusṭāṭ* and *fustāṭ*, with a *tā'* instead of a *ṭā'*. *Fussāṭ* with a *shadda* on the *sīn*, and the *fā* being with *ḍamma* or *kasra* [*fussāṭ*, *fissāṭ*].It means a camp or a stop.

al-Dawiyy: With a *fatḥa* on the *dāl* and *kasra* on the *waw* and a *shadda* on the *yā'*. A sound that is not understood.

al-Nakha'ī: With a *fatḥa* on the nūn and *khā'*. Ascribed to al-Nakh'a, the grandfather of a tribe.

Ḥalab shāh: With a *fatḥa* on the *lām*, and it is permissible with a *sukūn* in a rare dialect [*ḥalb*].

al-Raqāshī: With a *fatḥa* on the *rā'* and the *qāf* being light.

al-Qadhā: Like *'ūd*, pottery crumbs, and the like; things that are swept from the mosque.

Sulaymān ibn Yasār: With double-dotted underneath *yā*, then a vowel-less *sīn*.

Abū Usayd: With a *ḍamma* on the *hamza*, and a *fatḥa* on the sīn. His name is Mālik ibn Rabī'a. He participated in Badr.

Tanṭiḥunī: With a *kasra* and *fatḥa* on the *ṭā'* [*tanṭiḥunī*, *tanṭaḥunī*].

Muntashir jiddān: With a *kasra* on the *jīm*. It is a gerund.

Ushnān: With a *ḍamma* or *kasra* on the *hamza* [*ushnān*, *ishnān*], two dialects. Abū 'Ubayda and Ibn al-Jawālīqī mentioned them both. It is a Persian word which is Arabized. In Arabic, it is *al-maḥḍa ḥurḍ*. The *hamza* of *ashnān* is part of its root.

Karāsī aḍrāsih: It is permissible to put a *shadda* on the *yā'* or to lighten it [*karāsīy*, *karāsī*]. And likewise, everything derived from it, where its singular is with a *shadda*, it is permissible in its plural to put a *shadda* or to lighten it.

al-Ruwyānī: With a *ḍamma* on the *rā'* , a *sukūn* on the *waw*. Ascribed to Ruwyān: the well-known land.

'Alā ḥasab ḥālih: It is with a *fatḥa* on the *sīn*, meaning, in accordance to his ability.

al-Ḥammām: It is known. The word is masculine according to the lexicographers.

al-Ḥushūsh: Latrines. Its singular is *ḥush* with a *ḍamma* or *fatḥa* on the *ḥa* [*ḥush*, *ḥash*]: two pronunciations.

Ḥajr al-insān: With a *fatḥa* or *kasra* on the *ḥa* [*ḥajr*, *ḥijr*].

al-Jināza: With a *kasra* or *fatḥa* on the *jīm* [*jināza*, *janāza*]. From the root *j-n-z*: when something is covered.

Bahz ibn Ḥakīm: With a *fatḥa* on the single-dotted, with a *sukūn* on the *ha* and *zay*.

Zurāra: With a *ḍamma* on the *zay*.

Aḥmad ibn Abī al-Ḥawāriy: With a *fatḥa* on the *ḥa*, and a *kasra* on the *rā'*. Some put a *fatḥa* on the *rā'* [*ḥawārayy*]; our shaykh Abū al-Baqā' Khālid al-Nābulusī (God grant him mercy) mentioned this, and perhaps he preferred it. He was the great scholar of his time in this discipline with complete mastery in it. The name of Abū al-Ḥawārī is 'Abdallāh ibn Maymūn ibn 'Abbās ibn al-Ḥārith.

al-Jū'ī: With a *ḍamma* on the *jīm*.

Abū al-Jawzā': With a *fatḥa* on the *jīm* and *zay*. His name is Aws ibn 'Abdallāh or Aws ibn Khālid.

Ḥabtar: With a dot-less *ḥa* with a *fatḥa*, then a twice-dotted-above *tā'*, with a *fatḥa*, then a *rā'*.

al-Rajul al-ṣāliḥ: [The righteous man] is the one upholding the rights owed God Most High and the rights owed [His] servants. Al-Zajjāj, the author of *al-Maṭāli'*, and others said this.

Abū Dharr: His name is Jundub. Another opinion is that his name is Burayr, with a *ḍamma* on the single-dotted *bā'*, and the *rā'* repeating.

Ijtaraḥu al-sayyi'āt: He earned evil deeds.

Shi'ār: With a *kasra* on the *shīn*. A sign.

al-Shirāk: With a *kasra* on the *shīn*. It is the thin strap which is on the top of a sandal on the top of the foot.

Umm Salama: Her name is Hind. Another opinion is Ramlah, and it is baseless.

'Abdallāh ibn Mughaffal: With a *ḍamma* on the *mīm*, and a *fatḥa* on the single-dotted *ghayn* and *fā'*.

al-Laghaṭ: With a *fatḥa* or *sukūn* on the *ghayn* [*laghaṭ*, *laghṭ*]; two dialects. It is jumbling up sounds.

al-Jumu'a: With a *ḍamma*, *sukūn*, or *fatḥa* on the *mīm* [*jumu'a*, *jum'a*, *juma'a*]; al-Fara' and al-Wāḥidī said it.

al-Ma'wwidhitān: With a *kasra* on the *waw*.

al-Awzā'ī: His name is 'Abd al-Raḥmān ibn 'Amr. The Imām of Shām [Greater Syria] in his time. Ascribed to a place at the Farādīs Gate in Damascus, called al-Awzā'; or it is a tribe. There are other opinions.

'Arzab*:* With a dot-less *'ayn* with a *fatḥa*, then a *rā'* with a *sukūn*, then a *zay* with a *fatḥa*, then a single-dotted *bā'*.

Burayda ibn al-Ḥuṣayb: With a *ḍamma* on the *ḥā'*, a *fatḥa* on the *ṣād*—both of them dot-less.

Faāla: With a *fatḥa* on the *fā'*.

Lallāhi ashadd adhanā: With a *fatḥa* on the *hamza* and *dhāl*, meaning, with respect to listening.

al-Qayna: With a *fatḥa* on the *qāf*: a female singer.

Ṭūbā lahum: Meaning, goodness for them. This is what the lexicographers said.

al-A'mash: Sulaymān ibn Mahrān.

Abū al-'Āliya*:* With the *'ayn* dot-less. His name is Rufay', with a *ḍamma* on the *rā'*.

Abū Lubāba: The Companion g. With a *ḍamma* on the *lām*. His name is Bashīr; another opinion is that it is Rifa'a ibn 'Abd al-Mundhir.

'Aynāhu tadhrifān*:* Meaning, their tears were pouring. It is with a *fatḥa* on the two-dotted *tā'* from above, and *kasra* on the *rā'*.

Fa mā khaṭbukum: Meaning, *what's your errand?*

Ayyām al-ma'dūdāt: The three days of Tashrīq after the Day of Sacrifice.

Tashmīt al-'āṭis: It is with a *shīn* and *sīn* [*'āṭis*, *'āṭish*].

al-Qaffāl: The one mentioned here is al-Marwazī, 'Abdallāh ibn Aḥmad.

Yaqrun: With *ḍamma* on the *rā'* according to the pure dialect, and in a dialect with a *kasra* [*yaqrin*].

al-Baghawī: Ascribed to Bagh, a city between Harāt and Marw, it is also called Baghshūr. His name is al-Ḥusayn ibn Mas'ūd.

al-Aṣāl: The plural of *aṣīl*. It is the end of the day or the time between late afternoon and the setting of the sun.

Zubayd ibn al-Ḥārith: With a *ḍamma* on the *zay*, and then a singly dotted [*bā'*] with a *fatḥa*.

Subbūḥ quddūs: With a *ḍamma* in the first of the two, and a *fatḥa* [*sabbūḥ*, *qaddūs*]; two well-known dialects.

Abū Qilāba: With a *kasra* on the *qāf*, and lightness on the lām and single-dotted *bā'*. His name is 'Abdallāh ibn Zayd.

Yaḥyā ibn Waththāb: With a triple-dotted *thā'* with a *shadda*.

Mu'an ibn Rifā'a: With a *ḍamma* on the *mīm* and dot-less *'ayn*, and a *nūn* in the end.

al-Shikhkhīr: With a *kasra* on the *shīn* and the single-dotted *khā'*, and with a *shadda* on the *khā*.

al-Ḥakam ibn 'Utayba: He is with a double-dotted-above *tā'*, then with a double-dotted-below [*yā'*], then a single-dotted [*bā'*].

al-Maḥyā wa al-mamāt: Life and death.

Awzi'hum: Meaning, *inspire them*.

Ḥamdan yuwāfī ni'amahu: Meaning, *reaching and obtaining it*.

Yukāfi'mazīdahu: It is with a *hamza* in the end of *yukāfi'*, meaning, *it serves as thanks for the bounty that He has provided us with*.

Mujālid: The narrator from al-Sha'bī. With a *jīm* and *kasra* on the *lām*.

Abū al-Qāsim al-Ṣaymarī: With a *fatḥa* on the dot-less *ṣād* and *mīm*; or with a *ḍamma* on the *mīm* [*ṣaymurī*], but this is odd. I clarified it at length in *Tahdhīb al-Asmā' wa al-Lughāt*.

11

CONCLUDING REMARKS

This is the last of what God has facilitated for me with regard to this book. It is condensed and minute compared to [all that can be said about] the etiquette of reciters of the Quran. However, what I mentioned in the beginning of the book compelled me to make it condensed.

I ask God the Magnificent that it be a source of comprehensive benefit for me and my loved ones, for everyone who looks in it, and the rest of the Muslims—in the Two Abodes [this life and the next].

Praise is for God, Lord of the worlds—praise that reaches the measure of His bounties and matching His provision. May His complete prayers and blessings be upon our master Muḥammad, his folk, Companions, one and all.

All praise is for God, Lord of the worlds.

[The author (God grant him mercy) wrote]: I began compiling [this work] on Thursday the 12th of Rabīʿ al-Awwal, [the birthday of the Prophet (God bless him and give him peace)]; and I finished compiling it Thursday morning, the 3rd of Rabīʿ al-Thānī, 666 AH.

TRANSLATOR'S NOTES

AUTHORS INTRODUCTION

1. This is a reference to what God Most High said, *This day I have perfected your religion for you, and completed My favor upon you, and chosen Islam for you as the religion* (Quran, 5:3).

CHAPTER ONE

1. Bukhārī (5027), Adū Dāwūd (1452), Tirmidhī (2909), Dārimī (3341), Ibn Mājah (211), Aḥmad (1:412, 413, 500). Someone who learns and teaches the Quran has become the representative of God and His Messenger (God bless him and grant him peace) and beneficial to His servants. The person that is most beloved to God is the one most beneficial to His servants. See *al-Tāj al-Jāmi' li al-Uṣūl* (4:3).
2. Bukhārī (4937), Muslim (798), Tirmidhī (2906), Adū Dāwūd (1454), Aḥmad (6:48, 94, 98, 110, 170, 192, 239, 266), Dārimī (3371), Ibn Mājah (3779). Someone who has memorized the Quran, is skillful in it, and acts according to it is on the level of those noble angels. The one who recites it and wants to memorize it while it is difficult for him, has two rewards: the reward of recitation and the reward for trying to memorize it. See *al-Tāj al-Jāmi' li al-Uṣūl* (4:4).
3. The phrase "*Ṣaḥīḥayn*" refers to the collections of rigorously authenticated hadiths by Bukhārī and Muslim. The authenticity of a hadith found in both collections is considered very strong.

[The numerals in the parenthesis are to be understood as follows: those set off by a colon (e.g.: 5:234) refer to volume and page number of the source; the others are the hadith numbers, as they are arranged in the respective hadith compendiums.]

4. Bukhārī (5020, 5059, 5427, 7560), Muslim (797), Tirmidhī (2869), Abū Dāwūd (4830), Nasā'ī (4:397, 404; 8:124–25, 404, 408), Dārimī (3366), Ibn Mājah (214).
5. Muslim (817), Dārimī (3318), Ibn Mājah (218).
6. Muslim (804), Aḥmad (5:249).
7. Bukhārī (5025, 7529), Muslim (815, 267), Tirmidhī (1937), Aḥmad (2:9, 36, 88).
8. Bukhārī (73, 1409, 7141, 7316), Muslim (816), Ibn Mājah (4208).
9. Tirmidhī (2912), Dārimī (3311).
10. Regarding Tirmidhī's use of compound judgments with hadiths, Imām al-Nawawī says: "Tirmidhī and others saying 'this hadith is well-rigorously authenticated' is problematic since their definitions differ, so how are they reconciled? The answer: It is interpreted to mean that the hadith was narrated with two chains: one of them rigorously authenticated and the other well-authenticated. Shaykh Ibn Ṣalāḥ said, 'And it is possible that what is intended by the linguistic meaning of "well" is that which the self inclines towards.'" (*Irshād Ṭullāb al-Ḥaqā'iq*, p69.) The last explanation is considered weak. And God knows best.
11. Tirmidhī (2927), Dārimī (3359), *Fatḥ al-Bārī* (9:66).
12. Tirmidhī (2914), Aḥmad (1:223), Dārimī (3309), al-Ḥākim (1:554). A ruined house is void of goodness and inhabitants, and so someone who memorizes the Quran is full of goodness and steeped in excellence. See *al-Tāj al-Jāmi' li al-Uṣūl* (4:6).
13. Abū Dāwūd (1464), Tirmidhī (2915), Aḥmad (2:192), Ibn Ḥibbān (1789), al-Ḥākim (1:552–53).
14. Abū Dāwūd (1453), Aḥmad (3:440).
15. For the first half of the hadith, see Dārimī (3322–23); for the second half, see Dārimī (3310, 3326).
16. See the first footnote of this chapter.

CHAPTER TWO

1. The one with the most Quran is given precedence, even if the other person is a legist; this is the opinion of al-Aḥnaf, Ibn Sīrīn, and the Ḥanbalīs. But the majority say that the one with the most understanding regarding purification and Prayer is given precedence over the one who has merely memorized more Quran. Their proof is that the amount of Quran required for Prayer is limited, while what is needed for the study of Sacred Law is unlimited. Something may occur in the Prayer that is known only to a legist. Ibn Mas'ūd (God be

pleased with him) said, "If one of us memorized a chapter from the Quran, he did not leave it for the next until mastering the knowledge it contains and knowing what it permits and prohibits." This stresses the importance of Sacred Law over mere memorization. See *al-Tāj al-Jāmiʿ li al-Uṣūl* (1:253).

2. Muslim (673), Tirmidhī (235, 773), Abū Dāwūd (582–84), Nasā'ī (2:76–77), Aḥmad (4:118, 121).
3. Bukhārī (4642, 7286).
4. The superiority of reciting Quran is general. But whenever something has been appointed for a specific time or place by God or His Messenger (God bless him and give him peace), it is superior in that time or place.

CHAPTER THREE

1. Abū Dāwūd (4834).
2. Abū Dāwūd (4842).
3. Imām Muslim mentioned it in the introduction to his *Ṣaḥīḥ*. Imām al-Sakhāwī considered it well authenticated in his biography of Ibn Ḥajar.
4. Bukhārī (1343–45, 1347–48, 1353, 4078), Adū Dāwūd (3138), Tirmidhī (1036), Nasā'ī (4:62), Ibn Mājah (1514).
5. Bukhārī (6502).
6. Muslim (657), Aḥmad (4:312–13), Tirmidhī (222). It was not found in Bukhārī, and God knows best.

CHAPTER FOUR

1. Bukhārī (1, 54, 2529, 3898, 5070, 6689, 6953), Muslim (1907), Adū Dāwūd (2201), Tirmidhī (1647), Nasā'ī (1:59–60), Aḥmad (1:25, 43), Ibn Mājah (4227).
2. This is the first hadith in Imām al-Nawawī's *Forty Hadith*. Scholars differ in interpreting the phrase "Actions are only by their intentions," which on the surface equates actions and intentions. The Ḥanafīs say the *complete reward* for actions hinges on intention, while the Shāfiʿīs and Ḥanbalīs hold that the *soundness* of an action hinges on intention. This difference is part of the reason why the Ḥanafīs do not consider *intention* to be a condition for the soundness of ablution (*wuḍū'*), contrary to the Shāfiʿīs and Ḥanbalīs.
3. The remainder of the verse is: *...then We appoint for him Hell, which he will endure, disgraced and vanquished.*

4. Abū Dāwūd (3664), Ibn Mājah (252), Aḥmad (2:338), al-Ḥākim (1:85), Ibn Ḥibbān (89).
5. This means to turn their attention to him and to become well known among them: God will enter him into the fire unless he repents and singles out his intention for seeking knowledge. See *al-Tāj al-Jāmiʿ li al-Uṣūl* (1:74).
6. The chain from Anas (God be pleased with him): al-Bazzār (178). The chain from Ḥudhayfa (God be pleased with him): Ibn Mājah (259). The chain from Ka'b (God be pleased with him): Tirmidhī (2656). The hadith has supporting chains; see *Majmaʿ al-Zawā'id* (1:183–84).
7. Dārimī (388).
8. Tirmidhī (2652, 2653), Ibn Mājah (247).
9. This means that "religion is hinged upon sincerity," since religion and sincerity are not synonymous with one another. Other explanations include: "Religion in its *complete* form is sincerity," or "One of [religion's] conditions is sincerity."
10. This hadith expresses one of the foundations of Islam and is the seventh hadith in Imām al-Nawawī's *Forty Hadith*. It is related from Tamīm al-Dārī (God be pleased with him), in Muslim (55), Abḍ Dāwūd (4944), Nasā'ī (7:156), Aḥmad (4:102); and from Abū Hurayra (God be pleased with him) in Tirmidhī (1927) and Aḥmad (2:297). Sincerity%{Sincerity!hinged to religion} towards *God*: by believing in Him, establishing what is obligatory, thanking *Him*, and bringing people to do this. Sincerity towards *His Book*: by learning it, acting according to it, and guiding people to this. Sincerity towards *His Messenger*, Muḥammad ibn 'Abdallāh (God bless him and grant him peace): by following him, assisting him, and defending him. Sincerity towards *the leaders of the Muslims*, those responsible for their affairs: by respecting them and obeying their orders in what pleases God and His Messenger (God bless him and grant him peace) (*O you who believe! Obey God and obey the Messenger and those of you who are in authority* (Quran, 4:59)) and by correcting them when they err. Sincerity towards *their common folk*: by guiding them to what holds their happiness in this world and the Hereafter, and offering them assistance and protection. See *al-Tāj al-Jāmiʿ li l-uṣūl* (1:27–28).%{Sincerity!hinged to religion}
11. Bukhārī (13), Muslim (45), Nasā'ī (8:115), Aḥmad (3:176, 177, 206, 207, 251, 272, 275, 278, 289), Dārimī (2743), Ibn Mājah (66).
12. Bukhārī in *al-Adab al-Mufrad* (1145–46).

13. Al-Ḥāfiẓ al-ʿIrāqī *Takhrīj al-Iḥyā'* (3:176). Ibn al-Sunnī related it in *Riyā al-Mutaʿallimīn* with a weakly authenticated chain.
14. Imām al-Nawawī means that a teacher should not be compelled to go to a student to teach him or her. Rather, it is the proper etiquette for a student to go to a teacher to learn. It is said that Imām Mālik refused to go to the governor to teach him and insisted that the governor come to him, in order to preserve the dignity of knowledge.
15. Abū Dāwūd (4820), *al-Adab al-Mufrad* (1136), Aḥmad (3:18), al-Ḥākim (4:269).
16. Bukhārī (52, 205), Muslim (1599), Abū Dāwūd (3329–30), Aḥmad (4:267, 269, 271, 275), Dārimī (2524).
17. *Maʿrifa* is experiential knowledge of God.
18. Muslim (26 in the *Introduction*). A variation of this hadith is the last hadith in *al-Shamā'il al-Muḥammadiyya.*
19. See al-Khaṭīb al-Baghdādī, *al-Faqīh wa al-Mutaffaqih* (2:99).
20. *Al-Adab al-Mufrad* (1007–08), Aḥmad (2:230, 287, 439), Tirmidhī (2707), Abū Dāwūd (5208), Ibn Mājah (1931–32).
21. Dārimī (256), *Fatḥ al-Bārī* (1:166): Ibn Abī Shayba narrated it with a rigorously authenticated chain.
22. Abū Dāwūd (2606), Tirmidhī (1212), Aḥmad (3:416–17, 432; 4:384, 390–91), Ibn Mājah (2236).

CHAPTER FIVE

1. Aḥmad (3:428, 444), al-Haythamī *Majmaʿ al-Zawā'id* (4:73), al-Ṭabarānī in *al-Kabīr.*
2. Abū Dāwūd (830), Aḥmad (3:397).
3. One is censured for reciting the Quran and then begging for money—either by extending the hand as one recites or in the streets with the intention to beg. The Quran is the speech of God, not a trade-good for the perishing trinkets of this world. See *al-Tāj al-Jāmiʿ li al-Uṣūl* (4:12–13). See also Tirmidhī (2918), Aḥmad (4:432–33, 439).
4. See *Radd al-Muḥṭār* (2:334), *Hidā al-Ilāhiyya* (p.150).
5. *Ahl al-Ṣuffa* ("People of the Shelter") were poor Muslims who lived under a small awning in the Prophet's mosque (God bless him and grant him peace).
6. Abū Dāwūd (3416), Aḥmad (5:315), Ibn Mājah (2157).
7. Whoever recites the Quran in less than three nights does not understand what is required when reciting, since etiquette requires having ritual purity, sitting facing the *qibla*, reciting correctly, pondering

the meanings, being aware that God is observing him and answers each word, and intending to act according to its contents as long as he lives. See *al-Tāj al-Jāmiʿ li l-uṣūl* (4:13).

8. Abū Dāwūd (1394), Tirmidhī (2950), Dārimī (1501), Aḥmad (2:164–65, 189, 193, 195), Ibn Mājah (1347).
9. The 24-hour day begins with sunset, so "Friday night" starts with the sunset after Thursday afternoon until the dawn ushering Friday's Dawn Prayer.
10. *Iḥyā' ʿUlūm al-Dīn* (1:276).
11. Dārimī (3486).
12. Bukhārī (1122, 1157, 3739, 7016, 7029, 7031), Muslim (2478, 2479). ʿAbdallāh here is ʿAbdallāh ibn ʿUmar (God be pleased with him and his father). After hearing this he never left it.
13. Bukhārī (1152), Muslim (2:814, 185), Aḥmad (2:170), Ibn Mājah (1331).
14. What he means here is that at one time people were regularly busy reading the Quran, whereas the people of his day were not—as if the people were exempt of the fears that drove those of the past to recite so much.
15. Bukhārī (1145, 6321, 7494), Muslim (758), Abū Dāwūd (1315, 4733), Tirmidhī (446), Ibn Mājah (1366), Imām Mālik's *al-Muwaṭṭa* (1:214), Aḥmad (2:258, 267, 282, 419, 487, 504), Dārimī (1486–87).
16. Muslim (757), Aḥmad (3:313, 331, 348).
17. This most likely refers to the biography of Shaykh ʿAbd al-Qādir al-Jaylānī, authored by the Sufi scholar ʿAlī ibn ʿAbdallāh ibn al-Ḥasan ibn Jahdam al-Hamadhānī. It may also be Shaykh Abḍ al-Ḥusayn ʿAlī ibn al-Ḥusayn ibn Hamawayhī ibn Zayd, a Sufi who died in 374 AH. God have mercy upon them both.
18. Abū Dāwūd (1398), Ibn Mājah (662), Ibn Sunnī (703).
19. Bukhārī (5033), Muslim (791), Aḥmad (4:397, 411).
20. Bukhārī (5031), Muslim (789), *al-Muwaṭṭa* (1:202), Nasā'ī (2:154), Aḥmad (2:17, 64, 112), Ibn Mājah (3783).
21. Abū Dāwūd (461), Tirmidhī (2917). See also *Fatḥ al-Bārī* (9:86).
22. The severity of the sin here is not universal, but with respect to the sins associated with the Quran itself. The connection between picking up trash in the mosque and forgetting Quran is that the mosque is a house of God, and the Quran is His speech. Just as there is reward associated with showing respect towards His house by removing trash from it, there is great sin associated with show-

ing disrespect letting part of His Quran be removed from memory. See *al-Futuḥāt al-Rabbāniyya* (3:252).

23. Aḥmad (5:327), Dārimī (3343), Abū Dāwūd (1474), *al-Futuḥāt al-Ilāhiyya* (3:253), *Fatḥ al-Bārī* (9:86).
24. The words *wird* and *ḥizb* refer to a specific amount of a selection of recitation, invocation, reading, or some other action.
25. Muslim (747), Abū Dāwūd (1313), Tirmidhī (581), Imām Mālik's *al-Muwaṭṭa* (1:200), Dārimī (1386), Ibn Mājah (1343).

CHAPTER SIX

1. This of course is a reference to the well-known hadith where Jibril (peace be upon him) teaches us about beliefs, actions, and perfection. It is the third hadith in Imām al-Nawawi's *Forty Hadith*. Bukhārī (50, 4499), Muslim (8, 9, 10).
2. That is, one opinion being that it is lawful and the other that it is prohibited.
3. The Māliki madhhab allows women who teach or study the Quran more interaction with the Quran than the other three schools. Some of the rulings apply to all women, while others are specifically for students and instructors. Muḥammad Bashīr al-Shafaqah writes:

> [Menstruation and postpartum bleeding] prevent touching the *muṣḥaf* as long as she is not an instructor or a student.
>
> It is permissible for a woman who is menstruating or has postpartum bleeding to recite the Quran—even while blood is flowing—from memory or from the *muṣḥaf* without touching it, whether or not she fears forgetting it, and whether or not she is in the state of major ritual impurity because of intercourse, and to do so after the blood has stopped but before making the purificatory both if she is not [also] in the state of major ritual impurity because of intercourse.
>
> A woman who is menstruating may touch and write on a board for the sake of instruction, whether she is teaching or learning, and she may also do whatever is associated with this, such as carrying it back to or taking it from its place. It is also permissible for a menstruating woman who a teacher or a student to touch the complete *muṣḥaf*. (See *Fiqh al-'Ibādāt*, p.131)

It must be stressed that only the second paragraph applies to all women, and that the first and third are specifically for women who are in the process of studying and teaching the Quran itself. We must all remember that just as doing what God has ordered us to do is obedience for which we are rewarded, stopping at the limits that He has set is also obedience for which we are rewarded. And God knows best.

4. Linguistically, *naskh* (abrogation) means *removing* and *transporting*. Its meaning in the *Sharī'a* is to raise a legal judgment after it

was revealed. Abrogation can occur with respect to the wording of the Quran, its meaning, or both. It occurs in the Quran in three ways: 1. abrogating the phrase and the meaning together; 2. abrogating the phrase but not the meaning; 3. abrogating the meaning but not the phrase. Abrogation is a complex matter discussed in books of jurisprudence and Quranic sciences.

5. See *Radd al-Muḥṭār* (1:254).
6. Abū Ya'lā, al-Ṭabarānī in *al-Awsaṭ*.
7. Bukhārī (297, 7549), Muslim (301), Abū Dāwūd (260), Nasā'ī (1:191), Aḥmad (6:96), Ibn Mājah (634).
8. The Quran's 9th chapter, called al-Tawba, or 'Repentance.'
9. Imām al-Dhahabī considered this account to be sound.
10. The remainder of the verse is: *and if you forgive them, You, indeed You, are the August, the Wise.* See Nasā'ī (2:177), Ibn Mājah (1350).
11. The remainder of the verse is: *...the same in life and death? Bad judgments indeed!.*
12. Ibn Mājah (4196).
13. *Ihya' 'Ulūm al-Dīn* (1:277).
14. Abū Dāwūd (1466), Tirmidhī (2924), Nasā'ī (3:214), Aḥmad (6:294, 300).
15. Bukhārī (4281, 4835, 5034, 5047, 7540), Muslim (794), Abū Dāwūd (1467).
16. Bukhārī (775, 4996, 5043), Muslim (822), Aḥmad (1:380, 417, 427).
17. Muslim (772), Aḥmad (5:384, 397), Abū Dāwūd (871, 874), Nasā'ī (2:176, 177; 3:225–26).
18. See *Fatḥ Bāb al-'Ināyah* (1:200).
19. Bukhārī (4326).
20. This paragraph has been abridged as it contains some things that are not present at this time.
21. See *Radd al-Muḥṭār* (1:325), *Badā'i al-Ṣanā'i* (1:298–99).
22. The seven canonical recitations in which there is consensus, are named after the following *imāms* of recitation: 'Abdallāh ibn Kathīr al-Darī al-Mākkī (d 120 AH); 'Abdallāh ibn 'Amr al-Yashabī al-Shāmī (d 118 AH); 'Āsim ibn Abī al-Najud al-Asdī al-Kūfī (d 127 AH); Abū 'Amr Zabbān ibn al-'Alā' al-Baṣrī (d 154 AH); Ḥamza ibn Ḥabīb al-Zayyāt al-Kūfī (d 156 AH); Nāfi' ibn 'Abd al-Raḥmān ibn Abī Na'īm al-Madanī (d 169 AH); and Abū al-Ḥasan 'Alī ibn Ḥamza al-Kisā'ī—the grammarian—al-Kūfī (d 189 AH).

23. Imām al-Nawawi uses the opening verse of a sura to identify it. But for the sake of clarity and immediate sense, I identify the sura by its conventional name.
24. Muslim (879), Abū Dāwūd (1074), Tirmidhī (520), Nasā'ī (2:159).
25. Muslim (891), *al-Muwaṭṭa* (1:180), Abū Dāwūd (1154), Tirmidhī (534), Nasā'ī (3:183–84).
26. Muslim (726), Abū Dāwūd (1256), Nasā'ī (2:155–56).
27. These last two are commonly referred to together as the "*mua'wwidhatayn*". In the translation they are referred to by chapter name and number. As for the hadith, see Abū Dāwūd (1424), Tirmidhī (463), Nasā'ī (2:244–45), al-Hakim (1:305).
28. Ibn Ḥajar said that he did not find the evidence for this, and perhaps it is a matter of not disagreeing with those who say it is obligatory. See *al-Futuḥāt al-Rabbāniyyah* (2:202).
29. *Al-Futuhat al-Rabbaniyyah* (2:203).
30. *Ihya' 'Ulūm al-Dīn* (1:279).
31. Muslim (2700), Tirmidhī (3375), Aḥmad (2:447; 3:33, 49, 92, 94).
32. Muslim (2701), Abū Dāwūd (1455), Aḥmad (2:252, 407, 447).
33. Muslim (2701), Aḥmad (4:92), Tirmidhī (3376), Nasā'ī (8:298).
34. Dārimī (3370).
35. See: Muslim (1893), Aḥmad (4:120, 5:274), Abū Dāwūd (5129), Tirmidhī (2673).
36. Bukhārī (2942, 3009, 3701, 4210), Muslim (2406), Aḥmad (5:333).
37. *Ihya 'Ulūm al-Dīn* (1:278–279).
38. Bukhārī (5023, 7482, 7544), Muslim (792), Abū Dāwūd (1473), Nasā'ī (2:180), Aḥmad (2:271, 285, 450), Dārimī (1499, 3493–94).
39. Muslim (793), Aḥmad (5:349, 351, 359).
40. Ibn Mājah (1340), Aḥmad (6:19, 20), Ibn Ḥibbān (659), al-Ḥākim (1:570), al-Bayhaqī (10:230).
41. Bukhārī (4232), Muslim (2399).
42. Abū Dāwūd (1467), Nasā'ī (2:179–180), Dārimī (3503), Aḥmad (4:283, 285, 296, 304), Ibn Mājah (1342), al-Ḥākim (1:575).
43. Abū Dāwūd (1333), Tirmidhī (2920), Nasā'ī (5:80), Aḥmad (4:151, 158).
44. Hadith Abū Lubabah (God be pleased with him): Abū Dāwūd (1471). The chain from Sa'd ibn Abī Waqqāṣ (God be pleased with him): Abū Dāwūd (1470), Aḥmad (1:172, 175, 179), Ibn Mājah (1337), Dārimī (1498). Hadith Abū Hurayrah (God be pleased with him): Bukhārī (7527).
45. Bukhārī (767, 769, 4952, 7549), Muslim (464).
46. Abū Dāwūd (1471).

47. Bukhārī (4582, 5049–50, 5055–56), Muslim (800), Tirmidhī (3027–28), Abū Dāwūd (3668), Aḥmad (1:380, 433), Ibn Mājah (4194).

48. Dārimī (3496)

49. Quran, 4:23–24:

﴿إِنَّ ٱللَّهَ كَانَ غَفُورًا رَّحِيمًا ﴿٢٣﴾ ۞ وَٱلْمُحْصَنَٰتُ مِنَ ٱلنِّسَآءِ إِلَّا مَا مَلَكَتْ أَيْمَٰنُكُمْ﴾

50. Quran, 12:52–53:

﴿ذَٰلِكَ لِيَعْلَمَ أَنِّى لَمْ أَخُنْهُ بِٱلْغَيْبِ وَأَنَّ ٱللَّهَ لَا يَهْدِى كَيْدَ ٱلْخَآئِنِينَ ﴿٥٢﴾ ۞ وَمَآ أُبَرِّئُ نَفْسِىٓ ۚ إِنَّ ٱلنَّفْسَ لَأَمَّارَةٌۢ بِٱلسُّوٓءِ إِلَّا مَا
رَحِمَ رَبِّىٓ ۚ إِنَّ رَبِّى غَفُورٌ رَّحِيمٌ ﴿٥٣﴾﴾

51. Quran, 27:55–56:

﴿أَئِنَّكُمْ لَتَأْتُونَ ٱلرِّجَالَ شَهْوَةً مِّن دُونِ ٱلنِّسَآءِ ۚ بَلْ أَنتُمْ قَوْمٌ تَجْهَلُونَ ﴿٥٥﴾ ۞ فَمَا كَانَ جَوَابَ قَوْمِهِۦٓ إِلَّآ أَن
قَالُوٓا۟ أَخْرِجُوٓا۟ ءَالَ لُوطٍ مِّن قَرْيَتِكُمْ ۖ إِنَّهُمْ أُنَاسٌ يَتَطَهَّرُونَ ﴿٥٦﴾﴾

52. Quran, 33:30–31:

﴿يَٰنِسَآءَ ٱلنَّبِىِّ مَن يَأْتِ مِنكُنَّ بِفَٰحِشَةٍ مُّبَيِّنَةٍ يُضَٰعَفْ لَهَا ٱلْعَذَابُ ضِعْفَيْنِ ۚ وَكَانَ ذَٰلِكَ عَلَى ٱللَّهِ يَسِيرًا ﴿٣٠﴾
۞ وَمَن يَقْنُتْ مِنكُنَّ لِلَّهِ وَرَسُولِهِۦ وَتَعْمَلْ صَٰلِحًا نُّؤْتِهَآ أَجْرَهَا مَرَّتَيْنِ وَأَعْتَدْنَا لَهَا رِزْقًا كَرِيمًا ﴿٣١﴾﴾

53. Quran, 36:27–28:

﴿بِمَا غَفَرَ لِى رَبِّى وَجَعَلَنِى مِنَ ٱلْمُكْرَمِينَ ﴿٢٧﴾ ۞ وَمَآ أَنزَلْنَا عَلَىٰ قَوْمِهِۦ مِنۢ بَعْدِهِۦ مِن جُندٍ مِّنَ ٱلسَّمَآءِ وَمَا كُنَّا
مُنزِلِينَ ﴿٢٨﴾﴾

54. Quran, 41:46–47:

﴿مَّنْ عَمِلَ صَٰلِحًا فَلِنَفْسِهِۦ ۖ وَمَنْ أَسَآءَ فَعَلَيْهَا ۗ وَمَا رَبُّكَ بِظَلَّٰمٍ لِّلْعَبِيدِ ﴿٤٦﴾ ۞ إِلَيْهِ يُرَدُّ عِلْمُ ٱلسَّاعَةِ ۚ وَمَا تَخْرُجُ مِن
ثَمَرَٰتٍ مِّنْ أَكْمَامِهَا وَمَا تَحْمِلُ مِنْ أُنثَىٰ وَلَا تَضَعُ إِلَّا بِعِلْمِهِۦ ۚ وَيَوْمَ يُنَادِيهِمْ أَيْنَ شُرَكَآءِى قَالُوٓا۟ ءَاذَنَّٰكَ مَا مِنَّا مِن
شَهِيدٍ ﴿٤٧﴾﴾

55. Quran, 39:47–48:

﴿وَلَوْ أَنَّ لِلَّذِينَ ظَلَمُوا۟ مَا فِى ٱلْأَرْضِ جَمِيعًا وَمِثْلَهُۥ مَعَهُۥ لَٱفْتَدَوْا۟ بِهِۦ مِن سُوٓءِ ٱلْعَذَابِ يَوْمَ ٱلْقِيَٰمَةِ ۚ وَبَدَا لَهُم مِّنَ ٱللَّهِ
مَا لَمْ يَكُونُوا۟ يَحْتَسِبُونَ ﴿٤٧﴾ وَبَدَا لَهُمْ سَيِّـَٔاتُ مَا كَسَبُوا۟ وَحَاقَ بِهِم مَّا كَانُوا۟ بِهِۦ يَسْتَهْزِءُونَ ﴿٤٨﴾﴾

56. Quran, 51:30–31:

﴿وَبَدَا لَهُمْ سَيِّـَٔاتُ مَا كَسَبُوا۟ وَحَاقَ بِهِم مَّا كَانُوا۟ بِهِۦ يَسْتَهْزِءُونَ ﴿٤٨﴾ ۞ قَالَ فَمَا خَطْبُكُمْ أَيُّهَا ٱلْمُرْسَلُونَ ﴿٣١﴾﴾

57. Quran, 2:202–03:

﴿أُو۟لَٰٓئِكَ لَهُمْ نَصِيبٌ مِّمَّا كَسَبُوا۟ ۚ وَٱللَّهُ سَرِيعُ ٱلْحِسَابِ ﴿٢٠٢﴾ ۞ وَٱذْكُرُوا۟ ٱللَّهَ فِىٓ أَيَّامٍ مَّعْدُودَٰتٍ ۚ فَمَن تَعَجَّلَ
فِى يَوْمَيْنِ فَلَآ إِثْمَ عَلَيْهِ وَمَن تَأَخَّرَ فَلَآ إِثْمَ عَلَيْهِ ۚ لِمَنِ ٱتَّقَىٰ ۗ وَٱتَّقُوا۟ ٱللَّهَ وَٱعْلَمُوٓا۟ أَنَّكُمْ إِلَيْهِ تُحْشَرُونَ ﴿٢٠٣﴾﴾

58. Quran, 3:14–15:

﴿زُيِّنَ لِلنَّاسِ حُبُّ ٱلشَّهَوَٰتِ مِنَ ٱلنِّسَآءِ وَٱلْبَنِينَ وَٱلْقَنَٰطِيرِ ٱلْمُقَنطَرَةِ مِنَ ٱلذَّهَبِ وَٱلْفِضَّةِ وَٱلْخَيْلِ
ٱلْمُسَوَّمَةِ وَٱلْأَنْعَٰمِ وَٱلْحَرْثِ ۗ ذَٰلِكَ مَتَٰعُ ٱلْحَيَوٰةِ ٱلدُّنْيَا ۖ وَٱللَّهُ عِندَهُۥ حُسْنُ ٱلْمَـَٔابِ ﴿١٤﴾ ۞ قُلْ أَؤُنَبِّئُكُم بِخَيْرٍ
مِّن ذَٰلِكُمْ ۚ لِلَّذِينَ ٱتَّقَوْا۟ عِندَ رَبِّهِمْ جَنَّٰتٌ تَجْرِى مِن تَحْتِهَا ٱلْأَنْهَٰرُ خَٰلِدِينَ فِيهَا وَأَزْوَٰجٌ مُّطَهَّرَةٌ وَرِضْوَٰنٌ
مِّنَ ٱللَّهِ ۗ وَٱللَّهُ بَصِيرٌۢ بِٱلْعِبَادِ ﴿١٥﴾﴾

59. Muslim (2995), Abū Dāwūd (5026–27), Aḥmad (3:37, 93, 96).

60. Quran, 9:30:

﴿ وَقَالَتِ ٱلْيَهُودُ عُزَيْرٌ ٱبْنُ ٱللَّهِ وَقَالَتِ ٱلنَّصَـٰرَى ٱلْمَسِيحُ ٱبْنُ ٱللَّهِ ۖ ذَٰلِكَ قَوْلُهُم بِأَفْوَٰهِهِمْ ۖ
يُضَـٰهِـُٔونَ قَوْلَ ٱلَّذِينَ كَفَرُوا۟ مِن قَبْلُ ۚ قَـٰتَلَهُمُ ٱللَّهُ ۚ أَنَّىٰ يُؤْفَكُونَ ﴿٣٠﴾ ﴾

61. Quran, 5:64:

﴿ وَقَالَتِ ٱلْيَهُودُ يَدُ ٱللَّهِ مَغْلُولَةٌ ﴾

62. Quran, 19:88:

﴿ وَقَالُوا۟ ٱتَّخَذَ ٱلرَّحْمَـٰنُ وَلَدًا ﴿٨٨﴾ ﴾

63. Quran, 33:56:

﴿ إِنَّ ٱللَّهَ وَمَلَـٰٓئِكَتَهُۥ يُصَلُّونَ عَلَى ٱلنَّبِىِّ ۚ يَـٰٓأَيُّهَا ٱلَّذِينَ ءَامَنُوا۟ صَلُّوا۟ عَلَيْهِ وَسَلِّمُوا۟ تَسْلِيمًا ﴿٥٦﴾ ﴾

64. Quran, 95:8:

﴿ أَلَيْسَ ٱللَّهُ بِأَحْكَمِ ٱلْحَـٰكِمِينَ ﴿٨﴾ ﴾

65. Abū Dāwūd (887), Tirmidhī (3344), Aḥmad (2:249)
66. Quran, 75:40:

﴿ أَلَيْسَ ذَٰلِكَ بِقَـٰدِرٍ عَلَىٰٓ أَن يُحْـِۧىَ ٱلْمَوْتَىٰ ﴿٤٠﴾ ﴾

67. Quran, 7:185:

﴿ أَوَلَمْ يَنظُرُوا۟ فِى مَلَكُوتِ ٱلسَّمَـٰوَٰتِ وَٱلْأَرْضِ وَمَا خَلَقَ ٱللَّهُ مِن شَىْءٍ وَأَنْ عَسَىٰٓ أَن يَكُونَ قَدِ ٱقْتَرَبَ أَجَلُهُمْ ۖ فَبِأَىِّ حَدِيثٍۭ
بَعْدَهُۥ يُؤْمِنُونَ ﴿١٨٥﴾ ﴾

68. An alternative name for Sūrat al-Isrā'.
69. The Muḥakkimah were one of the sects of Khawārij, people who seceded from following 'Alī (God be pleased with him). They are known for their literal interpretation of the verse "*Judgment is reserved solely for God*" (Quran, 6:57). See *Refutation Of The Innovator Of Najd* and *Kitāb al-Milal wa al-Nihal* (1:157)
70. The monograph's title is *Kitāb al-Tarkhīṣ fī al-Ikrām bi'l-Qiyyām lī Dhawi al-Faḍl wa'l-Mazziya min AHl al-Islām 'alā Jihat al-Birr wa al-Taqwā wa al-Iḥtirām lā 'alā Jihat al-Riyā' wa'l-I'ẓām*. Imām al-Nawawī refers to this again later on in the text. There is a rebuttal of this monograph by Ibn al-Ḥājj, and Ibn Ḥajar has written a counter-rebuttal of Ibn al-Ḥājj's work.
71. See *Radd al-Muḥṭār* (1:360), *Fatḥ Bāb al-'Ināyah* (1:227, 231, 234).
72. Ibn Ḥibbān (457), Ibn Khuzaymah (490).
73. "New" refers to Imām al-Shāfi'ī's school after going to Egypt. "Old" refers to the previous formulation. As for the issue here, Imām al-Nawawi considers the old opinion to be the strongest one. See *Mughnī al-Muḥtāj* (1:159–60).
74. Abū Dāwūd (798, 799), Nasā'ī (2:164).
75. There are three views on what the latecomer does after the imām concludes the Prayer. One, the latecomer makes up what he had

missed of the Prayer (the Ḥanafī and Ḥanbalī view); the second is that he completes what he had started (the Shāfi'ī); and the third is a mix of the previous two (the Mālikī). So someone following the Ḥanafī or Ḥanbalī school will read additional verses after al-Fātiḥa in the two *rak'a*s that he prays because he is now making up for the two *rak'a*s that he prays because he is now making up for the two *rak'a*s that he missed, whereas the Shāfi'ī will not because the two *rak'a*s that he will pray will be considered the concluding *rak'a*s of the Prayer, in which only al-Fātiḥa is recited.

76. Bukhārī (5043), Muslim (822), Aḥmad (1:380, 417, 427).
77. Imams Mālik and Aḥmad differ here, making them both audible.
78. This is crucial concerning obligatory invocations during the Prayer. As for other invocations, Imām al-Nawawi mentions in the beginning of *al-Adhkār* that invocation [*dhikr*] can occur by the heart or by the tongue, and the best of all is when both are joined. He also mentions that making invocations using the tongue and the heart together should never be left out of fear of showing off [*ri'ā*] since leaving actions for others is showing off while doing them for others is associating partners with God [*shirk*], and that abandoning the good out of fear of the false thoughts that other may have is not the way of those who have knowledge of God. And God knows best. (See the beginning of *al-Adhkār*).
79. Imām al-Nawawī uses the term "*imālah*" in describing this pronunciation of "*Āmīn,*" in which the *alif* is articulated a *yā'*.
80. Bukhārī (780–82, 4475, 6402), Muslim (409), Abū Dāwūd (936), Tirmidhī (250), Nasā'ī (2:143–44), Dārimī (1248–49), Aḥmad (2:233, 238, 270, 459).
81. See *Radd al-Muḥtār* (1:515), *Fatḥ Bāb al-'Ināyah* (1:373–74).
82. Bukhārī (1077).
83. Bukhārī (1072), Muslim (577), Abū Dāwūd (1404), Tirmidhī (576), Nasā'ī (2:160), Dārimī (1480), Aḥmad (5:183, 186).
84. Bukhārī (1071, 4862), Muslim (575–76), Abū Dāwūd (1406), Nasā'ī (2:160), Aḥmad (1:388, 401, 437, 443, 462), Dārimī (1473).
85. Bukhārī (1069, 3422), Abū Dāwūd (1409), Tirmidhī (577), Nasā'ī (2:159), Dārimī (1475), Aḥmad (1:279, 360, 364).
86. See *Radd al-Muḥtār* (1:513),*Fatḥ Bāb al-'Ināyah* (1:375).
87. See *Radd al-Muḥtār* (1:513), *Fatḥ Bāb al-'Ināyah* (1:377).
88. Quran, 41:37:

﴿وَمِنْ ءَايَٰتِهِ ٱلَّيْلُ وَٱلنَّهَارُ وَٱلشَّمْسُ وَٱلْقَمَرُ ۚ لَا تَسْجُدُوا۟ لِلشَّمْسِ وَلَا لِلْقَمَرِ وَٱسْجُدُوا۟ لِلَّهِ ٱلَّذِى خَلَقَهُنَّ إِن كُنتُمْ إِيَّاهُ تَعْبُدُونَ ﴿٣٧﴾﴾

89. Quran, 27:25:

﴿أَلَّا يَسْجُدُوا لِلَّهِ الَّذِي يُخْرِجُ الْخَبْءَ فِي السَّمَاوَاتِ وَالْأَرْضِ وَيَعْلَمُ مَا تُخْفُونَ وَمَا تُعْلِنُونَ ﴿٢٥﴾﴾

90. The reliable opinion is that it is obligatory for a person to make the prostration upon hearing one of these verses. See *Radd al-Muḥtār* (1:516), *Fatḥ Bāb al-'Ināyah* (1:373).

91. Yaḥyā ibn Abī al-Khayr. He memorized al-Shirāzī's *al-Muhadhdhab* and explained it in his work *al-Bayān*. He died in Yemen in 558 AH.

92. See *Radd al-Muḥtār* (1:520), *Fatḥ Bāb al-'Ināyah* (1:372).

93. Al-Ruwyani.

94. The relied upon position with the Ḥanafīs is Abū Ḥanīfa's. See *Radd al-Muḥtār* (1:522).

95. The term Persian [*Fārisī*] is sometimes used to refer to all languages other than Arabic.

96. See *Radd al-Muḥtār* (1:514).

97. See *Radd al-Muḥtār* (1:518).

98. See *Fatḥ Bāb al-'Ināyah* (1:381).

99. 'Abd al-Raḥmān ibn Ma'mūn. He was a Shāfi'ī scholar, known as "al-Mutawwalī," who was born in Nīsābūr in 427 AH. He was assigned head of the Niẓāmiyya School in Baghdad, where he died in 487 AH. God have mercy upon him.

100. Al-Ḥusayn ibn Mas'ūd.

101. Evidence for gender-related differences associated with Prayer are found in a genre of literature known as the *muṣannafāt*. Books of this genre include accounts of the Prophet (God bless him and grant him peace), his Companions (God be pleased with them), and the first generations of Successors. 'Abd al-Razzāq al-Ṣan'ānī—the great hadith master and instructor of Imām Aḥmad—mentioned these hadiths in a section right before the chapter on Friday Prayer (3:126–51).

102. Tirmidhī (579), Ibn Mājah (1053), Ibn Khuzaymah (562), Ibn Mājah (691), al-Ḥākim (1:219–20).

103. Bukhārī (823), Abū Dāwūd (844), Tirmidhī (287), Nasā'ī (243).

104. See *Majma' al-Zawā'id* (1:160): al-Ṭabarānī related it in *al-Kabīr*.

105. Muslim (2687).

106. Bukhārī (1461).

107. Bukhārī (4612), Muslim (177), Tirmidhī (3070), Aḥmad (6:49–50).

108. Bukhārī (324, 351, 971, 974, 980–81, 1652), Muslim (890), Abū Dāwūd (1136–1139), Tirmidhī (539–40), Nasā'ī (3:180–81).

109. Dārimī (3475), see *al-Futuḥāt al-Rabbāniyyah* (3:243).

110. Dārimī (3484), see *al-Futuḥāt al-Rabbāniyyah* (3:246).

111. A sounder account is related from Ibn 'Abbās (God be well pleased with them both): Tirmidhī (2949), Dārimī (3479). Every time one

finishes the Quran's recitation, he should immediately begin again. The Quran is the most superior worship—after the things required of a person—bringing the servant close to his Lord Most High. It is related from Imām Aḥmad (God be well pleased with him) that he saw in his sleep his Lord a number of times and said, "By God, if I see Him another time I am going to ask Him which thing brings servants closer to Him." So he saw his Lord and said, "O Lord! By what thing does the servant draw closer to You?" He said, "By reciting My speech, O Aḥmad." He said, "If he understoods the meaning or if he does not understand, O Lord?" He said, "Whether he understood the meaning or not." See *al-Tajj al-Jami' li al-Uṣūl* (4:7).

CHAPTER SEVEN

1. This verse is mentioned since there is consensus that here it is a verse of the Quran, while there is difference of opinion whether the preceding "*Bismillahi al-Raḥmāni al-Raḥīm*" is intended as a verse or not.
2. This obviously refers to the very last verse in the Quran, thus emphasizing without ambiguity that the whole of the Quran, without exception, is considered from God and revealed to the Prophet (God bless him and grant him peace) through the agency of the noble Angel Gabriel (peace be upon him) (Jibrīl).
3. These are matters known and communicated via *naql*, transmitting what other qualified scholars have said. This would include such things as abrogation and circumstances for a particular revelation.
4. Abū Dāwūd (4603), Aḥmad (2:258, 286, 424, 475, 478, 494, 503, 528).
5. Bukhārī (5032, 5039), Muslim (790), Tirmidhī (2943), Nasā'ī (2:154), Aḥmad (1:382, 417, 423, 429, 438, 449, 463), Dārimī (2248, 3350).
6. Bukhārī (5037–38, 5042, and 2655, 6335), Muslim (788), Adū Dāwūd (1331), Aḥmad (6:138). Forgetting means abandoning, something which is not suitable with the Quran. See *al-Tāj al-Jāmi' li al-Uṣūl* (4:8).
7. [According to the majority of scholars, what is intended here is the Arabic text itself, not necessarily a translation of its meanings.
8. This is in reference to the *muṣḥaf*, that is, the actual Arabic text of the Quran in one bound volume. It does not refer to translations of the Quran's meanings.
9. One opinion being permissibility and the other prohibition.

10. The reciter recites the Quran and puffs out his breath gently on the sick person. This is one way in which the Quran is used for healing and protection.
11. Bukhārī (5016–17, 5748, 6319), Muslim (2192), Adū Dāwūd (3902), Tirmidhī (3399), Ibn Mājah (3529), Aḥmad (6:104, 114, 124, 166, 181, 256, 263).

CHAPTER EIGHT

1. Ubaydullāh ibn Abī Rafī': Muslim (877); Abū Dāwūd (1124); and Tirmidhī (519). Samura ibn Jundub: Abū Dāwūd (1125) and Nasā'ī (3:111–12).
2. Abū Dāwūd (1424), Tirmidhī (463), Nasā'ī (2:244–45), al-Ḥākim (1:305).
3. Dārimī (3410), al-Bayhaqī (3:239), al-Ḥākim (2:368).
4. Dārimī (3407).
5. Abū Dāwūd (1523), Tirmidhī (2905), Nasā'ī (3:68), Aḥmad (4:201).
6. Bukhārī (4008, 5008–09, 5040, 5051), Muslim (808), Adū Dāwūd (1397), Tirmidhī (2884), Aḥmad (4:118, 121, 122), Ibn Mājah (1369), Dārimī (1495, 3391).
7. Dārimī (3381).
8. Aḥmad (4:158). See also *Majma' al-Zawā'id* (7:149).
9. Sūrat Banī Isrā'īl is an alternative name for Sūrat al-Isrā' (17). As for the hadith, see Tirmidhī (2921), Aḥmad (6:68), and al-Ḥākim (2:434).
10. Bukhārī (4569), Muslim (763).
11. Bukhārī (2276, 5007, 5736, 5749); Muslim (2201); Adū Dāwūd (3418); Tirmidhī (2064); Ibn Mājah (2156); and Aḥmad (3:2, 10, 44). The hadith tells of the occasion when a few of the Companions of the Prophet (God bless him and grant him peace) were traveling and a girl ran up to them and said that the chief of her clan was stung, presumably by a scorpion, and needed help. "Are any of you a healer?" she asked. One of the Companions went with her and recited Sūrat al-Fātiḥa over the chief, who then recovered. When he rejoined the other Companions and informed them of what had happened, they asked him if he had ever healed like this before. He said, "No. I only recited [Sūrat al-Fātiḥa] over him." When they returned to the Prophet (God bless him and grant him peace) and narrated to him the event, he approved.
12. *Sharḥ Aṣḥāb al-Ḥadīth* (189).

13. The majority of scholars understand this to mean someone on the brink of death, while others understand this to mean someone who has died.
14. Abū Dāwūd (3121), Nasā'ī (1074), Aḥmad (5:26–27), Ibn Mājah (1448), Ibn Ḥibbān (720), al-Ḥākim (1:565).

CHAPTER NINE

1. Bukhārī (4987).
2. Dārimī (3353).
3. Bukhārī (2290), Muslim (1869), Abū Dāwūd (2610), Ibn Mājah (2879).
4. The author of this book is al-Baghawī.

APPENDIX ONE

SUPPLICATIONS UPON COMPLETING THE QURAN

الْحَمْدُ للهَ رَبِّ العالَمِيْنَ حَمْدًا يُوافِي نِعَمَهُ وَيُكَافِىءُ مَزِيدَهُ، اللَّهُمَّ صَلِّ وَسَلِّمْ عَلَى مُحَمَّدٍ وَعَلَى آلِ مُحَمَّدٍ كَمَا صَلَّيْتَ عَلَى إِبْرَاهِيْمَ وَعَلَى آلِ إِبْرَاهِيْمَ وَبَارِكْ عَلَى مُحَمَّدٍ وَعَلَى آلِ مُحَمَّدٍ كَمَا بَارَكْتَ عَلَى إِبْرَاهِيْمَ وَعَلَى آلِ إِبْرَاهِيْمَ فِي العَالَمِيْنَ إِنَّكَ حَمِيْدٌ مَجِيْدٌ.

Al-Ḥamdu lillāhi rabbi-l-ʿālamīn ḥamdan yuwāfī niʿamahu wa yukāfi'u mazīdah. Allāhumma ṣalli wa sallim ʿalā Muḥammadin wa ʿalā āli Muḥammadin, kamā ṣallayta ʿalā Ibrāhīma wa ʿalā āli Ibrāhīma, wa bārik ʿalā Muḥammadin wa ʿalā āli Muḥammadin, kamā bārakta ʿalā Ibrāhīma wa ʿalā āli Ibrāhīma fi-l-ʿalamīna innaka ḥamīdun majīd.

***

اللَّهُمَّ أَصْلِحْ قُلُوْبَنَا وَأَزِلْ عُيُوْبَنَا وَتَوَلَّنَا بِالْحُسْنَى وَزَيِّنَا بِالتَّقْوَى وَاجْمَعْ لَنَا خَيْرَيِ الآخِرَةِ وَالأُوْلَى وَارْزُقْنَا طَاعَتَكَ مَا أَبْقَيْتَنَا.

Allāhumma aṣliḥ qulūbanā, wa azil ʿuyūbana, wa tawallanā bi-l-ḥusnā, wa zayyinnā bi-l-taqwā, wa-jmaʿ lanā khayrayi-l-akhirati wa-l-ūlā, wa-rzuqnā ṭāʿataka mā abqaytanā.

***

اللَّهُمَّ يَسِّرْنَا لِلْيُسْرَى وَجَنِّبْنَا العُسْرَى وَأَعِذْنَا مِنْ شُرُوْرِ اَنْفُسِنَا وَسَيِّئَاتِ

أَعْمَالِنَا وَأَعِذْنَا مِنْ عَذَابِ النَّارِ وَعَذَابِ القَبْرِ وَفِتْنَةِ المَحْيَا وَالمَمَاتِ وَفِتْنَةِ
المَسِيْحِ الدَّجَّالِ.

Allāhumma yassirnā li-l-yusrā, wa jannibnā al-‘usrā, wa a‘idhnā min shurūri anfusinaa wa sayyi‘āti a‘mālinā, wa a‘idhnā min ‘adhāb al-nāri wa ‘adhaaab al-qabri, wa fitnati al-maḥyā wa al-mamāt, wa fitnat al-masīḥ al-dajjāl.

* * *

اللَّهُمَّ إِنَّا نَسْأَلُكَ الهُدَى وَالتَّقْوَى وَالعَفَافَ وَالغِنَى.

Allāhumma innā nas’aluka al-hudā wa al-tuqā wa al-‘afafā wa al-ghinā.

* * *

اللَّهُمَّ إِنَّا نَسْتَوْدِعُكَ أَدْيَانَنَا وَأَبْدَانَنَا وَخَوَاتِيْمَ أَعْمَالِنَا وَأَنْفُسَنَا وَأَهْلِيْنَا
وَأَحْبَابَنَا وَسَائِرَ المُسْلِمِيْنَ وَجَمِيْعَ مَا أَنْعَمْتَ بِهِ عَلَيْنَا وَعَلَيْهِمْ مِنْ أُمُوْرِ
الآخِرَةِ وَالدُّنْيَا.

Allāhumma innā nastawdi‘uka adyānanā wa abdānanā, wa khawātīma a‘mālinā wa anfusanā, wa AHlīnā wa aḥbābana wa sā’iri al-muslimīna, wa jamī‘ mā an‘amta bihi ‘alaynā wa ‘alayhim min umūr al-ākhirati wa-l-dunyā.

* * *

اللَّهُمَّ إِنَّا نَسْأَلُكَ العَفْوَ وَالعَافِيَةَ فِي الدِّيْنِ وَالدُّنْيَا وَالآخِرَةِ وَاجْمَعْ بَيْنَنَا
وَبَيْنَ أَحْبَابِنَا فِي دَارِ كَرَامَتِكَ بِفَضْلِكَ وَرَحْمَتِكَ.

Allāhumma innā nas‘aluka al-‘afwa wa al-‘afiyati fi-l-dīn wa al-dunyā wa al-ākhira, wajma‘ baynā wa baynā aḥbābinā fī dār karamātika bi faḍlika wa raḥmatika.

* * *

اللَّهُمَّ أَصْلِحْ وُلَاةِ الْمُسْلِمِيْنَ وَوَفِّقْهُمْ لِلْعَدْلِ فِي رَعَايَاهُمْ وَالإِحْسَانِ إِلَيْهِم وَالشَّفَقَةِ عَلَيْهِم وَالرِّفْقِ بِهِمْ وَالاعْتِنَاءِ بِمَصَالِحِهِمْ وَحَبِّبْهُمْ إِلَى الرَّعِيَّةِ وَحَبِّبَ الرَّعِيَّةَ إِلَيْهِم وَوَفِّقْهُمْ لِصِرَاطِكَ الْمُسْتَقِيْمِ وَالعَمَلِ بِوَظَائِفِ دِيْنِكَ القَوِيْمِ.

Allāhumma aṣliḥ wulāta al-muslimīn, wa waffiqhum li-l-ʿadl fī raʿāyahum wa al-iḥsān ilayhim wa al-shafaqa ʿalayhim, wa al-rifq bihim wa al-iʿtināʾ bi maṣāliḥihim, wa ḥabbibhum ilā al-raʿiyyati wa ḥabib al-raʿiyyata ilayhim, wa waffiqhum li-ṣiraṭika al-mustaqīm, wa al-'amal bi waẓāʾif dīnika al-qawīm.

***

اللَّهُمَّ الْطُفْ بِعَبْدِكَ سُلْطَانِنَا وَوَفِّقْهُ لِمَصَالِحِ الدُّنْيَا وَالآخِرَةِ وَحَبِّبْهُ إِلَى رَعِيَّتِهِ وَحَبِّبْ الرَّعِيَّةَ إِلَيْهِ.

Allāhumma ulṭuf bi ʿabdika sulṭāninā, wa waffiqhu li maṣāliḥ al-dunyā wa al-ākhira, wa ḥabbibhu ilā raʿiyyatihi, wa ḥabbib al-raʿiyyata ilayhi.

***

اللَّهُمَّ احْمِ نَفْسَهُ وَبِلَادَهُ وَصُنْ أَتْبَاعَهُ وَأَجْنَادَهُ وَانْصُرْهُ عَلَى أَعْدَاءِ الدِّيْنِ وَسَائِرِ الْمُخَالِفِيْنَ وَوَفِّقْهُ لِإِزَالَةِ الْمُنْكَرَاتِ وَإِظْهَارِ المَحَاسِنِ وَأَنْوَاعِ الخَيْرَاتِ وَزِدِ الإِسْلَامَ بِسَبَبِهِ ظُهُوْرًا وَأَعِزَّهُ وَرَعِيَّتَهُ أَعْزَازًا بَاهِرًا.

Allāhumma iḥmi nafsahu wa bilādahu, wa ṣun atbā'ahu wa ajnādahu, wanṣurhu 'alā aʿdāʾi al-dīn wa sāʾiri al-mukhālifīn, wa waffiqhu li-izālat al-munkarāt wa iẓhār al-maḥāsini wa anwāʿ al-khayrāt, wa zid al-islāma bi-sababihi ẓuhūran, wa aʿizzahu wa raʿiyyatahu iʿzāzan bāhiran.

***

اللَّهُمَّ أَصْلِحْ أَحْوَالَ الْمُسْلِمِيْنَ وَأَرْخِصْ أَسْعَارَهُمْ وَآمِنْهُمْ فِيْ أَوْطَانِهِمْ

وَاقْضِ دُيُوْنَهُمْ وَعَافِ مَرْضَاهُمْ وَانْصُرْ جُيُوْشَهُمْ وَسَلِّمْ غُيَّابَهُمْ وَفُكَّ أَسْرَاهُمْ وَاشْفِ صُدُوْرَهُمْ وَأَذْهِبْ غَيْظَ قُلُوْبِهِمْ وَأَلِّفْ بَيْنَهُمْ وَاجْعَلْ فِي قُلُوْبِهِمُ الإِيْمَانَ وَالحِكْمَةَ وَثَبِّتْهُمْ عَلَى مِلَّةِ رَسُوْلِكَ صَلى الله عَلَيْهِ وَسَلَّمْ وَأَوْزِعْهُمْ أَنْ يُوْفُوْا بِعَهْدِكَ الَّذِي عَاهَدْتَهُمْ عَلَيْهِ وَانْصُرْهُمْ عَلَى عَدُوِّكَ وَعَدُوِّهِمْ إِلَهَ الحَقِّ وَاجْعَلْنَا مِنْهُمْ.

Allāhumma aṣliḥ aḥwāl al-muslimīna wa arkhiṣ as'ārahum, wa āminhum fī awṭānihim, wa-qḍi duyūnahum, wa 'āfi marḍāhum, wa-nṣur juyūshahum, wa sallim ghuyyābahum, wa fukka asrāhum, wa-shfi ṣudūrahum, wa adhhib ghayẓa qulūbihim, wa allif baynahum, wa-j'al fī qulūbihim al-imān wa al-ḥikma, wa thabbithum 'alā millati rasūlika ṣall allāhu 'alayhi wa sallam wa awzi'hum an yūfū bi-'ahdika alladhī 'āhadtahum 'alayhi, wanṣurhum 'alā 'adūwwika wa 'adūwwihim ilāha al-ḥaqqi wa-j'alnā minhum.

* * *

اللَّهُمَّ اجْعَلْهُمْ آمِرِيْنَ بِالْمَعْرُوْفِ فَاعِلِيْنَ بِهِ نَاهِيْنَ عَنِ الْمُنْكَرِ مُجْتَنِبِيْنَ لَهُ مُحَافِظِيْنَ عَلَى حُدُوْدِكَ دَائِمِيْنَ عَلَى طَاعَتِكَ مُتَنَاصِفِيْنَ مُتَنَاصِحِيْنَ.

Allāhumma-j'alhum āmirīnā bi-l-ma'rūfi fā'ilīnā bihi, nāhīna 'an al-munkari mujtanibīna lahu, muḥāfiẓīna 'alā ḥudūdika, dā'imīna 'alā ṭā'atika mutanāṣifīna mutanāṣiḥīn.

* * *

اللَّهُمَّ صُنْهُمْ فِي أَقْوَالِهِمْ وَأَفْعَالِهِمْ وَبَارِكْ لَهُمْ فِي جَمِيْعِ أَحْوَالِهِمْ.

Allāhumma ṣunhum fī aqwālihim wa af'ālihim wa bārik lahum fī jamī' aḥwālihim.

* * *

الحَمْدُ للهِ رَبِّ العَالَمِيْنَ حَمْدًا يُوَافِي نِعَمَهُ وَيُكَافِئُ مَزِيْدَهُ، اللَّهُمَّ صَلِّ وَسَلِّمْ

عَلَى مُحَمَّدٍ وَعَلَى آلِ مُحَمَّدٍ كَمَا صَلَّيْتَ عَلَى إِبْرَاهِيْمَ وَعَلَى آلِ إِبْرَاهِيْمَ وَبَارِكْ عَلَى مُحَمَّدٍ وَعَلَى آلِ مُحَمَّدٍ كَمَا بَارَكْتَ عَلَى إِبْرَاهِيْمَ وَعَلَى آلِ إِبْرَاهِيْمَ فِي العَالَمِيْنَ إِنَّكَ حَمِيْدٌ مَجِيْدٌ.

Al-Ḥamdu lillāhi rabbi-l-ʿālamīn ḥamdan yuwāfī niʿamahu wa yukāfiʾu mazīdah. Allāhumma ṣalli wa sallim ʿalā Muḥammadin wa ʿalā āli Muḥammadin, kamā ṣallayta ʿalā Ibrāhīma wa ʿalā āli Ibrāhīma, wa bārik ʿalā Muḥammadin wa ʿalā āli Muḥammadin, kamā bārakta ʿalā Ibrāhīma wa ʿalā āli Ibrāhīma fi-l-ʿālamīna innaka ḥamīdun majīd.

APPENDIX TWO

VERSES OF PROSTRATION

﴿وَلِلَّهِ يَسْجُدُ مَن فِي ٱلسَّمَٰوَٰتِ وَٱلْأَرْضِ طَوْعًا وَكَرْهًا وَظِلَٰلُهُم
بِٱلْغُدُوِّ وَٱلْءَاصَالِ ۩ ﴿١٥﴾ ﴾

Quran, 13:15

﴿وَلِلَّهِ يَسْجُدُ مَا فِي ٱلسَّمَٰوَٰتِ وَمَا فِي ٱلْأَرْضِ مِن دَآبَّةٍ
وَٱلْمَلَٰٓئِكَةُ وَهُمْ لَا يَسْتَكْبِرُونَ ﴿٤٩﴾ يَخَافُونَ رَبَّهُم مِّن فَوْقِهِمْ
وَيَفْعَلُونَ مَا يُؤْمَرُونَ ۩ ﴿٥٠﴾ ﴾

Quran, 16:49-50

﴿قُلْ ءَامِنُوا۟ بِهِۦٓ أَوْ لَا تُؤْمِنُوٓا۟ ۚ إِنَّ ٱلَّذِينَ أُوتُوا۟ ٱلْعِلْمَ مِن قَبْلِهِۦٓ إِذَا يُتْلَىٰ
عَلَيْهِمْ يَخِرُّونَ لِلْأَذْقَانِ سُجَّدًا ﴿١٠٧﴾ وَيَقُولُونَ سُبْحَٰنَ رَبِّنَآ إِن كَانَ
وَعْدُ رَبِّنَا لَمَفْعُولًا ﴿١٠٨﴾ وَيَخِرُّونَ لِلْأَذْقَانِ يَبْكُونَ وَيَزِيدُهُمْ
خُشُوعًا ۩ ﴿١٠٩﴾ ﴾

Quran, 17:107-109

﴿ أُوْلَٰٓئِكَ ٱلَّذِينَ أَنْعَمَ ٱللَّهُ عَلَيْهِم مِّنَ ٱلنَّبِيِّـۧنَ مِن ذُرِّيَّةِ ءَادَمَ وَمِمَّنْ
حَمَلْنَا مَعَ نُوحٍ وَمِن ذُرِّيَّةِ إِبْرَٰهِيمَ وَإِسْرَٰٓءِيلَ وَمِمَّنْ هَدَيْنَا وَٱجْتَبَيْنَآ
إِذَا تُتْلَىٰ عَلَيْهِمْ ءَايَٰتُ ٱلرَّحْمَٰنِ خَرُّوا۟ سُجَّدًا وَبُكِيًّا ۩ ﴿٥٨﴾ ۞ ﴾

Quran, 19:58

﴿ أَلَمْ تَرَ أَنَّ ٱللَّهَ يَسْجُدُ لَهُۥ مَن فِى ٱلسَّمَٰوَٰتِ وَمَن فِى ٱلْأَرْضِ
وَٱلشَّمْسُ وَٱلْقَمَرُ وَٱلنُّجُومُ وَٱلْجِبَالُ وَٱلشَّجَرُ وَٱلدَّوَآبُّ
وَكَثِيرٌ مِّنَ ٱلنَّاسِ ۖ وَكَثِيرٌ حَقَّ عَلَيْهِ ٱلْعَذَابُ ۗ وَمَن يُهِنِ ٱللَّهُ
فَمَا لَهُۥ مِن مُّكْرِمٍ ۚ إِنَّ ٱللَّهَ يَفْعَلُ مَا يَشَآءُ ۩ ﴿١٨﴾ ﴾

Quran, 22:18

﴿ يَٰٓأَيُّهَا ٱلَّذِينَ ءَامَنُوا۟ ٱرْكَعُوا۟ وَٱسْجُدُوا۟ وَٱعْبُدُوا۟
رَبَّكُمْ وَٱفْعَلُوا۟ ٱلْخَيْرَ لَعَلَّكُمْ تُفْلِحُونَ ۩ ﴿٧٧﴾ ﴾

Quran, 22:77

﴿ وَإِذَا قِيلَ لَهُمُ ٱسْجُدُوا۟ لِلرَّحْمَٰنِ قَالُوا۟ وَمَا ٱلرَّحْمَٰنُ أَنَسْجُدُ لِمَا
تَأْمُرُنَا وَزَادَهُمْ نُفُورًا ۩ ﴿٦٠﴾ ﴾

Quran, 25:59-60

﴿ إِنَّمَا يُؤْمِنُ بِـَٔايَٰتِنَا ٱلَّذِينَ إِذَا ذُكِّرُوا۟ بِهَا خَرُّوا۟ سُجَّدًا
وَسَبَّحُوا۟ بِحَمْدِ رَبِّهِمْ وَهُمْ لَا يَسْتَكْبِرُونَ ۩ ﴿١٥﴾ ﴾

Quran, 32:15

﴿وَمِنْ ءَايَٰتِهِ ٱلَّيْلُ وَٱلنَّهَارُ وَٱلشَّمْسُ وَٱلْقَمَرُ ۚ لَا
تَسْجُدُوا۟ لِلشَّمْسِ وَلَا لِلْقَمَرِ وَٱسْجُدُوا۟ لِلَّهِ ٱلَّذِى خَلَقَهُنَّ
إِن كُنتُمْ إِيَّاهُ تَعْبُدُونَ ٣٧ فَإِنِ ٱسْتَكْبَرُوا۟ فَٱلَّذِينَ
عِندَ رَبِّكَ يُسَبِّحُونَ لَهُۥ بِٱلَّيْلِ وَٱلنَّهَارِ وَهُمْ لَا يَسْـَٔمُونَ ۩
٣٨﴾

Quran, 41:37-38

﴿فَٱسْجُدُوا۟ لِلَّهِ وَٱعْبُدُوا۟ ۩ ٦٢﴾

Quran, 53:62

﴿إِنَّ ٱلَّذِينَ عِندَ رَبِّكَ لَا يَسْتَكْبِرُونَ عَنْ عِبَادَتِهِۦ وَيُسَبِّحُونَهُۥ
وَلَهُۥ يَسْجُدُونَ ۩ ٢٠٦﴾

Quran, 7:206

﴿وَإِذَا قُرِئَ عَلَيْهِمُ ٱلْقُرْءَانُ لَا يَسْجُدُونَ ۩ ٢١﴾

Quran, 84:21

كَلَّا لَا تُطِعْهُ وَٱسْجُدْ وَٱقْتَرِب ۩ ١٩

Quran, 96:19

APPENDIX THREE

BRIEF BIOGRAPHIES OF PERSONS CITED IN THE TEXT

(Dates are according to the Islamic calendar, unless otherwise indicated.)

'Abbād ibn Ḥamza ibn 'Abdallāh ibn al-Zubayr. A Successor who has hadiths in Muslim's *Ṣaḥīḥ*, al-Nasā'ī's *Sunan*, and Bukhārī's *al-Adab al-Mufrad*.

'Abdallāh ibn 'Abbās ibn 'Abd al-Muṭṭalib, Abū al-'Abbās (d. 68). Son of the paternal uncle of the Prophet (God bless him and give him peace). One of his aunts was Maymūna bint Ḥārith, a wife of the Prophet (God bless him and give him peace). He was born three years before the Hijra. The Prophet (God bless him and give him peace) supplicated that God bless him with understanding of the religion, wisdom, and understanding of the Quran. He saw Jibrīl (peace be upon him) twice. He was 13 years old at the death of the Prophet (God bless him and give him peace). In spite of his young age, 'Umar ibn al-Khaṭṭāb (God be pleased with him) sought his counsel. He lost his eyesight at the end of his life. He died at 70 years of age.

'Abdallāh ibn 'Abd al-Raḥmān ibn al-Fał, Abū Muḥammad al-Dārimī (181–255). A great hadith master, exegete, and legist. He authored a book of Sunan which some of the Scholars put above Ibn Mājah's *Sunan* in reliability.

'Abdallāh ibn Abī al-Hudhayl, Abū al-Mughīra. A Successor and trustworthy narrator.

'Abdallāh ibn Abī Zayd ibn 'Abd al-Raḥmān, Abū Muḥammad (310–386). A Mālikī legist and exegete of the Quran.

'Abdallāh ibn Aḥmad al-Marwazī, Abū Bakr al-Qaffāl (d. 417). The chief Shāfi'ī scholar, master of hadith, and ascetic of his day.

'Abdallāh ibn 'Amr ibn al-'Āṣ, al-Sahmī, al-Qurashī. A Companion who possessed vast knowledge, memorized the Quran, and devoted himself to worship. He asked for and received permission from the Prophet (God bless him and give him peace) to record hadith.

'Abdallāh ibn Ḥabīb ibn Rabī'a, Abū 'Abd al-Raḥmān al-Sulamī (d. 74). A Successor and son of a Companion. He was born during the life of the Prophet (God bless him and give him peace). He was a trustworthy and accurate narrator, and the great Quran reciter of Kūfa. He said, "We learned the Quran from people who whenever they learned ten verses of the Quran, they would not move on to ten more until they knew what those [ten] contained. So we would learn Quran and act according to it. After us, a people will inherit the Quran: they drink it just as they drink water [and thus give it little respect], and it will not go beyond their throats [because they do not act according to it]."

'Abdallāh ibn Mas'ūd ibn Ghāfil, al-Hudhalī, Abū'Abdal-Raḥmān (d. 32). An early convert to Islam and an emigrant to both Abyssinia and Medina. He was one the Companions in whom the Prophet (God bless him and give him peace) would confide secrets. 'Umar assigned him to overlook courts and the Muslim common fund (*bayt al-māl*) in Kūfa. He died in Medina, in 32 AH, and was over sixty years old.

'Abdallāh ibn al-Mubārak ibn Wā, Abū 'Abd al-Raḥmān (118–181). Ḥadīth master, *mujtahid,* merchant, and traveler. He combined hadith, *fiqh,* Arabic, history, bravery, and generosity. He was the first to author a work devoted to jihād, and he died returning from battling Rome.

‘Abdallāh ibn Mughaffal ibn ‘Abd Ghanam (d. 60). A Companion whom ‘Umar (God be pleased with him) sent to teach in Baṣra.

‘Abdallāh ibn Muḥammad ibn ‘Ubayd, Abū Bakr ibn Abī Dunyā (208–281). An author of more than 164 works. He was born and died in Baghdad.

‘Abdallāh ibn Muslim ibn Qutayba, Abū Muḥammad (213–276). Born in Baghdad, he resided in Kūfa and was appointed as judge of al-Daynūr. He wrote many works on the subjects of Quran and hadith, as well as other disciplines.

‘Abdallāh ibn Qays ibn Salīm al-Ash‘arī, Abū Mūsā (d. 52). An early convert to Islam who emigrated to Abyssinia. During ‘Umar’s caliphate he was assigned to command the city of Baṣra.

‘Abdallāh ibn Sulaymān ibn al-Ash‘ath, Abū Bakr (230–316). Son of the great hadith master Imām Abū Dāwūd. He was a hadith master and a legist. He authored several works concerning the Quran and hadith, including: *Kitāb al-Maṣāḥif, al-Musnad, al-Sunan, al-Tafsīr, al-Qirā’āt,* and *al-Nāsikh wa al-Mansūkh*. He died during the month of Dhū’l-Ḥijja at 87 years of age.

‘Abdallāh ibn ‘Ubayd ibn ‘Abdallāh ibn Abī Mulayka (d. 117). A Successor who met thirty of the Companions.

‘Abdallāh ibn al-Zubayr (God be pleased with them both) (God be pleased with them both) assigned him to be a judge and to make the Call to Prayer. He was a legist and hadith master from the same generation as ‘Aṭā. His narrations are included in the six major hadith collections.

‘Abdallāh ibn ‘Umar ibn al-Khaṭṭāb, Abū ‘Abd al-Raḥmān (d. 73). He was born one year before the revelation began. He and his father entered Islam in Mecca while he was young. He was known for his knowledge, piety, and carefulness in both his personal actions and when giving legal judgments. He died in 73 AH at the age of 84.

'Abdallāh ibn 'Uthmān, Abū Bakr ibn Abī Quḥāfa al-Ṣiddīq (d. 13). He was a life-long Companion of the Prophet (God bless him and give him peace) and the first adult male to enter Islam. Many entered Islam through him, including: 'Uthmān ibn 'Affān, Ṭalḥa ibn 'Ubaydullāh, al-Zubayr ibn al-'Awwām, Sa'd ibn Abī Waqqāṣ, and 'Abd al-Raḥmān ibn 'Awf. He died in Medina on Tuesday night, eight days before the end of Jumāda al-Ākhira, in the year 13 AH, between the Sunset and Night Prayers. He was 63 years old. His wife Asmā' ibn 'Umays washed him, and 'Umar prayed the Funeral Prayer over him. He was buried next to the Prophet (God bless him and give him peace) in his daughter 'Ā'isha's house.

'Abdallāh ibn Wahb ibn Muslim, Abū Muḥammad (125–197). A colleague of Imām Aḥmad who combined fiqh, hadith, and worship. When he was offered to become a judge, he hid himself and did not leave his house.

'Abdallāh ibn Yazīd ibn Hurmūz (d. 148). A legist from Medina.

'Abdallāh ibn Yūsuf ibn Muḥammad, Abū Muḥammad al-Juwaynī (d. 438). Imām al-Ḥaramayn's father. He was an accomplished Shāfi'ī scholar knowledgeable in exegesis, *fiqh,* and lexicography.

'Abdallāh ibn Zayd ibn 'Amr, Abū Qilāba (d. 104). He was offered a judgeship but fled from it. He was a trust worthy narrator who narrated many hadiths.

'Abd al-Ḥamīd ibn 'Abd al-Raḥmān al-Ḥammānī, Abū Yaḥyā (d. 202). A trustworthy narrator who has narrations included in Bukhārī, Muslim, and other primary sources.

'Abd al-Karīm ibn Hawāzin ibn 'Abd al-Mālik, Abū al-Qāsim al-Qushayrī (376–465). The Shaykh of Khurāsān during his age. He was a Shāfi'ī legist, hadith scholar, commentator of the Quran, theologian, and a great Sufi. His most famous work is *al-Risālatal-Qushayriyya,* a central work concerning *taṣawwuf.*

ʿAbd al-Karīm ibn Muḥammad ibn ʿAbd al-Karīm, Abū al-Qāsim al-Rāfiʿī (557–623). One of the greatest Shāfiʿī legists ever.He died in Qizwin.

ʿAbd al-Malik ibn ʿAbdallāh ibn Yūsuf, Imām al-Ḥaramayn al-Juwaynī (419–478). The most knowledgeable of all late scholars of the Shāfiʿī *madhhab,* "the Glory of Islam, absolute Imām of all Imāms, main authority in the Law, whose leadership is agreed upon East and West, whose immense merit is the consensus of Arabs and non-Arabs, upon the like of whom none set eyes before or after" (Ibn ʿAsākir), "whose work forms the connecting link between the respective methods of the Salaf and Khalaf" (al-Kawtharī).

ʿAbd al-Malik ibn Marwān ibn al-Ḥakam (d. 86). The well-known Umayyad caliph and legist. He resided in Greater Syria. He saw ʿUthmān ibn ʿAffān and narrated hadith from Abū Hurayra (God be pleased with them both). He remained the caliph for 14 years after killing ʿAbdallāh ibn al-Zubayr. He was 58 when he died.

ʿAbd al-Raḥmān ibn ʿAmr, al-Awzāʿī (88–157). He was born in Baʿlbak, Lebanon, and became the Imām of Greater Syria of his time. When offered a judgeship, he refused. He once said, "If God wishes evil for a people, He opens up to them the paths to argument and bars them from deeds." He died in Beirut where four communities attended his funeral: the Muslims carried his bier, followed by the Jews, the Christians, and the Copts. Al-Shāfiʿī said: "I never saw a man whose *fiqh* resembled his hadith [in rigor] more than al-Awzāʿī."

ʿAbd al-Raḥmān ibn Maʾmūn ibn ʿAlī al-Ābiwardī, al-Mutawallī (d. 478). A Shāfiʿī legist and jurisprudent who was assigned head of the Niẓāmiyya School in Baghdad. He authored *Tatimmat al-Ibāna fī Fiqh al-Shāfiʿī,* the completion of the unfinished *Ibāna* of Imām Abū al-Qāsim ʿAbd al-Raḥmān ibn al-Furānī (d. 461)

'Abd al-Raḥmān ibn Ṣakhr, Abū Hurayra (d. 57). He received his nickname "Abū Hurayra" because of a cat he carried in his sleeve. He entered Islam late during the year of Khaybar. After entering Islam he spent as much time as possible with the Prophet (God bless him and give him peace) and became one of the greatest hadith narrators of the Companions. More than eight hundred Companions and Successors narrated from him, including: Ibn 'Abbās, Ibn 'Umar, Jābir, Anas, and Wathila ibn al-Asqa' (God be well pleased with them all). Among the supplications of the Prophet (God bless him and give him peace) on his behalf: "O God! Make Your little servant Abū Hurayra and his mother beloved to Your believing servants."

'Abd al-Raḥmān ibn Shibl ibn 'Amr. A Companion who died during the Caliphate of Mu'āwiya.

'Abd al-Raḥmān ibn Yazīd, Abū Bakr al-Nakha'ī (d. after 80). The brother of al-Aswad ibn Yazīd. Some considered him a trustworthy narrator.

'Abd al-Wāḥid ibn al-Ḥusayn ibn Muḥammad, Abū al-Qāsim al-Ṣaymarī (d. 387 or 405). A Shāfi'ī legist and resident of Baṣra.

'Abd al-Wāḥid ibn Ismā'īl ibn Aḥmad ibn Muḥammad al-Ruwyānī (415–501). A Shāfi'ī legist. A top scholar in *fiqh* and jurisprudence. He once said that if all of the works of Imām al-Shāfi'ī were burned he could dictate them from memory.

'Abdata ibn Abī Lubāba, Abū al-Qāsim (d. 127). A resident of Damascus.

Abū 'Abd al-Raḥmān al-Sulamī = Abdallāh ibn Ḥabīb ibn Rabī'a

Abū 'Abd al-Raḥmān al-Sulamī = Muḥammad ibn al-Ḥusayn

Abū al-Aḥwaṣ = 'Awf ibn Mālik

Abū al-'Āliya = Rafī' ibn Mahrān

Abū 'Amr [al-Baṣrī] = Zabbān ibn 'Ammār

Abū ʿAmr al-Dānī = ʿUthmān ibn Saʿīd

Abū Bakr ibn Abī Dāwūd = ʿAbdallāh ibn Sulaymān

Abū Bakr al-Kindī = Muḥammad ibn Yūsuf

Abū Bakr al-Ṣiddīq = ʿAbdallāh ibn ʿUthmān

Abū Dardā' (d. 32). A companion known by this agnomen. (Dardā' was his daughter.) He was the last of his household to enter Islam. He was knowledgeable and wise, and one of the Companions to give legal opinions. He resided in Greater Syria and died in Damascus.

Abū Dāwūd = Sulaymān ibn al-Ashʿath

Abū Dharr = Jundub ibn Junāda

Abū Ḥāmid al-Ghazālī = Muḥammad ibn Muḥammad

Abū Ḥanīfa = Al-Nuʿmān ibn Thābit

Abū Hārūn al-ʿAbdī = ʿAmmāra ibn Juwayn,

Abū Ḥātim al-Sajistānī = Sahl ibn Muḥammad

Abū Hurayra = ʿAbd al-Raḥmān ibn Ṣakhr

Abū Isḥāq al-Marwazī = Ibrāhīm ibn Aḥmad

Abū Jaʿfar al-Naḥḥās = Aḥmad ibn Muḥammad

Abū al-Jawzā' = Aws ibn ʿAbdallāh

Abū Juḥayfa = Wahb ibn ʿAbdallāh

Abū Lubāba = Rifāʿa ibn ʿAbd al-Mundhir

Abū Maysara = ʿAmr ibn Sharaḥbīl

Abū Muḥammad al-Juwaynī = ʿAbdallāh ibn Yūsuf

Abū Mūsā al-Ashʿarī = ʿAbdallāh ibn Qays

Abū al-Qāsim al-Ṣaymarī = ʿAbd al-Wāḥid ibn al-Ḥusayn

Abū Qilāba = ʿAbdallāh ibn Zayd ibn ʿAmr

Abū al-Rabī‘ = Sulaymān ibn Dāwūd ibn Ḥammād

Abū Rajā’ = ‘Imrān ibn Mulḥān

Abū Sa‘īd al-Khudrī = Sa‘d ibn Mālik

Abū Salama = Sulaym ibn ‘Itr

Abū Ṣāliḥ = Dhakwān ibn ‘Abdallāh

Abū Sulaymān al-Khaṭṭābī = Ḥamd ibn Muḥammad

Abū Ṭalḥa = Zayd ibn Sahl

Abū Thawr = Ibrāhīm ibn Khālid

Abū Umāma al-Bāhilī = Ṣudī ibn ‘Ujlān

Abū ‘Umar ibn ‘Abd al-Barr = Yūsuf ibn ‘Abdallāh

Abū Usayd = Mālik ibn Rabī‘a

Abū ‘Uthmān ibn al-Ḥāddād = Sa‘īd ibn Muḥammad

Abū ‘Uthmān al-Maghribī = Sa‘īd ibn Salām

Abū Yūsuf = Ya‘qūb ibn Ibrāhīm

Aḥmad = Aḥmad ibn Muḥammad

Aḥmad al-Dawraqī = Aḥmad ibn Ibrāhīm

Aḥmad ibn ‘Abdallāh ibn Maymūn, Abū al-Ḥasan (d. 246) His sayings include, "Whoever does anything without following a sunna: his actions are in vain [*bāṭil*]," and "Whoever looks at this world with desire and love, God removes light and certainty from his heart."

Aḥmad ibn ‘Alī ibn Thābit, Abū Bakr al-Baghdādī (392–463). Historian and hadith master. He was the most important early codifier of the sciences of hadith. When his death drew near he gave away all of his property and declared his works an endowment for all Muslims. His more than 56 works include: *Tarīkh Baghdād, al-Nukhala’, al-Kifāya fī ‘Ilm al-Riwāya,*

Taqyīd al-ʿIlm, and *Sharaf Aṣḥāb al-Ḥadīth.* He died in Baghdad in 463 AH.

Aḥmad ibn ʿAmr ibn ʿAbd al-Khāliq, al-Baṣrī, Abū Bakr al-Bazzār (210–292). A hadith master who transmitted hadith in Isfahan, Baghdad, Egypt, Mecca, and Ramla. He compiled a *musnad* of hadith.

Aḥmad ibn Ḥanbal = Aḥmad ibn Muḥammad

Aḥmad ibn al-Ḥawārī = Aḥmad ibn ʿAbdallāh ibn Maymūn

Aḥmad ibn Ibrāhīm ibn Kathīr al-Dawraqī (d. 242). A trustworthy hadith master.

Aḥmad ibn Manṣūr ibn Sayyār ibn Maʿārak, Abū Bakr al-Rammādī (182–265). A hadith master and trustworthy narrator.

Aḥmad ibn Muḥammad ibn Ḥanbal, Abū ʿAbdallāh al-Shaybānī (164–241). Founder of the Ḥanbalī school of law, the epitome of hadith masters, and champion of the sunna. Imām al-Shāfiʿī said, "I have left no one in Baghdad with more understanding and knowledge, and more scrupulous and ascetic than Aḥmad ibn Ḥanbal."

Aḥmad ibn Muḥammad ibn Ibrāhīm, Abū Isḥāq al-Thaʿlabī (d. 427). The great Quranic exegete and historiographer.

Aḥmad ibn Muḥammad ibn Ismāʿīl, Abū Jaʿfar al-Naḥḥās (d. 338). An exegete and litterateur.

Aḥmad ibn Mūsā ibn al-ʿAbbās ibn Mujāhid, Abū Bakr (245–324). One of the great scholars of canonical recitation.

Aḥmad ibn Shuʿayb ibn ʿAlī, al-Nasāʾī, Abū ʿAbd al-Raḥmān (215–303). The great Shāfiʿī and Mālikī hadith master. He authored many works, and his Sunan is included as one of the six major compilations of hadith. It has the highest criteria for authenticity among them after the two *Ṣaḥīḥ*s.

Aḥmad ibn ʿUmar ibn Surayj, Abū al-ʿAbbās (239–306). The hadith master and Shāfiʿī legist, the "peerless admonisher" (*wāʿiẓ*) of his time and a fierce debater known as the "Swooping Falcon" (*al-Bāz al-Ashhab*). Ibn al-Subkī also calls him "the Fierce Lion Against the Dissenters of the Madhhab of al-Shāfi'ī." He is said to have authored 400 works. The nickname "the Little Shāfi'ī"was given to him by Abū Ḥafṣ al-Muṭawwi'ī. Ibn Surayj is listed by al-Dhahabī in the *Siyar* among "Those who are imitated in Islam" in the generation of *Imām al-A'imma* (the Imām of all Imāms) Ibn Khuzayma and Imām al-Ṭabarī.

'Ā'isha bint Abī Bakr al-Ṣiddīq (d. 57). The third and youngest wife of the Prophet (God bless him and give him peace). She was "absolutely the most knowledgeable woman in the Umma or, rather, among humankind" (al-Dhahabī); "comprehensive in her knowledge, unique in her understanding, a *mujtahida*, indeed the epitome of learning and teaching" (al-Suyūṭī). She was the daughter of the first successor of the Prophet (God bless him and give him peace) and dearest of men to him—Abū Bakr al-Ṣiddīq— and Umm Rūmān the daughter of 'Āmir ibn Uwaymir ibn 'Abd Shams ibn Attāb ibn Udhayna al-Kinaniyya. She was known for her knowledge in religious matters, medicine, eloquence, and Arab lore. She was 19 years old at the death of the Prophet (God bless him and give him peace).

'Alī al-Azdī = 'Alī ibn 'Abdallāh

'Alī ibn 'Abdallāh al-Azdī. From the same generation as al-Ḥasan al-Baṣrī.

'Alī ibn Abī al-Ṭālib, Abū al-Ḥasan (d. 40). Fourth of the Rightly Guided Caliphs. He was the first male youth to embrace Islam. He was the nephew of the Prophet (God bless him and give him peace) and his son in law. He participated with the Prophet (God bless him and give him peace) in all battles except for Tabūk, when the Prophet (God bless him and give him peace) delegated him to oversee his own family. He received the caliphate in 35 AH after 'Uthmān ibn 'Affān. He was stabbed during Ramaān in the city of Kūfa. He died three days later, at the age of 63. He was Caliph for four years and nine months.

'Alī ibn Aḥmad ibn Ḥamd, Abū Ḥasan al-Wāḥidī (d. 468). The great exegete of the Quran and scholar of fine literature. He authored many works concerning the Quran, including three separate exegeses entitled *al-Basīṭ, al-Wasīṭ,* and *al-Wajīz*. He also wrote *Asbāb al-Nuzūl,* concerning the circumstances of individual instances of revelation. He also wrote a commentary on the beautiful names of God Most High and several books concerning literature.

'Alī ibn Ḥamza ibn 'Abdallāh, Abū al-Ḥasan al-Kisā'ī (d. 189). One of the seven great Imāms of canonical recitations, and a great Imām in Arabic lexicography and grammar. He was a teacher of Hārūn al-Rashīd and his son.

'Alī ibn Hibatullāh, Abū al-Qāsim ibn 'Asākir (499–571). The great Shāfi'ī hadith master of Greater Syria. He was born and died in Damascus. He authored many works, including *Tarīkh Damashq al-Kabīr,* a history of Damascus.

'Alī ibn Muḥammad ibn Ḥabīb, Abū al-Ḥasan al-Mawardī (364–450). The great Shāfi'ī Imām. He was put in charge of the courts of Baghdad. During the 'Abbasid caliphate of al-Qā'im bi-amri-llāh he was made the head judge. The term "Mawardī" is a reference to selling rose water. His many works include *al-Ḥāwī* and *al-Aḥkām al-Sulṭāniyya*. He died in Baghdad.

'Alī ibn Sa'd ibn 'Abd al-Raḥmān, Abū al-Ḥasan (d. 493). A master legist and a master of jurisprudence. He died in Baghdad.

'Alqama ibn Qays ibn 'Abdallāh, Abū Shibl al-Nakha'ī (d. 61). A Successor who participated in the Battle of Ṣiffīn and the campaigns in Khurāsān. He died in Kūfa.

al-A'mash = Sulaymān ibn Mihrān

'Āmir ibn Sharāḥīl, Abū 'Amr al-Sha'bī (19–103). A Successor who was the epitome of memorization. He was born and died in Kūfa.

'Ammāra ibn Juwayn, Abū Hārūn al-'Abdī (d. 134). A narrator whose hadiths are rejected. He was accused of being a liar and having extreme partisanship for 'Alī (God be pleased with him).

'Amr ibn Murra ibn 'Abdallāh, Abū 'Abdallāh (d. 118). A trustworthy narrator of hadith.

'Amr ibn Sharaḥbīl, Abū Maysara (d. 63). Ibn Ḥibbān mentioned that his knees were as callused as a camel's from the frequency and length of his prayer. He died from the plague.

Anas ibn Mālik ibn al-Nuḍr (d. 91). For ten years he acted as a servant for the Prophet (God bless him and give him peace). He moved to Baṣra during the caliphate of 'Umar (God be well pleased with them) in order to teach. He was the last of the Companions to die in Baṣra at the age of 103 years old. He left 100 offspring.

Asmā' bint Abī Bakr al-Ṣiddīq, Umm 'Abdallāh (d. 73). She was older than her sister 'Ā'isha by ten years. One of the earliest converts to Islam. She married al-Zubayr ibn 'Awwām in Mecca and bore his son 'Abdallāh. She died in Mecca at the age of 100, ten days after her son's death.

'Aṭā ibn Abī Rabāḥ Aslam (27–115). He was a Makkan Successor and one of the illustrious legists. He died in Mecca at the age of 88.

'Awf ibn Mālik ibn Naḍla, Abū al-Aḥwaṣ. The Khawārij killed him during the days of al-Ḥajjāj ibn Yūsuf. Some of his narrations are found in Bukhārī's *al-Adab al-Mufrad,* Muslim's *Ṣaḥīḥ,* and the four *Musnad*s.

Aws ibn 'Abdallāh, Abū al-Jawzā' (d. 83). A trustworthy narrator who has hadiths in the six major collections of hadith.

al-Awzā'ī = 'Abd al-Raḥmān ibn 'Amr

Ayyūb al-Sakhtiyānī = Ayyūb ibn Abī Tamīma

Ayyūb ibn Abī Tamīma Kaysān, Abū Bakr al-Sakhtiyānī (131–166). A Successor. He was his age's chief legist, a hadith master, and ascetic.

al-Baghawī = Al-Ḥusayn ibn Mas'ūd

Bahz ibn Ḥakīm ibn Mu'āwiya ibn Ḥayda (d. after 140) al-Barā' ibn 'Āzib ibn al-Ḥārith. He participated with 'Alī ibn Abī Ṭālib (God be pleased with him) in the battles of the Camel, Ṣiffīn, and Nahrawān. He died in Kūfa during the time of Mus'ab ibn al-Zubayr.

Bashīr ibn Abī Mas'ūd 'Uqba ibn 'Amr. It is disputed whether he was a Companion or a Successor.

al-Bazzār = Aḥmad ibn 'Amr

al-Bukhārī = Muḥammad ibn Ismā'īl

Burayda ibn al-Ḥusayb ibn 'Abdallāh, Abū Sahl (d. circa 62). A Companion. He resided in Medina and then moved to Baṣra, and then left on the campaigns to Khurāsān. He died in Merv during the caliphate of Yazīd ibn Mu'āwiya. His narrations are found in the six major collections.

al-TMaḥḥāk ibn 'Abd al-Raḥmān ibn 'Azrab, al-Ash'arī, al-Ṭabarānī, Abū 'Abd al-Raḥmān (d. 105). He was 'Umar ibn 'Abd al-'Azīz's deputy in Damascus.

al-Dārimī = 'Abdallāh ibn 'Abd al-Raḥmān

Dāwūd = Dāwūd ibn 'Alī ibn Khalaf

Dāwūd ibn 'Alī ibn Khalaf, Abū Sulaymān al-Ṭāhirī ["the Literalist"] (201–270). He was a *mujtahid* Imām and founder of the Ẓāhirī school of jurisprudence. He was known for sticking to the literal meaning of the Quran and Sunna, and avoiding interpretation and analogical reasoning.

al-Dāwūdī = Muḥammad ibn Dāwūd

Dhakwān ibn 'Abdallāh, Abū Ṣāliḥ (d. 101). A freed-slave of the Mother of the Faithful Juwayriya (God be well pleased with her). He was born during the caliphate of 'Umar (God be pleased with him).

Dhū'l-Nūn = Thawbān ibn Ibrāhīm

Faāla ibn 'Ubayd ibn Nāfidh (d. 53). A Companion. He moved to Damascus. He died there during the caliphate of Mu'āwiya.

Fuḍayl ibn 'Amr, Abū al-Naḍar (d. 110). A trustworthy narrator of hadith.

al-Fuḍayl ibn 'Iyāḍ ibn Mas'ūd, al-Khurāsānī, Abū 'Alī (105–187). His repentance for being a highway robber was to travel seeking knowledge and spend the rest of his life near the Ka'ba. Many Imāms took knowledge and hadith from him, including Imām al-Shāfi'ī.

al-Ghazālī = Muḥammad ibn Muḥammad

Ḥabīb ibn Abī Thābit = Ḥabīb ibn Qays ibn Dinār

Ḥabīb ibn Qays ibn Dinār, Abū Yaḥyā (d. 119). A legist and narrator of some 200 hadiths. Some of them are included in the six major collections of hadith.

Ḥafṣā bint 'Umar ibn al-Khaṭṭāb (d. 45). A wife of the Prophet (God bless him and give him peace). She died during the month of Sha'bān at 60 years of age.

al-Ḥākim = Muḥammad ibn 'Abdallāh

al-Ḥakm ibn 'Utayba, Abū Muḥammad (or Abū 'Abdallāh) (50–115)

Ḥamd ibn Muḥammad ibn Ibrāhīm, Abū Sulaymān al-Khaṭṭābī (319–388). A Shāfi'ī legist, hadith master, and master of the Arabic language. He was born and died in Bust, located in modern day Afghanistan. His works include: *Ma'ālim al-Sunan, Bayān I'jāz al-Qur'ān, Iṣlāḥ Ghalaṭ al-Muḥaddithīn,* and his masterpiece *Gharīb al-Ḥadīth*. Among his sayings: "*īmān* is speech, which neither increases nor decreases; it is deeds, which increase and decrease; and it is conviction, which increases and does not decrease; if conviction decreases, *īmān* disappears."

Ḥamza ibn Ḥabīb ibn 'Ammāra (80–156). One of the seven great Imāms of canonical recitations. Sufyān al-Thawrī said, "Ḥamza did not recite a single letter from the Quran without having a transmitted account [to support it]."

al-Ḥārith ibn Asad, Abū 'Abdallāh al-Muḥāsibī (d. 243). The Shāfi'ī legist, expert in kalām, and Ṣūfī master whose words moved Imām Aḥmad to tears although the latter's opposition to him resulted in the people's desertion of al-Muḥāsibī who died in complete isolation. His name means "he who calculates his actions" or "he who excels in the examination of his conscience." One of the earliest authors of *ṣūfī* treatises and the teacher of al-Junayd, he also wrote rebuttals against the Mu'tazila. One of his better known works is *Risālat al-Mustarshidīn*. Among his sayings: "Intellect is the light of instinct together with trials, and it increases and becomes stronger through knowledge and good character."

al-Ḥārith al-Muḥāsibī = Al-Ḥārith ibn Asad al-Ḥasan ibn al-Ḥusayn

Ibn Abī Hurayra, Abū 'Alī (d. 345). The famous Shāfi'ī legist and Imām of the Iraqi Shāfi'īs.

al-Ḥasan al-Baṣrī = Al-Ḥasan ibn Yasār

al-Ḥasan ibn Yasār, Abū Sa'īd al-Baṣrī (21–110). A Successor born in Medina who became the Imām of Baṣra. He escaped unscathed from his many encounters with al-Ḥajjāj ibn Yūsuf al-Thaqafī. He died in Baṣra.

Ḥassān ibn 'Aṭiyya, Abū Bakr (d. circa 130 AH).

Hind bint Abī Umayya Suhayl ibn al-Mughīra, Umm Salama (d. 59). A wife of the Prophet (God bless him and give him peace). She died at the age of 84.

Hishām ibn Ḥassān, Abū ʿAbdallāh (d. circa 147). He was one of the most trustworthy narrators from Ibn Sīrīn. His narrations are included in the six major collections.

Hishām ibn Ismāʿīl ibn Hishām (d. 87). At one time the governor of Medina. His daughter married ʿAbd al-Malik ibn Marwān.

Ḥudhayfa ibn Qatāda al-Marʿashī. A companion of Sufyān al-Thawrī who related knowledge from him. He once said that the greatest of all calamities is the hardening of hearts.

Ḥudhayfa ibn al-Yamān (d. 35 or 36). Both he and his father (Ḥusayl ibn Jābir) emigrated to the Prophet (God bless him and give him peace) sometime near the Battle of Badr. He was the protector of the secrets of the Prophet (God bless him and give him peace). He died in Madā'in, in modern day Iran, some forty days after ʿUthmān (God be pleased with him) was assassinated.

Ḥujjat al-Islām = Muḥammad ibn Muḥammad Abū Ḥāmid al-Ghazālī

Ḥukaym ibn Saʿd, Abū Yaḥyā. A Successor from the same generation as al-Ḥasan al-Baṣrī. He was a trustworthy narrator whose narrations are included in Bukhārī's *al-Adab al-Mufrad* and Nasā'ī's *al-Sunan*.

Ḥumayd al-Aʿraj = Ḥumayd ibn Qays

Ḥumayd ibn Qays, Abū Ṣafwān al-Aʿraj (d. 130). A reciter.

Ḥusayn ibn Aḥmad ibn ʿAbd al-Ghaffār, Abū ʿAlī al-Fārisī ibn al-Kātib (288–377). The well-known grammarian. His writings include: *Al-Ḥujjat fī ʿIlal al-Qira'āt al-Sabʿa* and *al-īāḥ* in Arabic linguistics. He died in Baghdad.

al-Ḥusayn ibn al-Fałibn ʿUmayr, al-Bajalī (178–282). An exegete of the Quran. When he moved to Naysābūr the governor of the city, ʿAbdallāh ibn Ṭāhir, bought a house for him so he could teach. He did so for 65 years.

al-Ḥusayn ibn Mas'ūd, Abū Muḥammad, Abū Muḥammad al-Baghawī (d. 516). A Shāfi'ī legist, hadith master,and exegete. He is the author of *al-Tahdhīb fī Fiqh al-Imām al-Shāfi'ī* in four large tomes, an emendation of al-Qāḍī Ḥusayn's *al-Ta'līqa*, from which al-Nawawī frequently quotes in his *Rawḍ.*

Ḥusayn ibn Muḥammad ibn Aḥmad, al-Qāḍī (d. 462). A judge and a great Shāfi'ī scholar. The title "al-Qāḍī" refers to him in the Shāfi'ī school.

Ibn 'Asākir = 'Alī Ibn Hibatullāh

Ibn 'Abd al-Barr = Yūsuf Ibn 'Abdallāh

Ibn Abī Dāwūd = 'Abdallāh Ibn Sulaymān

Ibn Abī Dunyā = 'Abdallāh Ibn Muḥammad Ibn 'Ubayd

Ibn Abī Hurayra = Al-Ḥasan Ibn al-Ḥusayn

Ibn Abī Mulayk = 'Abdallāh Ibn 'Ubayd

Ibn Abī Zayd = 'Abdallāh Ibn Abī Zayd

Ibn al-Kātib = Ḥusayn Ibn Aḥmad

Ibn Mājah = Muḥammad Ibn Yazīd

Ibn al-Mubārak = 'Abdallāh Ibn al-Mubārak

Ibn Mujāhid = Aḥmad Ibn Mūsā Ibn al-'Abbās

Ibn al-Mundhir = Muḥammad Ibn Ibrāhīm

Ibn Muqla = Muḥammad Ibn 'Alī Ibn al-Ḥusayn

Ibn Qutayba = 'Abdallāh ibn Muslim

Ibn Rāhūyah = Isḥāq ibn Ibrāhīm

Ibn al-Ṣalāḥ = 'Uthmān ibn 'Abd al-Raḥmān

Ibn Shanbūdh = Muḥammad ibn Aḥmad ibn Ayyūb

Ibn Surayj = Aḥmad ibn 'Umar

Ibn Wahb = 'Abdallāh ibn Wahb

Ibrāhīm = Ibrāhīm ibn Yazīd

Ibrāhīm ibn Aḥmad ibn Ismā'īl, Abū Isḥāq al-Khawwāṣ (d. 291). A Sufi and one of the companions of Junayd. "Al- Khawwāṣ" refers to selling *khawṣ*, the leaves of certain trees.

Ibrāhīm ibn Aḥmad, Abū Isḥāq al-Marwazī (d. 340). A Shāfi'ī legist who headed the Shāfi'īs in Iraq after Ibn Surayj. He died in Egypt.

Ibrāhīm ibn Khālid ibn Abī al-Yamān, Abū Thawr (170–240). One of the greatest Imāms in *fiqh*. He was known for his knowledge, scrupulousness, and generosity.

Ibrāhīm ibn Sa'd ibn Ibrāhīm, Abū Isḥāq al-Zuhrī (d. 183). The great hadith narrator and chief judge of Baghdad.

Ibrāhīm ibn Yazīd ibn Qays, Abū 'Imrān al-Nakha'ī (d. 96). A Successor from Kūfa. He encountered some of the Companions and saw 'Ā'isha (God be pleased with them all), but he did not transmit hadith from any of them. He died while hiding from al-Ḥajjāj.

Ibrāhīm al-Khawwāṣ = Ibrāhīm ibn Aḥmad

Ibrāhīm al-Nakha'ī = Ibrāhīm ibn Yazīd

'Ikrima ibn Abī Jahl 'Amr ibn Hishām ibn al-Mughīra (d. 13). He entered Islam upon the conquest of Mecca in 8 AH and made good his Islam. He fought in the Battle of Yarmūk during the caliphate of 'Umar (God be pleased with him). He was 62 years old.

'Ikrima, Abū 'Abdallāh (27–107). A freed slave of Ibn 'Abbās (God have mercy upon him). He was one of the great legists of Mecca and an extensive traveler.

Imām al-Ḥaramayn = 'Abd al-Malik ibn 'Abdallāh ibn Yūsuf

'Imrān ibn Ḥuṣayn, Abū Najīd (d. 52). One of the more knowledgeable Companions (God be well pleased with them). He died in Kūfa.

'Imrān ibn Mulḥān, Abū Rajā' (d. 105). He embraced Islam after the conquest of Mecca, but never encountered the Prophet (God bless him and give him peace). He was over 120 years old when he died.

Isḥāq ibn Ibrāhīm ibn Mukhallad, Abū Ya'qūb Ibn Rāhūyah (161–238). A great hadith master and the scholar of Khurasān in his age. He traveled in search of hadith, and studied under Imāms Aḥmad ibn Ḥanbal, Bukhārī, Muslim, Tirmidhī, Nasā'ī, and others. He taught Ibn Qutayba. Abū Qudāma considered him greater than Imām Aḥmad in memorization of hadith, a remarkable assessment considering Aḥmad's knowledge of 700,000 to a million narrations according to his son 'Abdallāh's and Abū Zur'a al-Rāzī's estimations. Aḥmad himself named him "Commander of the Believers in Hadith," the highest grade in hadith Mastership, owned by no more than thirty Masters in Islamic history. He did not reach the same stature in *fiqh*.

Ismā'īl ibn Aḥmad ibn 'Abdallāh, Abū 'Abd al-Raḥmān (d. 430 AH) A Shāfi'ī scholarandQuranicexegete.

'Iyā ibn Mūsā ibn 'Iya Abū al-Fałal-Qāḍī (476–544). The great Andalusian scholar of hadith and its associated sciences, and a scholar of Arabic. His well-known works include *al-Shifā* and a commentary on *Ṣaḥīḥ Muslim* which serves as a base for Imām al-Nawawī's commentary.

Jābir ibn 'Abdallāh ibn 'Amr (d. 74). One of the most famous Companions and a transmitter of many hadith. He was one of the last Companions to die in Medina. He lived 94 years.

Ja'far ibn Muḥammad al-Bāqir ibn 'Alī Zayn al-'Ābidīn ibn al-Ḥusayn ibn 'Alī ibn Abī Ṭālib, Abū 'Abdallāh al-Ṣādiq (80–148). A descendent of the Prophet (God bless him and give him peace).

A Successor and one of the greatest Imāms of AHl al-Sunna. He was born and died in Medina. His mother was Umm Farwa bint al-Qāsim ibn Muḥammad ibn Abī Bakr the daughter of Asmā' bint 'Abd al-Raḥmān ibn Abī Bakr, hence he used to say: "Abū Bakr al-Ṣiddīq is twice my father." In another narration he says: "What man curses his own grandfather? May the intercession of Muḥammad (God bless him and give him peace) not include me if I do not consider Abū Bakr and 'Umar my leaders! I repudiate whoever repudiates them." Al-Dhahabī stated that the latter statement is *mutawātir* from Ja'far.

Ja'far al-Sādiq = Ja'far ibn Muḥammad al-Bāqir

al-Jū'ī = Al-Qāsim ibn 'Uthmān

al-Junayd ibn Muḥammad ibn al-Junayd, Abū al-Qāsim (d. 297). Some scholars consider him to be the founder of *taṣawwuf* because of his strict adherence to the Quran and *sunna*, and because he is free from blameworthy beliefs, extremism, and everything the Sharī'a demands be avoided. He was born and died in Baghdad. He made the Pilgrimage on foot thirty times. He defined *taṣawwuf* as "the upholding of every high manner and the repudiation of every low one."

Jundub ibn Junāda, Abū Dharr (d. 32). He was the first to greet the Prophet (God bless him and give him peace) with Islam's greeting: *Al-Salāmu 'alaykum* ("Peace be upon you"). He converted to Islam at an early date, and then returned to his tribe.

al-Juwaynī = 'Abd al-Malik ibn 'Abdallāh

Ka'b ibn Mālik ibn 'Amr (d. 50). He was a poet who used his immense skill for the Prophet (God bless him and give him peace). He was one of the three to stay back from the Battle of Tabūk. His repentance and its acceptance is recorded in the Quran. He died at the age of 77.

al-Khaṭīb Abū Bakr al-Baghdadī = Aḥmad ibn 'Alī ibn Thābit

al-Khaṭṭābī = Ḥamd ibn Muḥammad

Khaythama ibn Sulaymān ibn Ḥaydara, Abū al-Ḥasan (250–343). The great Syrian hadith master of his time. He died in Tarāblus, Syria.

al-Kisā'ī = 'Alī ibn Ḥamza

al-Layth ibn Sa'd ibn 'Abd al-Raḥmān, Abū al-Ḥārith (94–175). The chief scholar of Egypt in his age. Imām al-Shāfi'ī considered him superior to even Imām Mālik.

Ma'qil ibn Yasār ibn 'Abdallāh (d. after 60). A Companion who has narrations in the six major collections of hadith.

Makḥūl ibn 'Abdallāh (d. 112). The top legist of Damascus during his time. Al-Zuhrī praised him, saying that "there are [only] four scholars: Sa'īd ibn al-Musayyib in Medina, al-Sha'bī in Kūfa, al-Ḥasan in Baṣra, and Makḥūl in Greater Syria."

Mālik ibn Anas (93–179). The great Madinan Imām and founder of the school of jurisprudence that bears his name. When the Caliph Hārūn al-Rashīd (God be pleased with him) ordered him to come to relate hadith to him, his reply was, "Knowledge is something that is sought, not brought." He authored *al-Muwaṭṭa* in response to the Caliph Manṣūr's request for a book of prophetic hadith. Imām al-Shāfi'ī, who studied under him, praised him saying that "Mālik is God's proof over His creation."

Mālik ibn Rabī'a ibn al-Badan, Abū Usayd (d. circa 40). He carried the standard of Banī Sa'īda on the day that Mecca was conquered. He has narrations in the six major books of hadith.

Manṣūr ibn Zādhān, Abū al-Mughīra (d. 131). He was born during the life of Ibn 'Umar (God be pleased with him).

Masrūq ibn al-Ajda' ibn Mālik, Abū 'Ā'isha (d. 63). A Successor who was alive during the time of the Prophet (God bless him and give him peace) but entered Islam after his death (God bless him and give him peace).

al-Mawardī = 'Alī ibn Muḥammad ibn Ḥabīb

Mu'ādh ibn Anas al-Juhanī. Included among the people of Egypt.

Mu'ān ibn Rifā'a, Abū Muḥammad (d. after 150). From the same generation as Imāms Mālik and Sufyān al-Thawrī. He is a somewhat weak narrator.

Mu'āwiya ibn Qurra ibn Iyyās, Abū Iyyās (d. 113). A scholar and trustworthy narrator. He died at the age of 76.

Mu'āwiya ibn Ṣakhr ibn Ḥarb (d. 60). A scribe for the Revelation and the founder of the Umayyid dynasty. He embraced Islam with his father Abū Sufyān on the day of Mecca's conquest, 8 AH. 'Umar (God be pleased with him) appointed him governor of Damascus, where he died.

Muḥammad = Muḥammad ibn al-Ḥasan

Muḥammad ibn 'Abdallāh al-Nīsābūrī, Abū 'Abdallāh al-Ḥākim (321–405). The well-known hadith scholar and legist. His more famous works include *Mustadrik 'alā al-Ṣaḥīḥayn,* and *Ma'rifāt 'Ulūm al-Ḥadīth.* The latter is one of the first books concerning hadith sciences.

Muḥammad ibn Aḥmad ibn Ayyūb ibn al-Ṣalat ibn Shanbūdh, Abū alḤasan (240(?)–328). One of the greatest Quran reciters in Baghdad. When the city's governor became aware of him spreading aberrant opinions regarding recitation, he called for him to debate the other masters of recitation. He declared the other scholars ignorant and grew angry with the governor. He repented and was banished. Imām al-Dhahabī indicates that in spite of his mistakes, he deserves the same respect owed all masters of the Quran.

Muḥammad ibn 'Alī ibn al-Ḥusayn ibn Muqlah, Abū 'Alī (272–) Poet, litterateur, and calligrapher. He served as an adviser to three separate rulers.

Muḥammad ibn Dāwūd ibn Muḥammad, Abū Bakr al-Ṣaydalānī alDāwūdī (d. 427). He was a Shafi'ī legist and hadith narrator.

Muḥammad ibn al-Ḥasan ibn Firqad, Abū 'Abdallāh (131–189). An Imām who studied under Abū Ḥanīfa and then under Abū Yūsuf. His books include *al-Jāmi' al-Kabīr* and *al-Jāmi' al-Ṣaghīr*.

Muḥammad ibn al-Ḥusayn ibn Muḥammad, Abū 'Abd al-Raḥmān al-Sulamī (325–415). The great Sufi scholar who was born and died in Naysābūr.

Muḥammad ibn Ibrāhīm ibn al-Mundhir, Abū Bakr (242–319). A Shāfi'ī legist and *mujtahid*. He was the chief scholar of the Meccan sanctuary in his time. He died in Mecca.

Muḥammad ibn Idrīs ibn al-'Abbās, Abū 'Abdallāh al-Shāfi'ī (150–205). The great legist and founder of the school bearing his name. As a youth he was excellent in marksmanship, language, poetry, and the history of the Arabs. He then took to fiqh and hadith, and became qualified to give religious verdicts by the time he was fifteen year sold. ImāmAḥmad praised him saying, "The likeness of al-Shāfi'ī to other people is as the likeness of the sun to the earth." His works include *al-Umm, al-Risāla, al-Musnad, Faā'il Quraysh, Ādāb al-Qāḍī,* and others. He died in Egypt.

Muḥammad ibn 'Īsā ibn Sawra ibn Mūsā ibn al-Dhahak al-Sulamī alTirmidhī, Abū 'Īsā (d. 279). The great blind hadith master and author of *al-Jāmi'*. The second most brilliant student of Bukhārī after Muslim.

Muḥammad ibn Ismā'īl ibn al-'Abbās, Abū Bakr al-Warrāq (293–378).

Muḥammad ibn Ismā'īl ibn Ibrāhīm al-Bukhārī, Abū 'Abdallāh (194–257). The hadith master of his generation. He authored his *Ṣaḥīḥ* choosing from over 600,000 hadiths which became the soundest book in Islam after the Quran.

Muḥammad ibn Muḥammad ibn Muḥammad ibn Aḥmad, Abū Ḥāmid al-Ghazālī, Hujjat al-Islām (450–505). A Shāfi'ī legist, Sufi, and theologian. His works include: *Iḥyā 'Ulūm al-Dīn,*

Tahāfūt al-Falāsifa, al-Muṣtaṣfā fī 'Ilm Uṣūl al-Fiqh, al-Wasīṭ, and *al-Iqtiṣād fī al-I'tiqād.*

Muḥammad ibn Muslim ibn 'Abdallāh ibn Shihāb, Abū Bakr al-Zuhrī (58–124). A Successor. One of the greatest of all jusrists and hadith masters ever. He is credited with being the first to systematically record hadith.

Muḥammad ibn Sīrīn, Abū Bakr (d. 110). A freed slave of Anas ibn Mālik (God be pleased with him) and a famous and illustrious Successor. He was a legist, transmitter of hadith, and an ascetic. He died at the age of 77.

Muḥammad ibn Yazīd, Abū 'Abdallāh Ibn Mājah (209–273). A great hadith master, legist, and Quranic exegete. His *Sunan* is among the six major collections of hadith.

Muḥammad ibn Yūsuf ibn Ya'qūb, Abū Bakr al-Kindī (283–355). The most knowledgeable historian of Egypt. He also had knowledge in hadith and lineage.

Mujāhid ibn Jabr, Abū al-Ḥajjāj (21–104). A Successor who studied exegesis from Ibn 'Abbās (God be pleased with him). He became the chief of the reciters and exegetes. He died while prostrate in Prayer.

Mujālid ibn Sa'īd ibn 'Umayr, Abū 'Amr (d. 144). A hadith narrator who was not strong. al-Musāyyib ibn Rāfi',Abūal-'Alā'(d.105). A blind legist.

Muslim ibn al-Ḥajjāj ibn Muslim al-Qushayrī, al-Naysābūrī, Abū al-Ḥusayn (204–261). The most brilliant student of Bukhārī and the author of the *Ṣaḥīḥ*, the third soundest book in Islam after the Quran and Bukhārī's *Ṣaḥīḥ*.

Muṭarrif ibn 'Abdallāh ibn al-Shikhkhīr, Abū 'Abdallāh (d. after 80). A Successor and great ascetic. It is said that he was born the year of the Battle of Badr or the year of Uḥud.

al-Mutawallī = 'Abd al-Raḥmān ibn Ma'min

Nāfi' = Nāfi' ibn Abī Na'īm

Nāfi' ibn Abī Na'īm'Abdal-Raḥmān, Abū Ruwaym (d. 169). One of the seven Imāms of canonical recitation. He was born during the caliphate of 'Abd al-Malik ibn Marwān. Although he is somewhat weak as a narrator of hadith, there is agreement that he is most trustworthy in narrating the Quran.

al-Nasā'ī = Aḥmad ibn Shu'ayb

Naṣr ibn Ibrāhīm ibn Naṣr, Abū al-Fatḥ al-Maqdisī (377–490). The head of the Shāfi'īs in Greater Syria in his age. He died in Damascus.

al-Naḥḥās = Aḥmad ibn Muḥammad

al-Nu'mān ibn Thābit ibn Zūṭā, Abū Ḥanīfa (80–150). The great legist and founder of the school bearing his name. He was known for his noble character, sound intellect, and beautiful appearance. Imām al-Shāfi'ī praised him saying, "All scholars depend on Abū Ḥanīfa in *fiqh*."

Qabīsa ibn Dhū'ayb, Abū Sa'īd (7–86). A child of one of the Companions (God be pleased with them). A legist with narrations in the six major collections of hadith. He died in Damascus.

al-Qāḍī Abū al-Ṭayyib = Ṭāhir ibn 'Abdallāh

al-Qāḍī Ḥusayn = Ḥusayn ibn Muḥammad ibn Aḥmad

al-Qāḍī 'Iyāḍ = 'Iyāḍ ibn Mūsā

al-Qaffāl = 'Abdallāh ibn Aḥmad

al-Qāsim = Al-Qāsim ibn Muḥammad

al-Qāsim ibn Muḥammad ibn Abī Bakr al-Ṣiddīq (d. 101). He was one of the seven great legists of Medina. He died in Qadīd.

al-Qāsim ibn 'Uthmān, al-Jū'ī (d. 248). Shaykh of the Sufis. "Al-Jū'ī" is a reference to *jū'*, that is, hunger.

Qatāda ibn Du'āma ibn Qatāda, Abū al-Khaṭṭāb (61–118). **The hadith master of his age and exegete. He was blind. Imām Aḥmad said:** "Qatāda has the best memorization of all in Baṣra." He died in Wāsiṭ from the plague.

Qays ibn Ḥabtar. He narrates from the older Sucessors. He is considered a trustworthy narrator and has hadiths in Abū Dāwūd's *Sunan.*

Rafī' ibn Mahrān, Abū al-'Āliya (d. 93). He saw the Prophet (God bless him and give him peace) but did not enter Islam until the caliphate of Abū Bakr (God be pleased with him).

al-Rabī' ibn Sulaymān ibn 'Abd al-Jabbār ibn Kāmil, Abū Muḥammad (174–270). A hadith Master and direct student of al-Shāfi'ī. He was born and died in Egypt.

al-Rāfi'ī = 'Abdal-Karīm ibn Muḥammad

al-Rammādī = Aḥmad ibn Manṣūr ibn Sayyār

Rifā'a ibn 'Abd al-Mundhir, Abū Lubāba. He died during the caliphate of 'Alī (God be pleased with him). His narrations are found in Bukhārī, Muslim, Abū Dāwūd, and Ibn Mājah.

al-Ruwyānī = 'Abd al-Wāḥid ibn Ismā'īl ibn Aḥmad

Sa'd ibn Abī Waqqāṣ = Sa'd ibn Mālik

Sa'd ibn Mālik ibn Sanān, al-Khazrajī, al-Anṣārī, al-Khudrī, Abū Sa'īd (d. 74). A Companion who narrated many hadiths. He died at 84 years of age.

Sa'd ibn Mālik ibn Wahb (d. 55). An early convert to Islam. His conversion was at the hand of Abū Bakr al-Ṣiddīq (God be pleased with him). He was the first to let loose an arrow in jihād and one of ten Companions told during their lives that they will enter Paradise. During 'Umar's caliphate and part of 'Uthmān's (God be well pleased with them) He was responsible for managing the city of Kūfa. He died on his property outside of Medina and was carried to Medina for burial in Baqī'.

Sa'd ibn 'Ubāda (d. 15). He carried the standard of the Messenger of God (God bless him and give him peace) on the day that Mecca was conquered. He died during the caliphate of 'Umar (God be pleased with him) in Huran, Syria.

Sahl ibn 'Abdallāh ibn Yūnis al-Tustarī, Abū Muḥammad (200–283). The well-known Sufi Imām. He used to practice perpetual fasting and prayed all night. He reached a point where he broke his fast only once every twenty-five nights on one dirham's worth of barley bread for twenty years. He recommended the study of hadith as the highest pursuit. Among his sayings: "People are all drunk except the scholars, and the scholars are all confused except those who practice what they know."

Sahl ibn Muḥammad ibn 'Uthmān, Abū Ḥātim al-Sajistānī (d. 248). One of the great scholars of lexicography and poetry. He was from Baṣra and authored several works.

Sahl ibn Sa'd ibn Mālik (d. 91). The last Companion to die in Medina.

Sa'īd ibn Jubayr, Abū 'Abdallāh (46–95). The most knowledgeable of the Successors. Imām Aḥmad ibn Ḥanbal said concerning him that "Al-Ḥajjāj killed Sa'īd, and there was not a single person on the face of the earth who did not need his knowledge."

Sa'īd ibn al-Musayyib ibn Ḥazn ibn Abī Wahb, Abū Muḥammad (d. 94). One of the seven great jurists of Medina. He was born two years after the beginning of the caliphate of 'Umar (God be pleased with him). He combined *fiqh,* hadith, abstinence, and scrupulousness. He was the most knowledgeable Successor concerning the judgments of 'Umar (God be pleased with him). He died in Medina.

Sa'īd ibn Salām, Abū 'Uthmān al-Maghribī (d. 373). A Sufi Shaykh. A saying of his is that "the delivery from delusion is adhering to the Sharī'a."

Sa'īd ibn Muḥammad ibn Ṣubayḥ, Abū 'Uthmān (219–303). A Mālikī legist and scholar of hadith who spent time with

Saḥnūn. He authored a book concerning difficult words in the Quran.

Sālim ibn 'Abdallāh ibn 'Umar ibn al-Khaṭṭāb (d. 106). He was one of the seven great legists of Medina. He died in Medina.

Salmān al-Anmāṭī = I could not locate him in my notes.

Salmān al-Fārisī, Abū 'Abdallāh (d. 34) The well-known and illustrious Companion who originally came from Persia.

al-Sarī ibn al-Mughallis al-Saqṭī, Abū al-Ḥasan (160 -253). A great Sufi. His sayings include, "Anyone incapable of disciplining himself is even less capable of disciplining others." He was al-Junayd's uncle.

al-Ṣaydalānī = Muḥammad ibn Dāwūd

al-Sha'bī = 'Āmir ibn Sharāḥīl

al-Shāfi'ī = Muḥammad ibn Idrīs

Shaqīq ibn Salama, Abū Wā'il (d. 82). A noble Successor who reached the Prophet (God bless him and give him peace) but did not see him. 'Āṣim ibn Abī al-Nujūd said, "I never heard Abū Wā'il curse a human being nor an animal."

Shurayḥ ibn al-Ḥārith ibn Qays ibn al-Jahm, Abū Umaya (d. 78). A Successor and famous early judge. He embraced Islam during the life of the Prophet (God bless him and give him peace) but did not see him. He was put in charge of the courts in Kūfa during the caliphates of 'Umar, 'Uthmān, 'Alī, and Mu'āwiya (God be well pleased with them one and all). He was a trustworthy narrator of hadith and trusted in judgments. He lived a long life.

Ṣudī ibn 'Ujlān al-Bāhilī, Abū Umāma (d. 81 or 86). A Companion who died in Ḥams, Syria at the age of 91. He was one of the last Companions (God be well pleased with them) to pass away in Greater Syria.

Sufyān ibn Sa'īd ibn Masrūq al-Thawrī, Abū 'Abdallāh (97–161). The premier Imām of hadith, jurisprudence, and piety for his time. He is, with Abū Ḥanīfa, the chief representative of the School of Kūfa. Aḥmad called him the Imām par excellence and Ibn al-Mubārak said, "I learned from eleven-hundred shaykhs, but none better than Sufyān."

al-Sulamī = Muḥammad ibn al-Ḥusayn

Sulaym ibn 'Itr, Abū Salama al-Tajībī (d. 75). A trustworthy narrator.

Sulaymān ibn Aḥmad ibn Ayyūb ibn Mutir, Abū al-Qāsim al-Ṭabarānī (260–360). He began listening to hadith in 273 AH. He gathered hadith from more than 1000 shaykhs and was a prolific writer and the hadith master of his age. He died in Isfahān.

Sulaymān ibn al-Ash'ath ibn Shidād, al-Azdī, al-Sajistānī, Abū Dāwūd (202–275). An Imām in jurisprudence, hadith, and other sciences, he was a student of Imām Aḥmad ibn Ḥanbal. He authored many works. His *Sunan* is one of the six canonical collections of hadith.

Sulaymān ibn Dāwūd ibn Ḥammād, Abū al-Rabī' (d. 253). Imāms Abū Dāwūd and al-Nasā'ī transmitted from him and declared him trustworthy. He is reported to have been a Mālikī legist.

Sulaymān ibn Mihrān, Abū Muḥammad al-A'mash (61–148). A master of Quran, hadith, and inheritance laws. He was nicknamed "the *muṣḥaf*" as an allusion to his truthfulness and reliability.

Sulaymān ibn Yasār, Abū Ayyūb (34–107). A free slave of Mother of the Faithful Maymūna (God be well pleased with her). He was born during the caliphate of 'Umar (God be pleased with him) and one of the seven great legists of Medina.

al-Ṭabarānī = Sulaymān ibn Aḥmad ibn Ayyūb

Ṭāhir ibn ʿAbdallāh ibn Ṭāhir al-Ṭabarī, Abū al-Ṭayyib (348–450). A legist and notable of the Shāfiʿīmadhhab.

Ṭalḥa ibn Muṣarrif ibn Kaʿb, Abū Muḥammad (d. 112). The best Quran reciter of his time. A trustworthy narrator with hadiths in the six major collections of hadith. He was known for his scrupulousness and Ṭpious deeds.

Tamīm ibn Aws ibn Khārija al-Dārī, Abū Ruqaya. A Christian who entered Islam in 9 AH. He resided in Medina and moved to Greater Syria after the assassination of ʿUthmān (God be pleased with him). He later returned to Medina, where he died.

Tamīm al-Dārī = Tamīm ibn Aws

Ṭāwūs ibn Kaysān, Abū ʿAbd al-Raḥmān (33–106). A legist and hadith narrator, and one of the greatest of the Successors. He was courageous in admonishing the caliphs and governors. He died while performing Hajj.

al-Thaʿlabī = Aḥmad ibn Muḥammad ibn Ibrāhīm

Thawbān ibn Ibrāhīm al-Ikhmīmī al-Miṣrī, Abū al-Faya Dhū'l-Nūn (d. 245). A freed slave of Nubian origin. He is one of the most famous of the early Sufis.

al-Tirmidhī = Muḥammad ibn ʿīsā

ʿUmar ibn ʿAbd al-ʿAzīz ibn Marwān ibn al-Ḥakam (61–101). Considered the fifth of the Rightly Guided Caliphs. He was a man of great knowledge, a hadith master, ascetic, and *mujtahid*. His mother was Laylā bint ʿĀṣim ibn ʿUmar ibn al-Khaṭṭāb, Umm ʿĀṣim. He was known for his fairness, abstinence, and Godfearingness. In 99 AH he succeeded Sulaymān ibn ʿAbd al-Malik as caliph.

ʿUmar ibn al-Khaṭṭāb, Abū Ḥafṣa (d. 23). Second of the Rightly Guided Caliphs. He was known for his fairness, judiciousness and strength. He was the first caliph to be given the title "Commander of the Faithful", the first person to base dates using the Hijra, the first to gather the Quran in one volume, and the first to gather the people together for Tarāwīḥ Prayer. He was murdered while leading the Dawn Prayer. He was 63 years old and had been caliph for ten and a half years. He was buried in the house of 'A'isha, near the Prophet (God bless him and give him peace).

'Ubādat ibn al-Sāmat ibn Qays, Abū al-Walīd (d. 34). 'Umar sent him to Greater Syria as a judge and teacher. He resided in Ḥams and then moved to Palestine. He died at the age of 72.

Ubay ibn Ka'b (d. 19). One of the scribes of the Revelation and one of six Companions to memorize the Quran during the life of the Prophet (God bless him and give him peace). He was the most skillful at reciting the Quran. He died in Medina.

Umm Salama = Hind bint Abī Umayya

'Uqba ibn 'Amr ibn Tha'laba, Abū Mas'ūd. A Companion who resided in Kūfa and died during the caliphate of 'Alī ibn Abī Ṭālib.

'Urwa ibn al-Zubayr ibn al-'Awwām, Abū 'Abdallāh (22–93). One of the seven great legists of Medina. He was knowledgeable, righteous, generous, and a trustworthy narrator. He abstained from engaging in the various dissentions [*fitan*]. He died in Medina.

'Uthmān ibn 'Abd al-Raḥmān ibn 'Uthmān, Abū 'Amr Ibn al-Ṣalāḥ (d. 643). The great Shafi'ī legist and hadith scholar. He served as a teacher in Dār al-Ḥadīth, in Damascus, where he dictated what has come to be one of the classic manuals on hadith sciences.

'Uthmān ibn 'Affān, Abū 'Abdallāh (d. 35). Third of the Rightly Guided Caliphs and one of those famed for reciting the entire Quran in a single *rak'a.* He married two of the daughters of the Messenger of God (God bless him and give him peace), Ruqayya and, after Ruqayya's death, Umm Kulthūm, and was thus given the nickname "he of the two lights." He gathered together the Quran which he had read in its entirety before the

Prophet's death (God bless him and give him peace). During his tenure as Caliph, Armenia, Caucasia, Khurāsān, Kirman, Sijistān, Cyprus, and much of North Africa were added to the dominions of Islam.

'Uthmān ibn Sa'īd ibn 'Uthmān, Abū 'Amr al-Dānī (371–444). An Andalusian Imām in the sciences of Quran, a hadith master, and an exegete. He authored over 100 works.

Wahb ibn 'Abdallāh, Abū Juḥayfa (d. 74). One of the younger Companions. 'Alī (God be pleased with him) put him in charge of the Muslim common fund in Kūfa, and he participated in all of 'Alī's battles (God be pleased with him). He died in Kūfa.

al-Wāḥidī = 'Alī ibn Aḥmad

al-Warrāq = Muḥammad ibn Ismā'īl

Yaḥyā ibn Abī al-Khayr Sālim ibn As'ad, Abū al-Khayr (d. 558). He memorized al-Shirāzī's *al-Muhadhdhab* and later commented on it in *al-Bayyān*.

Yaḥyā ibn Waththāb (d. 103). A Successor and the chief Quranic scholar in Kūfa during his time. He has few narrations even though he is a trustworthy narrator.

Ya'qūb ibn Ibrāhīm ibn Ḥabīb, Abū Yūsuf (113–182). A legist and hadith master. He studied under Imām Abū Ḥanīfa and was the first to spread his madhhab, as well as the first to record fiqh. He was appointed judge during the caliphates of al-Mahdī, al-Hādi, and al-Rashīd. Yazīd ibn Abān al-Raqāshī, Abū 'Amr. An ascetic. Some of his narrations are found in *al-Adab al-Mufrad,* al-Tirmidhī's *Jāmi',* and Ibn Mājah's *Sunan.*

Yazīd al-Raqāshī = Yazīd ibn Abān

Yūsuf ibn 'Abdallāh ibn Muḥammad ibn 'Abd al-Barr ibn 'Āṣim, Abū 'Umar (378–463). The great Andalusian hadith master, Mālikī scholar, Quran master, and historian. Al-Qurṭubī cites him about five hundred times in his *Tafsīr*. Among his masterpieces: *Al-Intiqā' fī Faḍā'il al-Thalāthat al-A'immat al-Fuqahā'*

Mālik wa'l-Shāfi'ī wa Abī Ḥanīfa (*The Hand Picked Excellent Merits of the Three Great Jurisprudent Imāms: Mālik, Shāfi'ī, and Abū Ḥanīfa*); *al-Istidhkār li Madhhab 'Ulamā' al-Amṣār fī mā Taḍammanahu al-Muwaṭṭa' min Ma'ānī al-Ra'ī wa'l-Āthār* (*The Memorization of the Doctrine of the Scholars of the World Concerning the Juridical Opinions and the Narrations Found in Mālik's Muwaṭṭa'*); *al-Istī'āb fī Asmā' al-Aṣḥāb* (*The Comprehensive Compilation of the Names of the Prophet's Companions*); *Jāmi' Bayān al-'Ilmī wa Faḍlihi wa mā Yanbaghī fī Riwāyatihi wa Ḥamlih* (*Compendium Exposing the Nature of Knowledge and Its Immense Merit, and What is Required in the Process of Narrating it and Conveying it*). Of his book *al-Tamhīd limā fi'l-Muwaṭṭa' min al-Ma'ānī wa'l-Asānīd* (*The Facilitation to the Meanings and Chains of Transmission Found in Mālik's Muwaṭṭa'*) his friend Ibn Ḥazm said: "I do not know of anything like it with regard to the superlative understanding of hadith, let alone better than it."

Zabbān ibn 'Ammār, Abū 'Amr al-Baṣrī (70–154). A scholar of lexicography and literature, and one of the seven Imāms of canonical recitation. He was born in Mecca, raised in Baṣra, and died in Kūfa.

Zayd ibn Thābit al-TMaḥḥāk ibn Zayd ibn Lawdhān (d. 45). One of the scribes of the Prophet (God bless him and give him peace). He was one of the legists of the Companions (God be pleased with them), and the most learned concerning inheritance laws. During the caliphate of Abū Bakr (God be pleased with him) he participated in gathering and writing the Quran. Then during the caliphate of 'Uthmān (God be pleased with him) he helped in copying it. He died in Medina at 56 years of age.

Zayd ibn Sahl ibn al-Aswad ibn Ḥarām, Abū Ṭalḥa (d. 31). A Companion who died at the age of 77.

Zubayd ibn al-Ḥārith ibn 'Abd al-Karīm, Abū 'Abd al-Raḥmān (d. 122). He was a hadith master with narrations in the six major collections.

Zufar ibn al-Hudhayl ibn Qays al-'Anbarī (110–157). The pious Mujtahid Imām and trustworthy hadith master of noble birth, "extremely scrupulous, sharp in his analogies, scarce in his writing, memorizing everything he writes" (Wakī'), "trustworthy and reliable" (Yaḥyā ibn Ma'īn), "a man of wisdom, religion, understanding, and scrupulous Godfearingness" (Ibn 'Abd al-Barr), "the Godly *Mujtahid Faqīh*... one of the oceans of *Fiqh* and the truly wise men of the time" (al-Dhahabī). A principal student of Abū Ḥanīfa and successor to Abū Yūsuf. He died in Baṣra, where he was the chief judge.

al-Zuhrī = Muḥammad ibn Muslim

Zurāra ibn Awfa, al-'Āmirī, al-Baṣrī, Abū Ḥājib (d. 93). The judge of Baṣra.

BIBLIOGRAPHY

al-'Asqalānī, Ibn Ḥajar, and Muḥammad ibn Ismā'īl al-Bukhārī. *Fatḥ al-Bārī bi Sharḥ Ṣaḥīḥ al-Bukhārī*. Edited by Muḥammad Fu'ād 'Abd al-Bāqī and Muḥibb al-Dīn al-Khaṭīb. 14 vols. Cairo: Maktabat al-Salafiyya, 1390 AH/1970 CE.

al-Bukhārī, Muḥammad ibn Ismā'īl. *Ṣaḥīḥ al-Bukhārī*. Hadith numbering according to *Fatḥ al-Bārī*.

——. *Al-Adab al-Mufrad*. Edited by Muḥammad Fu'ād 'Abd al-Bāqī. 3rd edition. Beirut: Dār al-Bashā'ir al-Islāmiyya, 1989 CE.

al-Dāramī, 'Abdallāh. *Al-Musnad al-Jāmi'*. Dār al-Fikr, 1978 CE.

al-Dhahabī, Muḥammad ibn Aḥmad. *Mizān al-I'tidāl fī Naqd al-Rijāl*. 4 vols. Reprint. Beirut: Dār al-Ma'rifa, n.d.

——. *Tadhkirat al-Ḥuffāẓ*. 4 vols in 2. Beirut: Dār al-Ma'rifa, n.d. al-Ghazālī, Abū Ḥāmid. Iḥyā' 'Ulūm al-Dīn. 4 vols. Cairo: Lajna Nashr al-Thaqāfa al-Islāmiyya, 1935 CE.

al-Ḥaddād, 'Alawī ibn Aḥmad. *Misbaḥ al-Anām wa Jalā' al-Ṭalam fī Radd Shubh al-Bid'ī al-Najdī Allatī Aḍlla biha al-'Awwām*. Translated as *Refutation Of The Innovator of Najd* by Gibril Fouad Ḥaddād. Damascus: Maktabat al-Aḥbāb, 1422 AH / 2002 CE.

al-Ḥākim, Abū 'Abdallāh. *Al-Mustadrak 'alā al-Ṣaḥīḥayn*. 4 vols. Hyderabad, 1334 AH / 1916 CE. Reprint (with index vol 5). Beirut: Dār al-Ma'rifa, n.d.

al-Haythami, Ibn Ḥajar. *Majma' al-Zawā'id*. Beirut: Dār al-Kitāb al'Arabī, 1967 CE.

Ibn 'Ābidīn, Muḥammad Amīn. *Radd al-Muḥtār 'alā al-Durr al-Mukhtār.* 5 vols. Bulāq 1272 AH / 1855 CE. Reprint. Beirut: Dār Iḥyā' al-Turāth al-'Arabī, 1407 AH / 1987 CE.

Ibn Ḥanbal, Aḥmad. *Al-Musnad.* 6 vols. Cairo: Mu'assasa Qurṭuba, n.d. Reprint. Beirut: Dār Iḥyā' al-Turāth al-'Arabī, n.d.

Ibn Mājah, Muḥammad. *Sunan Ibn Mājah.* Edited by Fu'ād 'Abd al-Bāqī. 2 vols. Beirut: Dār al-Fikr, n.d.

al-Kāsānī, Abū Bakr ibn Manṣūr. *Badā'i' al-Ṣanā'i' fī Tartīb al-Sharā'i'.* Edited by 'Adnān Darawīsh. 6 vols. Beirut: Dār Iḥyā' al-Turāth al'Arabī, 1419 AH / 1998 CE.

al-Maqdisī, Abū 'Abdallāh Muḥammad ibn Mufliḥ. *Al-Ādābal-Shar'iyya.* Editors: Shu'ayb al-Arna'ūṭ and 'Umar al-Qayyām. 4 vols. 3rd edition. Beirut: Mu'assisa al-Risāla, 1418 AH / 1997 CE.

Muḥammad ibn 'Allān, Abū Zakariyyā Yaḥyā ibn Sharaf al-Nawawī. *Al-Futuḥāt al-Rabbāniyya 'alā al-Adhkār al-Nawawīyya.* 5 vols. in 3. Reprint. Beirut: Dār al-Iḥyā' li al-Turāth al-'Arabī, n.d.

Muslim ibn al-Ḥajjaj. *Ṣaḥīḥ Muslim.* Edited by Muḥammad Fu'ād 'Abd al-Bāqī. 5 vols. Cairo: Maṭba'a 'īsā al-Bābī al-Ḥalabī 1376 AH / 1956 CE. Reprint. Beirut: Dār al-Fikr, 1403 AH / 1983 CE.

al-Nasā'ī, Abū 'Abd al-Raḥmān Aḥmad. *Al-Sunan al-Kubrā.* Beirut: Dār Iḥyā' al-Turāth al-'Arabī, n.d.

Nasīf, Manṣūr 'Alī. *Ghāyat al-Ma'mul Sharḥ al-Tāj al-Jāmi' li-l-Uṣūl fī Aḥadīth al-Rasūl.* 5 vols. Reprint [index in 6th vol]. Beirut: Dār Iḥyā' al-Turāth al-'Arabī, 1413 AH / 1993 CE.

——. *Irshād Ṭulāb al-Haqā'iq ilā Ma'rifat Sunan Khayr al-Khalā'iq.* Edited by Dr. Nūr al-Dīn 'Itr. 2nd edition. Beirut: Dār al-Bashā'ir al-Islāmiya, 1411 AH / 1991 CE.

——. *Al-Tibyān fī Ādāb Ḥamalat al-Qur'ān.* Edited by 'Abd al-Qādir alArna'ūṭ. 2nd edition. Damascus: Dār al-Bayan, 1414 AH / 1994 CE.

——. *Al-Tibyān fī Ādāb Ḥamalat al-Qur'ān*. Edited by by Bashīr Muḥammad 'Uyūn. Third edition. Damascus: Maktabat Dār al-Bayān, 1421 AH / 2000 CE.

——. *Al-Tibyān fī Ādāb Ḥamalat al-Qur'ān*. Edited by Ghālib Karīm. Damascus, 1422 AH / 2001 CE.

——. *Al-Tibyān fī Ādāb Ḥamalat al-Qur'ān*. Edited by Khālid Khādim al-Saruji. Damascus: Dār Ibn al-Qayyim, 1422 AH /2001 CE.

——. *Kitāb al-Tarkhīṣ fī al-Ikrām bi'l-Qiyām li Dhawī al-Faḍwa al-Maziyya min AHl al-Islām 'alā Jihat al-Birr wa al-Taqwā wa al-Iḥtirām lā 'alā Jihat al-Riyā' wa al-I'ẓām*. Beirut: Dār al-Bashā'ir al-Islāmiyya, 1409 AH / 1988 CE.

al-Qārī, 'Alī ibn Sulṭān Muḥammad al-Harawī. *Fatḥ Bāb al-'Ināya bi Sharḥ al-Nuqāya*. Edited by Muḥammad and Haytham Naẓār Tamīm. 3 vols. Beirut: Dār al-Qalam, 1417 AH / 1997 CE.

al-Sajistānī, Abū Dāwūd. *Sunan Abī Dāwūd*. Edited by Muḥammad Muḥyī al-Dīn 'Abd al-Ḥamīd. 4 vols. in 2. Beirut: Dār al-Fikr, n.d.

al-Ṣan'ānī, 'Abd al-Razzāq. *Al-Muṣannaf. Edited by Ḥabīb al-Raḥmān al-'Azām*. Beirut: al-Maktab al-Islām, 1403 AH / 1983 CE.

al-Shahrastānī, 'Abd al-Karīm. *Kitāb al-Milal wa al-Nihal*. Printed in the margins of Ibn Ḥazm's *Kitāb al-Faṣl fī al-Milal wa al-Ahwa' wa al-Nihal*. 5 vols. in 3. Baghdad: Maktabat al-Muthanna, n.d.

al-Sharbīnī, Muḥammad Khaṭīb. *Mughnī al-Muḥtāj ilā Ma'rifat Ma'ānī Alfāẓ al-Minhāj*. Beirut: Dār al-Fikr: n.d.

Shihāb al-Dīn, Aḥmad ibn 'Alī ibn Ḥajar. *Taqrīb al-Tahdhīb*. Edited by Muḥammad 'Awwāma. Beirut: Dār Ibn Ḥazm, 1420 AH / 1999 CE.

Sirāj al-Dīn, 'Abdallāh. *Tilāwat al-Qur'ān al-Majīd, Faā'iluhā, Adābuhā, Khaṣā'iṣuhā*. 4th edition. Aleppo: Dār al-Falāḥ, 1418 AH / 1997 CE.

al-Shafaqa, Muḥammad Bashīr. *Fiqh al-'Ibādāt*. 3rd edition. Damascus: Dār al-Qalam, 1412 AH / 1992 CE.

al-Suyūṭī, Jalāl al-Dīn 'Abd al-Raḥmān. *Al-Iṭqān fī 'Ulūm al-Qur'ān*. Edited by Muḥammad Abū al-FałIbrāhīm. 4 vols. in 2. Iranian reprint of an Egyptian edition. n.d.

al-Tirmidhī, Abū 'īsā. *Sunan al-Tirmidhī*. Edited by Muḥammad Fu'ād 'Abd al-Bāqī. 5 vols. Cairo, n.d. Reprint. Beirut: Dār Iḥyā' al-Turāth al-'Arabī, n.d.

DETAILED TABLE OF CONTENTS

FOREWORD, XI

PREFACE TO THE SECOND EDITION, XIII

TRANSLATOR'S INTRODUCTION, XV

BRIEF BIOGRAPHY OF IMĀM AL-NAWAWĪ, XX
Early Education and Teachers, xx
Curriculum and Daily Schedule, xxi
His Asceticism and Extremely Simple Living, xxii
His Superlative Mastership in Hadith and Jurisprudence, xxii
His Fearless Admonishing of Princes, xxiii
Headmastership of Dār al-Ḥadīth, xxiii
Select Bibliography of Shaykh al-Islām, xxiii
Imām al-Nawawī's Death, xxvi
Notes to the Biography, xxvi

IMĀM AL-NAWAWĪ'S INTRODUCTION, 1
Reasons for Writing the Book and Its Structure, 2
Using Weakly Authenticated Hadiths, 3

1. THE MERIT OF RECITING AND BEARING THE QURAN, 5

2. THE PRECEDENCE OF RECITATION AND OF THE RECITER, 8

3. HONORING THE FOLK OF THE QURAN, 9

4. THE ETIQUETTE OF TEACHERS AND STUDENTS, 11
The Intention of the Bearers of the Quran, 11
Not Seeking a Worldly Objective, 13
Not Objecting to Students Reciting With Others, 14

Molded by Good Qualities, 15
Invocations and Supplications, 15
Being Kind and Accommodating, 15
Sincerity Toward Students, 16
Not Possessed of Arrogance, 17
Disciplining the Student, 17
The Communal Obligation of Teaching, 18
Resolved to Teach, 18
Teaching in Order of Arrival, 19
Students with Unsound Intentions, 19
Not Fidgeting During Recitation, 19
Not Disgracing Knowledge, 19
Having a Spacious Assembly, 20
The Student's Etiquette, 20
Studying from the Best, 21
Respecting the Teacher, 21
Entering and Exiting the Lesson, 22
Sitting During the Lesson, 22
A Moody Shaykh, 22
Between Lessons, 23
When to Study, 24
Treating Envy and Pride, 25

5. THE ETIQUETTE OF THE BEARERS OF THE QURAN, 26
Reciting for Livelihood, 27
Taking Wages, 27
Continually Completing the Quran, 28
Reciting at Night, 31
The Importance of Retaining the Quran, 33
Sleeping Through One's *Wird* (or *Ḥizb*), 33

6. THE ETIQUETTE OF RECITATION, 35
The Toothstick [*Miswāk*], 35
When the mouth is filthy, 36
Ritual purity, 36
Dry Ablution, 37
In the Absence of Water and Earth, 38
The Place of Recitation, 39
Facing the Qibla, 40
Seeking Protection, 41
Saying *"Bismillāhi al-Raḥmān al-Raḥīm"*, 41
Humility and Pondering, 42

Repeating a Verse, 43
Weeping During Recitation, 44
Distinctly Reciting, 45
Reciting Rapidly, 45
Supplicating While Reciting, 46
Differences of Opinion, 47
Things from which to protect the Quran, 47
Fidgeting, Distractions, and the Unlawful, 48
Enjoining Right and Forbidding Wrong, 48
Reciting in a Foreign Language, 48
Permissible Recitations, 49
Switching Recitations, 49
Reciting in Order, 50
Reciting a Chapter of the Quran Itself in Reverse Order, 50
Reciting from the *Muṣḥaf* or from Memory, 51
Devotion to the Quran in a Group, 52
Reciting in Turns, 53
Reciting with a Raised Voice, 54
Reciting Quietly, 56
Summary, 56
Beautifying the Voice with Quran, 57
Reciting with a Melodious Fashion, 58
Seeking a Wholesome, Beautiful Recitation, 59
Reciting at Assemblies, 60
Reading What has Complete Meaning, 60
When It Is Offensive to Read the Quran, 61
During the Friday Prayer, 62
Reciting While Going Around the Ka'ba [*Ṭawāf*], 62
Rejected Innovations, 62
Miscellaneous Issues of Concern, 63
Things Said with Certain Verse, 63
Reciting the Quran Intending It to Be Speech, 64
A Reciter Giving Greetings, 65
Greeting a Reciter, 65
Sneezing During One's Recitation, 66
The Call to Prayer, 66
Replying to a Question, 66
Reciting and Standing for Someone, 67
Valuable Rulings Associated with Recitation During Prayer, 67
An Additional Verse, 68
The Latecomer, 68

The Follower in a Prayer, 69
The Funeral Prayer, 69
Supererogatory Prayers, 69
Saying *"Bismillāhi al-Raḥmāni al-Raḥīm"*, 69
Someone Unable to Recite al-Fātiḥa, 70
Several *Suras* in One *Rak'a,* 70
When a Recitation Should Be Audible, 70
Supererogatory Prayers, 71
Making up Prayers, 71
Guidelines for Recitation in Silence and Aloud, 71
The *Imām* pausing for Silence, 71
Saying *"Amin"*, 72
The Ruling Concerning *"Āmīn"*, 73
Its Utterance Being Simultaneous to the *Īmām*'s, 73
Prostration at the Recitation of Passages of the Quran, 74
The Number of Verses of Prostration and Their Places, 75
Locations of the Verses of Prostration, 76
Disagreement About Sūrat Fuṣṣilat, 76
Specific Rulings Concerning the Verses of Prostration, 77
About Sūrat Ṣād, 78
If the Imām Prostrates for [Sūrat] Ṣād, 78
For Whom it is Proper to Prostrate, 78
Prostrating in General, 79
Prostration in Detail, 80
Recitation Other Than the Imām's, 81
The Timing of Prostration, 81
Ritual Impurity, 81
Multiple Prostrations, 82
Wile Riding, 82
Reading a Verse of Prostration Before al-Fātiḥa, 83
Reading a Verse of Prostration in Persian or as an Explication, 83
Listeners Prostrating with a Reciter, 83
The Ruling Concerning an Imām Reciting a Verse of Prostration, 83
Prostration At Times When Prayer is Prohibited, 84
Bowing Instead of Prostrating, 84
The Description of the Prostration, 84
Standing or Sitting, 85
Etiquette and Manner, 85
Raising the Head and Saying the Closing Salutation, 87
Prostration of Recitation During Prayer, 88

The Prostration and Invocation, 88
Rising from Prostration, 88
Standing Erect, 89
Optimal Times for Recitation, 89
Losing One's Place During the Recitation, 90
Quoting the Quran, 90
The Etiquette of Completing the Quran, 91

7. THE ETIQUETTE OF ALL PEOPLE WITH THE QURAN, 96
What Muslims Must Believe Concerning the Quran, 96
Explicating the Quran, 98
Using Uninformed Opinion, 98
Knowledge of Arabic Is Not Sufficient, 99
Arguing and Debating Without Justification, 99
Asking About the Wisdom of a Verse, 100
Saying "I was caused to forget" Instead of "I forgot", 100
Referring to Suras, 101
Pronunciations of the Word *"Sūra"*, 101
Saying "The recitation of" So-and-So, 101
The Quran and Non-Muslims, 102
The Quran as Medicine, 102
The Quran as Decoration, 102
Puffing the Words of the Quran for Protective Purposes, 103

8. RECOMMENDED TIMES FOR RECITATION, 104
Specific Months and Specific Suras, 104
Suras Yā Sīn, al-Wāqi'a, and al-Mulk, 104
Friday and Eid Prayers, 104
Daily Prayers, 105
Recommended Recitations on Friday, 106
Frequently Reciting Ayat al-Kursī and the *Mu'awidhatayn*, 106
Reciting at Bedtime, 106
Upon Waking Up, 107
Reciting Quran in the Presence of Someone Ill, 108
Reciting Quran in the Presence of Someone on the Brink of Death, 108

9. WRITING THE QURAN AND RESPECTING THE MUṢḤAF, 110
After the Prophet (God bless him and grant him peace), 110
Why the Quran Was Not Completely Written Down Beforehand, 111
The Number of *Maṣāḥif* 'Uthmān (God be pleased with him) Dis-

patched, 111
Pronunciations of the Word "*Muṣḥaf*", 111
Writing the *Muṣḥaf* is a Recommended Innovation, 112
How and Where Quran Is Written, 112
Safeguarding and Respecting the *Muṣḥaf*, 112
The *Muṣḥaf* and Non-Muslims, 113
Selling the *Muṣḥaf* to Non-Muslims, 113
The Insane and the Young, 113
Ritual Impurity, 113
Major Ritual Impurity, 114
Writing the Quran While One Is Ritually Impure, 114
Touching Books Containing the Quran, 114
Garments Embroidered with the Quran, 115
Commentary of the Quran, 115
Books of Hadith, 115
Something Whose Recitation Has Been Abrogated, 116
Touching While Having Inexcusable Filth, 116
In the Absence of Water or Earth, 116
When Fearing Its Destruction, 117
The Guardian's Responsibilities, 117
Commercial Transactions, 117

10. IMĀM AL-NAWAWĪ'S LEXICON, 119

11. CONCLUDING REMARKS, 131

TRANSLATOR'S NOTES, 132

APPENDIX ONE: SUPPLICATIONS UPON COMPLETING THE QURAN, 148

APPENDIX TWO: VERSES OF PROSTRATION, 153

APPENDIX THREE: BRIEF BIOGRAPHIES OF PERSONS CITED IN THE TEXT, 156

BIBLIOGRAPHY, 190

DETAILED TABLE OF CONTENTS, 194

INDEX, 200

ABOUT THE TRANSLATOR, 206

INDEX

Adab (etiquette)
  key to learning, xii
Adhān (Call to Prayer), 66, 82
Amīn
  rules concerning the saying of, 72–4
Angel(s)
  accompanying a group of believers remembering God, 52–3
  Gabriel, 52, 90, 145
  praying for those who complete the Quran, 31, 92
  recording the deeds of people, 5, 121
  saying "Amin", 74
Arabic
  pronunciation of "Āmin", 72–3
  required for Quran recitation, 48–9
  requirement for explication, 99
  text of supplications, 148–52
Ayat al-Kursī
  recitation of, 106–7

Basmala
  in recitation of the Quran, 41–2
Bearers of the Quran
  etiquette of, 26–34
  honored, 5–7, 9
Books of Hadith
  handling of, 115–6

Charity
  giving of to gain knowledge, 21
  in private and public, 56
Commentary of the Quran
  conditions of, 98–9
  handling of, 115

Day of 'Arafa
  preferred day to recite, 89
Dhu'l-Ḥijja
  recitation in the first ten days of, 89, 104
Dry ablution, 77

Eid Prayer
  recitation of Quran therein, 50, 70–1, 104–5

Friday
  preferred day for recitation, 89, 104–6

Friday Prayers
recitation of the Quran therein, 62, 70, 105
Funeral Prayer
silent recitation therein, 70

Gabriel, 52, 90, 145, 148–51
Group recitation of the Quran, 52–4

Hypocrite
compared to a bitter plant, 6

Imam al-Nawawi
biography, xx–xxiii
works of, xxiii–xxvi
Innovations (unlawful)
concerning the Quran, 61–3
Intention(s)
before prostration, 84
behind actions, 134
of the bearers of the Quran, 11–3
of the student of the Quran, 19
of the teacher of the Quran, 13–4
Invocations
during Prayer, 143
during prostration, 86–7
frequent repetition of, 15
replacing the recitation of al-Fātiḥa, 70
Istikhāra (Prayer of guidance)
recitation therein, 105

Ka'ba, 62, 105
Khatma (completion of the Quran's recitation)
fasting the day of, 91
supplications thereafter, 92–4, 148–52
timing of, 91

Lunar eclipse
Prayer occasioned by, 70

Miswāk (toothstick)
use of before recitation, 35, 36
Monday
preferred day for recitation, 89
Morning Prayer
blessing of, 10
completing the Quran's recitation therein, 91
recitation therein, 50, 105
recitation therein, 50
reciting thereafter, 89
Mu'awwidhatayn (last two suras of the Quran)
recitation of, 50, 103, 106–7
Muṣḥaf. See also Quran
compilation of, 111
Muslim education
starting with Quran, xv

Night Prayer Vigil
recitation therein, 71
Non-Muslims
and the Quran, 102, 113

Persian
recitation therewith, 83
Prayer
completing the recitation of the Quran therein, 91
duties of the *imām* of, 71
making up of, 71
recitation of Quran therein, 8,

29, 42–4, 46–7, 50, 57, 61–2, 64, 67–9, 104–5
recitation prostration therein, 78–9, 88–9
ritual impurity therein, 38–9, 116–7
saying "*Āmīn*" therein, 72–4
sneezing therein, 66
standing long therein, 89
weeping therein, 44–5
Prostration. *See also* Recitation Prostration
offensiveness of reciting therein, 61

Qibla
decorated with Quranic writing, 102–3
facing toward while reciting Quran, 19, 40–1
prostrating in the direction of, 77, 85
Quran. *See* Bearers and Bearing the Quran; *See also* Etiquette with the Quran; *See* Recitation of the Quran
and knowledge of Arabic, 99
and non-Muslims, 102, 113
and ritual purity, 36–9, 113–17
as decoration, 102–3
as medicine, 102
basmala part of, 41–2
blessing of, xi
books containing passages of, 114–6
commentaries of, 115
explication of, 98–9
forgetting a verse of, 100–1
garments embroidered with, 115
honoring the people of, 9, 10
inimitability of, 51
love of, 7
protection of, 47–8, 117
puffing of for protection, 103
quoting of, 90–1
recording of, 110–1
referring to suras of, 101
required belief in, 96, 98
respect for, 112–7
retention of, 33
sales of, 117–8
sincerity toward, 96
the start of Muslim education, xv
writing of, 112, 114

Rain
prayer for, 70–1
Ramadan
completing the recitation of the Quran therein, 29
preferred days to recite therein, 89
recitation of the Quran therein, 62, 89, 104
Recitation of the Quran
and ritual purity, 36–9
at Bedtime, 106–7
at night, 31–3
beautifying one's voice therein, 57–60
completion of, 91–5
continual process of, 28–31
for livelihood, 27–8
from memory, 51–2
impermissible styles therein, 49
in a foreign language, 48
in a group, 52–3
in a melodious manner, 58–9

in a quiet manner, 56–7
in daily Prayers, 67–9
intended as speech, 64–5
interruptions therein, 65–6
in the presence of someone dying, 108–9
in the presence of someone ill, 108
losing one's place therein, 89
merit of, 5–7
of *Ayat al-Kursī*, 106–7
on Fridays, 106
optimal times of, 89
order of text therein, 50–1
repeating a verse therein, 42–4
supplications upon the completion of, 92–4, 148–52
things said in response to, 63–4
upon waking up, 107–8
weeping therein, 44–5
what to avoid therein, 48–51, 61–3
while traveling, 40
with a raised voice, 54–7
with distinction, 44–5
with humility and pondering, 42–3

Recitation Prostration
bowing instead of, 84
description of, 84–5, 87–9
during congregational Prayer, 80–1
during Prayer, 88–9
etiquette of, 85, 87, 88
for whom it is required, 78–9
invocations therein, 86–8
locations of verses thereof, 76
multiple prostrations thereof, 82
number of verses thereof, 75–6
posture of, 83–5, 88–9
reciting verse of before al-Fātiḥa, 83
ritual purity therein, 81–2
ruling of, 74–5
specific ruling thereof, 77
time of, 81
verses of, 153–5
when prohibited, 84
while riding, 82
while standing or sitting, 85

Ritual purity
and bearing or reciting the Quran, 36–9, 113–7
definition of, 36

Satan (Devil)
seeking protection from, 41, 47
seeking protection from when yawning, 63

Shādh (anomalous recitation), 49

Sincerity
of the reciter of the Quran, 35
of the teacher toward students, 16–7
toward God, 11–4
toward the Quran, 96

Solar eclipse
Prayer occasioned by, 70

Students of Quran
manners of, 20–5

Students of the Quran
A moody shaykh, 22–3
respecting teacher, 21
studying with the best, 21
Treating envy and pride, 25

Supererogatory Prayers
recitation therein, 71

Supplication

during prostration, 86
effectiveness of at night, 32
for seeking God's protection from Satan, 65
of al-Fatiḥa, 72
opening one's Prayer, 72
persistence therein, 92
while reciting the Quran, 46–7
Supplications upon completing the Quran's recitation, 92–4, 148–52
Sūrat al-A'lā
recitation of, 50, 105
Sūrat al-Baqara
recitation of, 50, 107, 109
Sūrat al-Falaq
recitation of, 50, 105, 107
Sūrat al-Falaq and Sārat al-Nās. *See* Mu'wadhatayn
Sūrat al-Fātiḥa
recitation of, 47, 50, 61, 67–8, 72, 83, 108
Sūrat al-Ghāshiya
recitation of, 105
Sūrat al-Ikhlāṣ
recitation of, 50, 105, 107
Sūrat Āl 'Imrān
recitation of, 50, 106–7
Sūrat al-Insān
recitation of, 50, 104
Sūrat al-Jumū'a
recited during Friday Prayer, 105
Sūrat al-Kāfirīn
recitation of, 105
Sūrat al-Kāfirūn
recitation of, 50
Sūrat al-Kahf
recitation of, 50, 106
Sūrat al-Mulk
recitation of, 104
Sūrat al-Munāfiqīn
recited during Friday Prayer, 105
Sūrat al-Nās
recitation of, 50, 106–7
Sūrat al-Qamr
recitation of, 50, 105
Sūrat al-Sajda
recitation of, 50, 104
Sūrat al-Wāqi'a
recitation of, 104
Sūrat al-Zumar
recitation of, 107
Sūrat Banī Isrā'īl
recitation of, 107
Sūrat Falaq
recitation of, 106
Sūrat Hūd
recitation of, 106
Sūrat Qāf
recitation of, 50, 105
Sūrat Yā Sīn
recitation of, 104, 108
Sūrat Yūsuf
recitation of, 50

Tarāwīḥ Prayers
recitation therein, 70
Tayammum (dry ablution), 77, 116–7
Teacher of Quran
communal obligation of, 18
disciplining students, 17
harboring no arrogance, 17
intention of, 11–4
manners of, 18–20
molded by good qualities, 15

not seeking worldly objective, 13–4
objects not to students learning elsewhere, 14
sincerity toward students, 16, 17
spacious assembly of, 20
Thursday
preferred day for recitation, 89
Tibyān
about the translation of, xviii–xix
editions of, xvi–xvii
translation of contribution to Islamic literature, ix
Torah, 97, 116

Witr Prayer
recitation therein, 70, 105

ABOUT THE TRANSLATOR

Musa Furber is qualified to issue Islamic legal edicts (*fatwas*). He received his license to deliver edicts from senior scholars at the Egyptian House of Edicts (Dār al-Iftā' al-Miṣriyya) including the Grand Mufti of Egypt Ali Gomaa. He studied traditional Islamic disciplines for over 15 years with numerous scholars in Damascus, Cairo, and elsewhere. He also holds a BA in Applied Linguistics from Portland State University, and an MPA from Dubai School of Government. He is currently a research fellow at the Tabah Foundation in Abu Dhabi, UAE.

11067462R00138

Printed in Great Britain
by Amazon.co.uk, Ltd.,
Marston Gate.